Diversity and Detective Fiction

Diversity and Detective Fiction

edited by

Kathleen Gregory Klein

Bowling Green State University Popular Press
Bowling Green, OH 43403

Library of Congress Cataloging-in-Publication Data
Diversity and detective fiction / edited by Kathleen Gregory Klein.
    p.   cm.
    ISBN 0-87972-795-0 (cloth). -- ISBN 0-87972-796-9 (pbk.)
    1. Detective and mystery stories, American--History and criticism.
2. Pluralism (Social sciences) in literature. 3. Difference (Psychology)
in literature. 4. Gender identity in literature. 5. Ethnic groups in
literature. 6. Sex role in literature. 7. Race in literature. I. Klein,
Kathleen Gregory, 1946-
PS374.D4D58   1999
813'.087209355--dc21   99-21878
                                                                  CIP

Cover design by Dumm Art

R & R

CONTENTS

INTRODUCTION

Despite attempts by some critics to find the roots of contemporary detective fiction in the mysteries of the Bible or the tragedies of ancient Greek theater, the genre as we know it draws its characteristics primarily from the second half of the modern period of history. The success of its conventions is located in

a. the primacy of investigation over religion's received wisdom,
b. the debates of scientific thinking,
c. the rise of industrialization and consequent development of urban centers, and
d. the dichotomy between public and private spheres.

Only two decades after the publication of Poe's germinal trio of stories, the middle of the nineteenth century also saw the publication of Marx's *Das Kapital* and Darwin's *Origin of the Species* as well as the earliest efforts for women's suffrage. The ratiocinative thinking which Poe introduced and Conan Doyle was later to valorize was unquestionably—in the semiotic sense—a sign of its times.

Contemporary examples of the genre reflect earlier established conventions. Not only is the same subject at the center of the novel (murder and seldom just one) but also the narrative structure prevails. The parameters of the genre are well known, widely accepted, easily accessible. Paradoxically, this also makes the genre ripe for innovation with authors delicately working out the balance between what remains the same and what might conceivably be different. The changes of the past 25 years are congruent with a variety of recent social movements. The current range of socially provoked innovations began with gender—most sharply delineated in the modern female private-eye novel—and moved then to introduce race and ethnicity.

Detective fiction's current integration of multicultural social concerns occurs as frequently in plot or setting as in characters or criminal investigation. Dana Stabenow, in her novels of Alaska, demonstrates how abrasive edges are exposed when Native Americans and whites are required to work together without acknowledging their distinct cultural standpoints. Barbara Neeley's Blanche White is an African American housekeeper in the south, triply invisible in contemporary society

1

because of her race, class and gender. Yet, White uses this trio of marked characteristics to solve a murder. More than 80 female private eyes created since 1975 have taken over the territory once ceded to Sam Spade and Travis McGee, changing both the genre and the cultural image of women in the process.

In this context, *Diversity and Detective Fiction* takes as its focus the convergence of two points: the increasing responsibility of educational institutions to address America's multicultural society and the often overlooked opportunities present in the cultural texts of detective fiction. Teachers, from elementary school through universities, are undertaking curricular reforms which will allow them academically legitimate rubrics for discussing social and cultural issues. Moving away from strategies which draw heavily on personal experience—students' or teachers'—they are looking for pedagogical approaches which use the full range of cultural materials. Detective fiction provides one striking option. Recent statistical surveys indicate that 20 to 22 percent of all books sold in the United States are some form of mystery or detective fiction; and, they are enjoyed equally by male and female readers from age seven to adults. Because of this widespread exposure, these novels are considered familiar, accessible, and unthreatening by readers who might be resistant to other texts. And, as the authors here demonstrate, much contemporary detective fiction explores issues of cultural interaction—race, class, gender, ethnicity, age, and more—as it moves through the investigation of serious crime.

This volume goes beyond the two or three automatic names—Sue Grafton, Walter Mosley, Tony Hillerman—to explore the many ways in which diversity is posed by contemporary writers exploring distinctive American subcultures. The distinguishing characteristic of the book is its mix of essays focusing on teaching cultural diversity in the classroom and illustrating diversity through the novels to general readers. It is the first collection to articulate the pedagogical strategies of using detective fiction texts to investigate the politics of difference.

Among the issues addressed in the following essays are definitions of diversity; what constitutes ethnicity or race, especially in terms of multiple subjectivities; how race, gender, and ethnicity are culturally constructed; and what part identity politics play. Pedagogical issues are considered both explicitly and by implication. Every essay invokes theorists and researchers in the field, providing readers with the background and data on the social construction of difference. As experienced classroom teachers, the authors offer specific suggestions about how to position the novels being discussed in relation to various aspects of diversity. No single essay encapsulates all the issues or every theoretical possibility; even the entire volume does not claim to have exhausted the topic. Instead, it participates in an ongoing debate about the difference, emphasizing the importance of bringing these conversations to both formal and informal education. Even the clustering of essays in groups around categories demarcating "gender," "ethnicity," and "race" ought to provoke questions about difference inasmuch as the essays themselves—like the novels and the characters in them—overlap all three categories. None exists in a vacuum; all are simultaneous.

Gender roles—as distinct from biological sex—constitute the first focus of the essays in this book. Working with three feminist detectives, Margaret Kinsman opens this collection with a clear articulation of the place of mystery fiction in the classroom, recognizing its usefulness in teaching and learning the theories and experience of difference. Shifting the genre focus, Manina Jones states flatly that the conventions of the detective film are unable to accommodate a woman detective with agency in the recent *V. I. Warshawski.* She concludes that the economics of Hollywood filmmaking clashed with the feminist implications of the Paretsky novels and their strong female protagonist. And, in their analysis of women's series fiction, Frances DellaCava and Madeline Engel find concern for prejudice against minorities frequently introduced, not necessarily as part of the solution to the crime but adding texture to the social world of the novels.

DellaCava and Engel's essay leads naturally into the second section with its attention on ethnicity as both socially and personally constructed identity. Focusing on definitions of ethnicity, Gina and Andrew Macdonald chart the parameters and variations through the span of contemporary American mystery fiction. Mary Jean DeMarr's investigation of Dana Stabenow's novels points to the cultural tensions and personal ambivalence which exist on the fault line between native peoples and the majority culture which threatens to overwhelm them. Priscilla Walton finds that April Smith's *North of Montana* and Rochelle Majer Krich's *Angel of Death* critique stereotypical cultural perceptions as they move to complicate racial and ethnic identity formulations. Both novels critique "normative" perceptions of race and ethnicity, lending themselves to investigations of subjectivity.

Bridging the sections on ethnicity and racism is Michael Cohen's essay. Posing the question "Is racism a necessary element in detective stories," he explores stereotyping of the "other" from *Who Framed Roger Rabbit?* to *The Moonstone.* Explicitly concerned with both race and gender manifestations, Nicole Décuré and Frankie Bailey interrogate the black woman detective. Décuré approaches the works of black women writers with black women protagonists through the dual lenses of gender and race, posing the question of which dominates: race consciousness or gender consciousness. Additionally, she finds a striking use of supportive secondary women characters by these authors, a difference she notes from typical white-authored crime fiction. Situating Barbara Neely's *Blanche on the Lam* in the context of African American women writers and detective fiction's portrayals of African Americans, Bailey discusses the uses of the novel as a springboard for classroom exploration of the intersection of race, class, and gender.

The dichotomies of black and white link two of the final three essays. Through an extended interview with crime writer Mike Phillips, Claire Wells explores how the difference between white and black perceptions of crime and punishment has become established. Her conclusions point to the subversion of the nominally conservative genre by previously marginalized writers. Liam Kennedy uses the early works of Walter Mosley to show how completely the conventions of the hardboiled have been structured around the consciousness of a white subject. He draws on the narrative representation of urban space to articulate the terms of the racial debate. Andrew Pepper raises the question of what the non-Anglo investigator from a socially marginalized group brings to the genre. And he concludes by moving from the constructed fiction to a United States where the constructions of race and ethnicity remain central cultural definitions.

"DIFFERENT AND YET THE SAME":
WOMEN'S WORLDS/WOMEN'S LIVES AND THE CLASSROOM

Margaret Kinsman

"[O]ur lives are all different and yet the same" wrote the young Anne Frank in her diary, expressing a direct, private and instinctive understanding of the diversity of human "being" and human experience. Some 40 years later, Audre Lorde, feminist scholar and writer, more formally theorized a necessity to "recognize differences among women who are our equals, neither inferior nor superior, and devise ways to use each others' difference to enrich our visions and our joint struggles" (122). She warned her readers about not pretending to "a homogeneity of experience covered by the word sisterhood that does not in fact exist" (116).

The university lecturer, poised in the final decade of the twentieth century and interested in promoting non-canonical texts, new ways of reading, and the understanding that we all speak and act from a diversity of gender-marked places, might profitably persuade herself to look to crime and mystery fiction for curriculum material. The genre has a great vitality at the end of this century, enjoying a second "Golden Age" of reader popularity, publishing success, and critical acclaim. Like the first Golden Age of 1930s' British crime writing, it is women writers, protagonists, and readers who play key roles in defining the vigor and variety to be found in today's crime fiction novel, and who constitute a critically significant response to Lorde's injunction to value difference.

Popular fiction tends to take society's rules and regulations and shake them by the scruff of the neck. The 19th-century sensation novel, focused on matters of love, marriage, money, and property and hugely popular with a burgeoning female readership, constituted a threat to Victorian values. One of the ways the sensation novel showed the shakiness of society under its veneer of propriety and order was to allow a place where women behaved badly, against societal expectation. In that same popular tradition, many of today's women writers of crime and mystery fiction create spaces/places where a variety of female charaters behave against the grains of both gender and genre, and survive, not doomed to death or otherwise punished for transgression. In its contemporary proliferation of difference vis-à-vis female characters, theme, setting, and resolution, crime and mystery fiction offers considerable scope in the higher education classroom for investigating the topic of women and fictions of women as well as questions of literary form and content. This paper considers, through the examples of a selection of contemporary women authors (Barnes, Paretsky, and Wilson), what feminist crime and mystery fiction has to offer to the study of contemporary representations of women and the social issues that affect them. For the attentive student, whether in a cultural studies classroom or a literature or sociology seminar, there is much to be gained, including enjoyment and entertainment, from studying writers such as Sara Paretsky, Barbara Wilson, and Linda Barnes.

The particular focus in this paper is on three protagonists of series and three novels published in 1989/90: Paretsky's V. I. Warshawski in *Burn Marks;* Wilson's Pam Nilson in *The Dog Collar Murders;* and Barnes's Carlotta Carlyle in *Coyote.* Located by their respective authors in networks of female relatives, friends, and colleagues, the characters are constructed both to provide a level of uniting vision, and to allow for diverse actions and viewpoints. Thus a range of female experience, independence, and autonomy is made authentic and legitimate. The key textual strategy to which this discussion will return is located in the writing, against genre expectation, of a female detective with a life which includes other women from different backgrounds and with different life experiences. While the demographic norm of these particular novels is largely white, middle class and college-educated, a dedication to the principle of diversity can be detected and appreciated as a source of classroom material.

The writers and novels selected here suggest both a particular moment in the genre (the end of the 1980s, a decade in which Maureen Reddy suggests "Feminist literary criticism, feminism as a social movement, and feminist crime novels have grown up together . . ." (Reddy, "Feminist" 174), and inevitably, personal preference. Most syllabus production and canon formation reflects a certain degree of such personal idiosyncracity—so it is wise to keep in mind the very much wider range of crime fiction texts available which yield a wealth of information for the purposes of developing students' interest in and theoretical/critical understanding of representations of contemporary women, their lives, and the worlds in which they live.

As a higher-education curriculum area, crime and mystery fiction in general is increasingly mapped. Critical accounts of crime fiction written by male writers are numerous (e.g. Julian Symons, John Cawelti, Robin Winks) and give attention to the genre's narrative stress on the characteristics of action and violence historically construed as masculinist. The more recent critical approaches of e.g. Carolyn Heilbrun, Maureen Reddy, Kathleen Klein, Maggie Humm, Sally Munt, and Derek Longhurst, among others, show greater sensitivity to issues of gender, ethnicity, class, and reader preference, demonstrating how newer writers are working to revise and resist the masculinist legacy. Particular critical attention is paid by Reddy, Klein, Humm, and Munt to the appearance of the female detective whose "feisty" place in the text presents a challenge to the gender norms of detective fiction with its emphasis on active men and passive women.

However, it is arguably still a relatively under-explored, under-valued, and under-represented area of study for the undergraduate student. If a curriculum is a design for a future—an imagined productive society that we wish to see brought about—then the placing and positioning of crime and mystery fiction on the academic map seems apt. The genre, particularly in its contemporary period of vigorous growth and narrative attention to social and demographic diversity, offers a breadth and depth of material that is aesthetically valuable and culturally salient in a world where cultural difference is an everyday demand and most telling in our everyday lives.

While it is beyond the scope of this essay to undertake a full overview of the ever-expanding output on contemporary feminisms and recent genre theory, it is nevertheless useful to identify some of the touchstones this discussion assumes in relation to the terms gender, genre, and feminism.

Catherine Stimpson's description of feminism is a useful starting point: "feminism offers an *analysis* of history and culture that foregrounds gender, its structures and inequities; a collective enterprise . . . [of] *resistance* . . . ; and . . . *visions* of a different, and better, future . . ." (173) (emphases mine). Analysis, struggle, and vision are common threads in the historical experience of western women's resistance and self-definition in circumstances of social inequality between men and women. Mary Wollstonecraft's (1759-1797) *Vindication of the Rights of Women* (1792), often cited as the key text in early feminist history, included analysis, resistance, and vision, as did other famous landmark texts and speeches of eighteenth- and nineteenth-century feminists and suffragists, who drew on ideas about natural rights, justice, and democracy. Broadly speaking, the hallmarks (individualistic, liberal, and bourgeois) of eighteenth- and early nineteenth-century feminist movements were those that marked one strand of the 1960s' movement as liberal feminism, characterized by Betty Friedan's *The Feminine Mystique.* Friedan's liberal feminism (belief in democratic reform to achieve equal rights for women, without the need for revolution) was to provide an enduring blueprint for the postwar second wave women's movements in both the United States and the United Kingdom. Other significant blueprints were found in the radical feminism that grew out of the American-born Women's Liberation Movement and the black feminism that emerged out of the conjunction of Women's Liberation with the Civil Rights Movement to challenge the oppression of white women's movements which glossed over issues of economic differences and racism.

Another trajectory for later twentieth-century feminism was located in the famous "One is not born a woman, one becomes one" statement of Simone de Beauvoir, in her seminal 1949 feminist tract *The Second Sex.* de Beauvoir's differentiation between sex as a biological fact determined at conception, and gender, a category constructed through cultural and social systems, underpins what is now, by the 1990s, the use of gender as a theoretical construct which has emerged from many academic disciplines (sociology, history, linguistics, psychology, anthropology, psychoanalysis). de Beauvoir's argument that the female destiny of marriage and motherhood constituted separateness/otherness and inferiority in a social system where a woman exists in man's world on his terms was taken up by the French feminist deconstructionists of the 1980s. Cixous, Irigaray, and Kristeva have drawn on de Beauvoir and on the philosophic work of Foucault, Derrida, and Lacan to elaborate and theorize the notion of sexual difference, arguing that the gender of the writer bears on linguistic expression and contrasting masculine with feminine.

As 1980s' and 1990s' theory caught up with 1960s' and 1970s' practice, enquiry in the academy turned to the study of gender roles, with attention on the assigned, rather than the determined, nature of gender. Using gender as a theoretical category has enabled academic disciplines, literary studies among them, to become more attentive to other categories of e.g. class, race, sexual orientation, nation, family type, and to theorize the intersections and the permeability of boundaries, of identities, of difference. Black feminist literary criticism flowered in the 1980s, with collections of essays by e.g. June Jordan, Alice Walker, and Audre Lorde, creating a body of work addressing itself to the importance of the concept of difference for black women in the formation of the self and in relation to others. Their attention to the triple oppression of gender, race, and class illuminated both the construct of difference and the practice of identity politics in challenging ways, asserting the dynamic connecting force of difference over separatist stances. These perspectives, in conjunction with the postmodern insistence that "all is plural, multiple and different" (Tong 223), has led to a wider understanding that there is no one "correct" or "universal" way of being a feminist, or doing feminism. A challenge this poses for contemporary feminisms is the need to reconcile an emphasis on difference and diversity with the pressure to present an integrated standpoint from which to make claims for action and change. The point to return to is that feminism, wherever one positions oneself within it, is a radical perspective because it challenges, rather than supports, the status quo. The fundamental challenge of feminism, and one that is highly visible in the novels of Paretsky, Barnes, and Wilson, is its constant and abiding awareness that women's experiences constitute different views of reality and offer different ways of making sense of the world.

The motif of difference/diversity is itself a major theme in the long story of feminism(s) from the eighteenth-century Wollstonecraft on. What recurrent waves of women's movements and theories about those movements have shared is a belief about the specificity of gender to the systematic social injustices that women suffer across divides of race, class, nationality, sexuality; commitment to action for change; and visions of better futures. As Dale Spender's book title so aptly put it, *There's Always Been a Women's Movement,* and it has always concerned itself with questions of equity in social systems that privilege male power and authority. Feminist inquiry today finds itself at a matrix of overlapping questions and positions that challenge a falsely universal description of women, where one's stance can occupy many places and can shift across constructs and categories. Denise Riley's *'Am I That Name?'* argues for a full recognition of the ambiguity of the category of women. She sugggests that feminism(s) cannot rely on an apparent continuity of the subject women. Whether applied collectively or individually, it is an unstable category, Riley argues, because "'women' is historically discursively constructed, and always relatively to other categories which themselves change" (1-2). The very terminology of feminism, gender, woman, women continues to prove open to re-examination and new theoretical, ideological and political possibilities. As bell hooks has suggested, feminist thought is always a "theory in the making."

Contemporary feminist literary theorists continue to address the vexed question of speaking, writing, theorizing in language(s) and discourse(s) where the woman is constructed as the other. While the complexities of this postmodernist strand and its often uneasy relationship to feminism is beyond the scope of this discussion, it is worth noting some of the work on autobiography emerging from this school of thought where it intersects with a strand of psychoanalytic feminism. Nicole Ward Jouve's and Nancy K. Miller's recent works on the autobiographical voice in critical writing focus on the emergence of the personal in feminist criticism, and argue for a loosening of the boundaries between theoretical and personal writing. Miller makes the point that theoretical writers as varied in personal voice and style as bell hooks and Rachel Blau dePlessis counteract the tendency of high theory to efface women as subjects. Ward Jouve advocates a recognition of the complex, multiple ways in which a writer engages with her subject matter (whether it is fiction or theory), and understands this process of engagement as a means of self-creation, enabling identity as movement and process as against a unified and fixed selfhood. The critical importance of locating one's authority comes across in her insistent statement about voice: "dare [to] conquer a voice of your own" (132).

The history of later twentieth-century women's movements efforts to find and raise their voices is a complex and significant one which has provoked a multitude of responses. It is difficult to think of any aspect of contemporary society that has not been affected, to a greater or lesser extent, by women's theoretical and political struggles for parity over the last 30 years. The discourse(s) of feminism are uncontestably part of the later twentieth-century political, social, and cultural landscape. Stimpson argues that such a multiplicity of perspectives mandates "a fidelity to complexity" (176), thus returning us to the motif of difference as leading, in the right context, to innovation. Relying therefore, on the idea of inscribing difference as of cultural, academic, and literary significance and the significance of voice, the subgenre of feminist crime fiction offers evidence of the innovative impulse by making more visible the diversity of contemporary women's lives and the social issues that affect them.

In common with many other of today's highly aclaimed crime fiction novelists (predominantly though not exclusively women writers), the effects of 30 years of contemporary feminism on women's lives is plainly evident in the canons of the writers under consideration here: Barbara Wilson, Sara Paretksy, and Linda Barnes. These writers' (and by no means only these) collected works constitute a rich source of information on the subject of diversity in relation to the categories of "women," "women's lives," "women's struggles," and "feminism." More specifically, writers such as these (and others) are foregrounding the diversities of female experience and identity that are reflective of today's pluralistic American and British towns and cities, providing a map of contemporary female identities, concerns, and engagements with social issues. A reader of Barnes, Paretsky, or Wilson will see the world differently—however momentarily—and from the feminist perspectives that are accorded narrative privilege. The expanding subgenre of feminist crime fiction is then, for students and teachers, a place of complexity, where both theoretical and practical experiences of and resistances to patriarchal systems can be read, alongside a variety of representations of women, their communities of inheritance, and their communities of alternativity.

The narrative space in crime fiction occupied by writers such as Paretsky, Barnes, and others can be read both as theoretical discourse and as literary endeavor. It is a narrative space that lends itself particularly well to the increasingly interdisciplinary nature of higher education where the fields of women's studies, English Literature, psychoanalysis, cultural studies, sociology, feminist theory, and popular culture share boundaries, classrooms, and questions about the representation of women.

By 1994, according to a Sisters in Crime (an advocacy caucus) statistic, women writers made up almost 40 percent of active U.S. crime writers. The remarkable numerical increase of female crime fiction writers in both the United States and the United Kingdom since the 1960s, featuring a diversity of women detectives and plots, has been critically annotated and explored at length by feminist theorists and teachers such as Knepper, Klein, Cranny-Francis, Humm, and Munt.

Kathleen Gregory Klein's preface to the third and fourth editions of *Twentieth Century Guide to Crime and Mystery Writers* draws attention to the ways in which recent critical approaches to the genre are less concerned with formulaic fixity and definitions of high/low culture, and more conscious of gender, class, ethnicity, and reader preference. As she suggests, a highy visible trend in the crime fiction genre in the last 30 years or so is the motif of "difference," elaborated for example in the variety of detective protagonists who are no longer white, loner, vaguely middle-aged men. Another elaboration of difference can be traced in the sorts of crime being written about—the exploitative employment practices of the modern corporate and business worlds for instance. Finally, resolution, in a genre built on a tradition of closure (wrapping up the loose ends), is also, in the hands of contemporary writers, a testimony to difference as stories end on more ambivalent and insecure notes.

In the last two decades, literary and cultural theorists mentioned earlier have re-examined and expanded both the history and the significance of the crime and mystery fiction genre with particular critical and analytical emphases on the intersections of race, gender, class, and polyculturalism. Here too the theoretical, ideological, and political terminology of genre is arguably "in the making" as the significance of black crime novelists such as Walter Mosley, Barbara Neely, Valerie Wilson Wesley, and an emerging Hispanic body of work, is registered and affirmed. (See Messent and Willett.)

Klein explored the history of the professional woman detective in fiction from 1860 to 1980, juxtaposing fictional representations with the reality of women's lives since 1864, and came to the conclusion that detective fiction is inherently conservative in its sexual politics. With the notable exceptions of Paretsky and a few others, Klein found a long history of authors who "maintain and reinforce a conservative political ideology toward sex/gender roles which accords with the conservative implications of the genre" (*Woman* 223). Munt's 1994 discussion concurs with Heilbrun's conviction that the form proves an attractive vehicle for oppositional politics; Munt credits the lesbian thriller subgenre with staking the most radical claim to inverting formulaic genre tradition. A feminist counter-tradition becomes clear, even while its past and future remain subjects of debate and interpretation.

Historically, crime fiction is an enormously varied genre with a constant power: that it deals with the unspeakable and controls it. The tension between generic repetition and innovation is a productive one and has been crucial to the genre even though it may lead outside the framework. Confusion about the mobility of the genre in the 1990s is everywhere—in publishers' blurbs, on review pages, and in booksellers' displays, reflecting the ways in which genre convention and cultural rules are changing all the time.

Paretsky and her sisters have contributed to the project of making the genre new by including in their novels: innovative constructions of a social argument about the assassin-like role of patriarchal pressures and misogyny; the expression of female outrage; a critique of traditional nuclear family constructs; and the acceptance of the ambiguity of truth alongside the paradoxical understanding of how insecure and anxious that ambiguity can make us. All of these emphases can be traced to the innovation of placing a female sleuth in the narrative center, who tells the story of how she solves the daily mystery of how to be as an intelligent, achieving woman in a misogynistic world, alongside her account of resolving the criminal investigation. The sister with a story is already a challenge to the impersonal, male hero orthodoxies of the crime fiction genre. What then do these texts clarify about diversity and women to the alert and reflective reader? How do they indicate a valuing of differences among women as empowering?

In a 1994 essay reflecting on the ways in which women strive to speak while our culture continues to silence women's voices, Paretsky, herself one of the most widely read and admired crime fiction practitioners today, described the proliferation of women writing mystery genre books with strong female characters as "an exciting epoch in women's story-telling" ("Protocols" 17). The female narrative voices in these detective novels tell us, once we start to read between the lines, about women's lives in the socially constructed gendered communities we inhabit. Paretsky recently explained that her protagonist, V. I., who is written in the autobiographical first person, is "a woman of action. But her primary role is to speak. She says those things which I—which many women—are not strong enough to say for ourselves . . . her success depends . . . on her willingness to put into words things that most people would rather remained unspoken" ("Sexy" 22).

The claim of a first-person narrative space (shared by Linda Barnes's Carlotta Carlyle and Barbara Wilson's Pam Nilson) would seem to represent, on one hand, an identification with the famous private eye voices of Sam Spade and Philip Marlowe, roaming their mean 1940s' city streets. But Paretsky points to the silences women have always experienced, and so shows us how, on the other hand, the voice she writes is more complex than an updated imitation of a formula. Writing in the first person is, for Paretsky and the others under discussion, not only about genre tradition, but about the possibility of female self offered by the autobiographical I. It seems more than coincidental that the last 20 years or so has seen a huge movement in literary autobiographical activity, much of it by women, and increasingly sophisticated critical and theoretical articulations of the concept of identity. Untold stories and silenced protagonists are being given voice and visibility through community publishing projects, reminiscence work, a re-emerging worker/writer movement. The vehicle of crime fiction has enabled constructions of female identity and self-hood, modeled on the autobiographical "I" which has always worked well in the hard-boiled American tradition, but interrogating the male "eye's" claim on the public domain, on the making and breaking of social codes, and on the exclusion of female subjectivity. Breaking genre taboos appears to have much in common with breaking the taboos of theoretical discourse.

Women have historically been excluded from making, enforcing, or interpreting society's laws and ideas. The voices of Carlotta, Pam, and V. I. work to explore female agency in public spaces and authorize female participation in a multiplicity of selves who are not confined to the domestic sphere. Because Carlotta, Pam, and V. I. are all constructed with remembered pasts and imagined futures, their self-hoods are portrayed not as unified and fixed, but as identities constantly in the process of formation with movement across boundaries of experience and realities. Diversity, in these novels, starts with the self of the detective figure and her multiplicity of identities as daughter, friend, detective, lover, colleague, and homemaker of sorts.

Consider the opening passages of Barnes's *Coyote,* and Paretsky's *Burn Marks,* for example. *Coyote* opens with a Yiddish saying which Carlotta attributes to three maternal generations back; she mirrors her own six-foot-one self in the "formidable . . . reputedly seven feet tall" (1) persona of her great-grandmother. In the first lines of *Burn Marks* (1990), V. I. wakes out of an insistent dream about her mother's long-ago flight from the fascists in her native Italy. Both V. I. and Carlotta possess a clear sense of where they have come from, in terms of their families of descent, identifiying themselves repeatedly as daughters of immigrant, working-class stock, and reiterating the values of hard work, honesty, and self-responsibility they grew up with. At the same time as the past is present in the memories and identities of these sleuths, it is also a reminder of how far away from their origins these characters have moved, and a reminder about how identity can change.

Pam Nilson, in the opening paragraph of *Dog Collar Murders,* similarly establishes an identity in her family of origin—"my twin sister was getting married to the man she loved and I was the bridesmaid" (3), which is immediately undercut by the information that this is no traditional wedding with a bride in blushes and white. Pam's wry observation "some things weren't quite the way we would have imagined them" draws attention to the changes she and her sister have made in their lives (particularly their sexual identities—Penny is marrying Pam's male ex-lover; Pam is at the wedding with her lesbian partner Hadley and a group of lesbian friends) since the childhood days when they used to play "weddings."

All three writers draw attention to the fluctuations of identity as the journey of self-discovery takes people in many different directions. The old melting-pot assimilation model of diversity on which American society is built, and which features the mother as the domestic center, is paid tribute to in the constructions of, for example, Carlotta's Jewish/Scots parentage, and V. I.'s Polish-Catholic paternal forebears and her maternal Italian-Jewish heritage. However, newer models of cultural diversity, where bi-lingualism is valued rather than suppressed in favor of English, are hinted at by Carlotta, who berates herself for not having taken up the study of Spanish earlier or with more assiduousness, and makes clear her understanding of what she can learn from Paolina. Carlotta sees Paolina for who she is, and not as the label "poor" or "victim" in need of rescue from a white, middle-class woman. Paretsky similarly hints at new models in *Burn Marks,* with reference to the politically aspiring Roz Fuentes, who speaks the language of her Hispanic constituency and moves in and out of Chicago's political and ethnic communities with ease and aplomb. This, however, makes her no less a casualty of Chicago's endemically corrupt political systems and of the easy, though bankrupt, promise of the American Dream.

The quest for self-knowledge and affirmation—the discovery and identification of self—appears as subtle subtext throughout these novels and occasionally surfaces to take precedence over the investigation of the crime. One such example of precedence is found in Wilson's *The Dog Collar Murders,* where Pam's uncertainty about her stance vis-à-vis the pornography debate is foregrounded through the device of a pornography conference. A substantial portion of the text is given over to exploring the conference workshops on sexist images of women in media, the use of pornography by rapists and child molesters, censorship, sadomasochism as a presence in the lesbian community. The text signals a diverse range of concerns and positions in the debate and follows Pam's conquering of self-doubt as she locates her own position.

In another instance of fluctuation in identity, Vic often refers to the brief period in her young adult life when she flirted with the persona of Yuppie Wife. Just out of law school, seemingly hungry to belong to Dick Yarborough's WASP world of privilege and ease, and believing he is drawn to her independence of mind and career aspirations as a public defender, she marries him—only to shed him some 14 months later when she comes to the realization that "some men can only admire independent women at a distance" (*Indemnity* 30).

Throughout all three series of novels, these protagonists continue to interrogate models of traditional womanhood. Pam explores different styles of domestic arrangements and variations on her sexual identity with a growing self-awareness. Both her lesbian-identified sexuality and her unconventional living arrangements cast her outside the norm. Similarly, V. I.'s self-aware choice to stay away from matrimony is a constant thorn in the side of her late father's best friend, policeman Bobby Mallory, whose role it is to remind Vic at every oppportunity what it is that society really expects and wants of her: to marry, settle down, produce children, and "butt out of investigating." Bobby embodies the patriarchal injunction directed at women to nurture others and stay at home. What he paradoxically cannot grasp is how this recipe is for his, and other males' benefit, and not for V. I.'s fulfillment. For Bobby, V. I.'s ventures into the public sphere are unnatural and threatening. For V. I., who refuses to accept there are places she cannot/should not go, the venture is life-enhancing.

Carlotta, too, is happily single, though not without her on-again, off-again relationship with Sam Gianelli, and her punk housemate-cum-keeper, Roz. The third member of Carlotta's eclectic "family" of choice is Paolina, growing up poor and Hispanic in a Boston slum. Carlotta's and Paolina's lives intersect when Carlotta volunteers as a Big Sister in an urban mentoring project. Neither are these sleuths' domestic arrangements regular, nor are the families of choice they construct for themselves. While one of the textual purposes of such irregularities is to reconfigure the traditional male loner detective, another is to demonstrate the differences and varieties of female identity in contexts of inclusion, rather than exclusion.

Carlotta's Big Sister relationship with the young Paolina growing up in urban poverty and V. I.'s troubled relationship with her alcoholic Aunt Elena (*Burn Marks*), growing old in urban poverty, both draw attention to the different economic situations of women today as well as to the vulnerability of the old and the young in a society that considers whole sections of the population to be throwaway. For neither Vic nor Carlotta nor Pam is the traditional female nurturing role an appealing one, nor when it presents itself in a variety of guises, is it an unproblematic one. In *Burn Marks,* Vic has to face up to some serious questions about filial duty and obligation, and arrives at a boundary for herself (she will not have Aunt Elena live with her, or stay as a temporary guest for more than one or two nights) that leaves her vulnerable to her own guilt and to harsh judgments from others. Carlotta has to work hard not to overprotect Paolina, and indeed not to overstep her Big Sister role into that of Substitute Mother—especially as Carlotta is not uncritical of Paolina's own mother. The connection to the past and the future implicit in the societal assumption that women will marry and bear children is something that Carlotta, V. I., and Pam locate in other kinds of relationships than marital and maternal, forging links across boundaries of generation, linguistic difference, political persuasion, sexuality, and personal experience.

Another social expectation—that women will nurture a host of others and not themselves—is also challenged in these texts. The autonomous self, the one for whom solitude is not a burden and who can nurture herself is explored in all three protagonists in resistance to the stereotype of single women as lonely, failed, and prone to selfishness. Pam Nilson and her lover Hadley arrive at a joint solution to their desire for separate but linked households and, by the end of *The Dog Collar Murders,* are having a housewarming party in an echo of the wedding party with which the novel opened. Vic engages in constant sparring with her dearest friend Dr. Lotty Herschel and with Mr. Contreras, the 70-year-old downstairs neighbor, not to mention various lovers as she struggles "to establish relationships that support without confining" (Trembley 268). Vic experiences her autonomy as choice and, like Carlotta who offers a hymn to the pleasures of a solitary evening at the end of Chapter 1 in *Coyote,* expresses the upbeat side of not being in a predictable kinship system. All three protagonists are skilled at looking after themselves, able to take pleasure in solitary dining, for example. When they want company, they find it.

Solitude is also, in these protagonists' lives, a source of inner strength and offers a space to recharge both physical and mental batteries. Vic always prefers to lick her wounds, the bodily ones and the psychic ones, in private and alone. Carlotta, who is a part-time cab driver, has a habit of driving her Boston streets alone late at night figuring things out. Rather than reading solitude as a selfish or failed betrayal of the female nurturing role, it can be read as a requisite for personal autonomy and the single-minded trajectory of the investigator's quest. For women fulfilling the traditional roles of wife and mother, solitude is a rare thing. Female protagonists who experience solitude as a given and as a source of intellectual, emotional, and physical renewal help draw our attention as readers to the ways in which patriarchal systems conspire against female fulfillment by disallowing them the very nurturing and privacy they are expected to extend to others.

Rather more explicit attention is drawn to traditional gender construction with the motif of the emblematic empty fridge possessed by all three of the example protagonists. In the urban private eye mode of the 1920s to 1940s, Marlowe and Spade live in efficiency hotel apartments, in a world where men don't occupy domestic spheres or own fridges, and where a cold beer or a meal is only a stroll away in a public bar or restaurant. Carlotta, V. I., and Pam not only own fridges (the contents of which are often sparse and frequently moldy), they own and occupy whole apartments or houses, sharing their space and attention only when they choose to and on their terms. None of them could be characterized as fussy housekeepers, and none of them could be described as overgenerous hostesses. Vic's main domestic concern is that her precious red wine goblets, a legacy from her mother Gabriella who carried them with her when she fled fascist Italy, should not be broken. Carlotta's anxiety focuses on whether or not Roz has managed a trip to the grocery store. Such concerns represent a liberation from the worries women are traditionally encouraged to entertain: is the laundry white enough and is the floor shiny enough? Such concerns also place these protagonists in beleagured positions, well outside society's contemporary rallying cry for a return to family values.

Another feature of these three protagonists which places them outside the norm is their resistance to the cultural expectation that female outrage should not be expressed. Women who voice discontent, frustration, anger in our society run the risk of being labeled as strident and written off as hysterical. Barnes, Paretsky, and Wilson are alert to issues of social justice and the corroding effects of inequality, which allows them to explore in their texts, female exploitation, female rage and to consider the problems that fragment sisterhood as well as the desires that build community rather than incite conflict. Barnes's *Coyote,* for example, takes up the issue of illegal immigrant sweatshop workers; Carlotta's investigation into the death of a woman with no papers and no identity raises questions about the sexual harrassment and economic exploitation immigrant women are subjected to. Carlotta's outrage about the state of affairs she uncovers is expressed in her determination to uncover the sweatshop/illegal papers connection and bring the perpetrators to justice. As Harper's recent discussion of Barnes points out, "Although Carlotta does not preach feminism extensively, she is always battling for women who, because of their sex or race, are being abused by the system" (Harper 31). Wilson's Pam is allowed to express frustration and anger over the divisions between feminists in relation to the pornography debate. Pam's sulks and quarrels are treated as creative, allowing Pam to progress her understanding and knowledge.

Unexpressed anger stagnates and paralyzes people. The protagonist who wisecracks her anger, as all of these three do, signifies both the genre tradition of "irreverance towards authority and institutional power" (Willett 7) and more notably, for female private eyes, constitutes "an assertion of autonomy, a defiant refusal to be browbeaten" (7). Where male anger in crime fiction is often expressed with a gun, the lippy female keeps up a running commentary that often works to defuse potentially dangerous and violent situations. In the cases of V. I., Carlotta, and Pam, a strong voice is a more reliable, useful, and potent weapon than a gun.

Paretsky's construction of V. I.'s expression of rage is a particularly complex one which incorporates the wisecracking voice, and also pays attention to other motifs of rage. V. I., for example, often displays her anger viscerally, with throbbing temples, raised body temperature, and clenched fists. She constantly registers these markers of discomfort and acts on such physical indicators as authentic sources of information that help tell her when to raise her voice, when to cool off, when to back off, and when to go for the throat. Another complexity in Paretsky's configuration of female rage is linked to her understanding that the illusion of helplessness is often the source of female rage. Institutions of domesticity and marriage render women dependent and helpless, providing a natural habitat for outrage. So while V. I.'s disregard for personal safety is absolutely necessary to bolster her claim to independence and self-reliance, Paretsky also shows how her anger at and fear of the domestic trap can result in unwelcome divisions from friends and colleagues, as for example, when Vic's and Lotty's relationship is tested. Lotty and Vic, bonded over their joint activism in the pro-choice movement and established in a rewarding and reciprocal friendship, are nevertheless divided by V. I.'s fierce passion for autonomy and her utter disregard for Lotty's safety at one crucial point. Wedges can drive as deep as bonds, and it is this price attached to the expression of female rage that Paretsky suggests needs to be considered more seriously than the annoyance of being called strident. What Paretsky's, Barnes's, and Wilson's protagonists with a voice collectively call attention to is the day-to-day courage it takes to embrace difference and diversity—both in relation to one's self (the reiteration of "I'm gay" or "I'm black" or "I'm single" in a generally homophobic, racist and sexist society is wearing) and in relation to one's significant others, who are crucial to the collective struggle and vision. Female anger becomes linked to courage and energy, configured as enabling against the societal dictat that rage is not only inexpressible but destructive.

These three authors then, and their three protagonists of series, tell women's stories that describe and stimulate change in female destiny. The presence of V. I., Carlotta, and Pam in their texts from nearly ten years ago, as autonomous, economically independent, and socially mobile women seems, from the perspective of the late 1990s, oddly prescient of the real demographic critical mass of single professional women in their thirties—who appear to be in no rush toward matrimony, parenthood, and a two-car household—that now marks both American and British culture and society. As Ostriker pointed out, in a discussion of women poets, "Women writers have always tried to steal the language [because] their intention is to subvert and transform the life and literature they inherit" (211). By making explicit in their novels aspects of women's independence, autonomy, oppression, and relationships to male patriarchy, sexuality, and the family, writers such as Barnes, Paretsky, and Wilson have occupied and shifted the centre of a genre noted more for its stereotypical glamorization and/or victimization of women characters. (See discussions by e.g. Heilbrun, Munt, Reddy, and Cranny-Francis.) Studying such novels in the higher education classroom offers students an opportunity to address detective fiction as "texts with hidden signs, disguised meanings, at once duplicitous and self-subverting" (Duncker 90) and to ask what it is they can learn from the particular sub-genre identified with feminism. Understanding and incorporating contradiction, plurality, and reflexivity has become part of the process for contemporary feminists—those who theorize it and those who write it into crime fiction novels. The project of finding and telling the truth about women's lives, as they are lived and as they are fictionalized, is, in the hands of these three authors, a challenge to conventional wisdom. And what, theoretically, is the classroom for, if not to interrogate wisdom?

Works Cited

Barnes, Linda. *Coyote*. New York: Delacorte, 1990.

Cawelti, John. *Adventure, Mystery and Romance: Formula Stories as Art and Popular Culture*. Chicago: University of Chicago Press, 1976.

Duncker, Patricia. *Sisters and Strangers: An Introduction to Contemporary Feminist Fiction*. Oxford: Blackwell, 1992.

Harper, Donna Waller. "Linda Barnes." *Great Women Mystery Writers*. Ed. Kathleen Gregory Klein. Westport, CT: Greenwood Press, 1994. 29-32.

Heilbrun, Carolyn. *Writing A Woman's Life*. New York: Ballantine Books, 1989.

hooks, bell. *Feminist Theory: From Margin to Center*. Boston: South End Press, 1984.

Humm, Maggie. *Border Traffic—Strategies of Contemporary Women Writers*. Manchester: Manchester Press, 1991.

Klein, Kathleen Gregory. Preface. *St. James Guide to Crime and Mystery Writers*. 4th ed. 1996.

——. Preface. *Twentieth Century Guide to Crime and Mystery Writers*. 3rd ed. 1991.

——. *The Woman Detective, Gender and Genre*. Chicago: University of Illinois, 1988.

Longhurst, Derek, ed. *Gender, Genre & Narrative Pleasure*. London: Unwin Hyman, 1989.

Lorde, Audre. *Sister Outsider*. Trumansburg, NY: The Crossing Press, 1984.

Messent, Peter, ed. *Criminal Proceedings, The Contemporary American Crime Novel*. Chicago & London: Pluto Press, 1997.

Miller, Nancy K. *Getting Personal*. London: Routledge, 1991.

Munt, Sally R. *Murder by the Book? Feminism and the Crime Novel*. London: Routledge, 1994.

Ostriker, Alicia. *Stealing the Language*. London: Women's Press, 1987.

Paretsky, Sara. *Burn Marks*. New York: Delacorte, 1990.

——. *Indemnity Only*. New York: Dial, 1982.

——. "Protocols of the Elders of Feminism." *Law/Text/Culture*. Vol. 1. University of Wollongong, 1994. 14-27.

——. "Sexy, Moral and Packing a Pistol." *The Independent* [London] 18 June 1997: 22.

Reddy, Maureen. "The Feminist Counter-Tradition in Crime: Cross, Grafton, Paretsky and Wilson." *The Cunning Craft: Original Essays on Detective Fiction and Contemporary Literary Theory*. Ed. Ronald G. Walker and June M. Frazer. Macomb: Western Illinois UP, 1990. 174-87.

——. *Sisters in Crime, Feminism and the Crime Novel*. New York: Continuum, 1988.

Riley, Denise. *'Am I That Name?' Feminism and the Category of 'Women.'* Basingstoke: MacMillan, 1988.

Spender, Dale. *There's Always Been a Women's Movement This Century.* London: Pandora Press, 1983.

Stimpson, Catherine. *Where the Meanings Are.* London: Routledge, 1988.

Symons, Julian. *Bloody Murder: From the Detective Story to the Crime Novel.* London: PaperMac, 1992.

Tong, Rosemarie. *Feminist Thought.* London: Routledge, 1992.

Trembley, Elizabeth A. "Sara Paretsky." *Great Women Mystery Writers.* Ed. Kathleen Gregory Klein. Westport, CT: Greenwood Press, 1994. 266-69.

Ward-Jouve, Nicole. *White Woman Speaks with Forked Tongue.* London: Routledge, 1991.

Willett, Ralph. *The Naked City, Urban Crime Fiction in the USA.* Manchester & New York: Manchester University Press, 1996.

Wilson, Barbara. *The Dog Collar Murders.* London: Virago, 1989.

Winks, Robin, ed. *Detective Fiction: A Collection of Critical Essays.* New Jersey: Prentice-Hall, 1980.

SHOT/REVERSE SHOT:
DIS-SOLVING THE FEMINIST DETECTIVE STORY
IN KANEW'S FILM *V. I. WARSHAWSKI*

Manina Jones

Sara Paretsky's eight detective novels, from *Indemnity Only* to *Tunnel Vision,* are widely regarded as part of a contemporary feminist "counter-tradition" of popular detective writing that invites readers to question their assumptions about the traditionally masculine genre of crime fiction (Reddy 176) and ideally, as Kathleen Gregory Klein puts it, work toward solving "not only the problem of the crime but also the problems of the social system" itself (227). Paretsky's foregrounding of gender issues in her novels begins with a "recasting" of the role of the male hard-boiled private eye with feminist investigator V. I. Warshawski, and extends, Priscilla Walton argues, to an exploration of the interstices of race, class, and gender as they have been constructed and homogenized within traditional exemplars of the genre (205). Equally important, Paretsky's novels led the way in the development of a crime fiction subgenre that has, since the early 1980s, opened up the field of hard-boiled detective fiction to an ever-increasing number of female authors (e.g. Marcia Muller, Sue Grafton, Linda Barnes, Lia Matera, Liza Cody), as well as a lucrative—and previously untapped—market of women readers. For instance, *Publishers Weekly*'s 1990 survey of the post-1980s' mystery fiction publishing boom notes that "Most every publisher has a Grafton or Paretsky on the way up, or in the making, or about to be signed, since the woman as tough professional investigator has been the single most striking development in the detective novel the past decade [sic]" (Anthony 28).[1]

Based on the popularity of the early Paretsky novels, and on growing sales of the "tough gal private eye" genre, in 1985 Tri Star Pictures optioned lifetime character rights on Paretsky's Warshawski series for what *Variety* estimates as a "modest amount—probably a low six-figure pickup" (Max, "Warshawski's Mysterious Journey" 71). The film that resulted, *V. I. Warshawski*, directed by Jeff Kanew and starring Kathleen Turner was released in the summer of 1991. *Variety*'s retrospective of that year identified *V. I. Warshawski* as part of the "usual" studio quest for summer blockbusters, which also included *Robin Hood: Prince of Thieves, Terminator 2: Judgement Day, Naked Gun 2 1/2: The Smell of Fear, Backdraft,* and *Hudson Hawk* (Wolf 361). But *V. I. Warshawski* was clearly different from these other summer releases. For one thing, it was a financially pared-down version of the blockbuster, with television-like production values, a single "name" actor (Turner, though Charles Durning also has a small role), and a largely unknown director.[2] It was also, in contrast to the season's other "big" releases, a star vehicle for a female actress, based on a series of novels written by a woman. As *Time* magazine's Richard Corliss perceived, the film was a conspicuous manifestation of the Hollywood machine trying to address a "lingering dilemma: how to get women into the summer movie mainstream" (66). This mainstream had, by and large, been driven by "the desires and tastes of what the marketing departments identified as the core consumer: the twenty-five year old male" on whom the studios could depend not just for the admission prices of action adventure stories, but also for "the lucrative spin-off merchandising which helps keep the film industry buoyant" (Francke 99).

In a sense, *V. I. Warshawski* was favorably positioned to succeed. Based on a series of well-received novels with fast-moving adventure-based plots and a feisty, engaging, and attractive female protagonist, it stood to capitalise on an under-exploited film audience in much the same way Paretsky's novels had attracted a new market of female (as well as male) readers to her variant of the hard-boiled detective novel. Indeed, when film critic Kathi Maio, well before the release of Kanew's film, wrote that "Women are hungry for our own forceful, resolute 'action' heroes. It's never been easy to find them" (99), the novelist she suggested as a model to rectify this problem was Sara Paretsky. *V. I. Warshawski* also made use of one of the only truly bankable female stars at a time when roles for women in Hollywood seemed to be at an all-time low: in 1989 Kathleen Turner was the only woman on the top ten list of box office moneymakers. She ranked number ten.[3] In fact, *V. I. Warshawski*'s producer capitalized on Hollywood's perceived dearth of strong female roles in the late 1980s and early 1990s in order to promote the film, boasting "My hope is that this film will be Hollywood's catching up with women in society" (cited in Turan 1). In addition, by the time of the film's release, Paretsky was becoming a more famously "hot" author: her novel *Bloodshot* had made the bestseller list, selling around

35,000 hardcover and 300,000 paperbacks, and *Burn Marks* did even better (Max, "Warshawski's Mysterious Journey" 71). The latter novel had also made an appearance on the *New York Times* bestseller list, where Sue Grafton's female private investigator series was also cropping up on a regular basis.

Kanew's *V. I. Warshawski* is an excellent example of Hollywood's attempt to use book trends to measure changes in American consumer attitudes and interests (Max, "Warshawski's Mysterious Journey" 71). Indeed, one reviewer called *V. I. Warshawski* "less a movie than a marketing concept, a pastiche stitched out of the best-seller lists" (Dargis 64). The film was, by all accounts, a box office flop, though according to Glenwood Irons, "it has been a steady success at the video stores" (xxiii). Its aesthetic inadequacies, and the ways it failed to gauge and engage the interest of its projected audience are, however, instructive and revealing because of the ideological conflicts the film's adaptation of Paretsky's winning formula dramatizes. *V. I. Warshawski*, perversely, represents a remarkable example of what Susan Faludi would call a conservative "backlash" against precisely the potentially progressive feminist publishing trends the film was optioned to exploit. Its efforts to capitalize on the economic potential of a female audience by drawing on these trends end up, paradoxically, by pandering to a voyeuristic male spectator. The male gaze thus oversees the figure of the female "private eye," keeping her under constant, controlling surveillance. Kanew's cinematic adaptation of Paretsky's novels strategically invokes and then revokes her revisions of the hard-boiled tradition, systematically reassimilating the figure of the feminist detective into a collection of conservative cultural norms. The film, in other words, takes over a subversive approach to a conservative genre, using it to reinstall a new conservatism. *V. I. Warshawski*, indeed, may be read as the site of contradictory representations of both gender and genre, a site that reveals anxieties within the Hollywood institution, not simply about the idea of a woman's detective agency, but, it might be argued, about detection as a figure for women's agency in general.

One of the distinguishing features of the hard-boiled variant of detective fiction is its orientation around an individual's subjectivity; the private "I" of the private eye is the focal point of the story. Its hero is often understood as an existential loner, an American individualist, a twentieth-century urban cowboy. This subjective focus is apparent in the use of the distinctive cynical first-person narrative voice used by Raymond Chandler's Philip Marlowe, Mickey Spillane's Mike Hammer, or Ross Macdonald's Lew Archer. It takes its most striking cinematic form in Robert Montgomery's 1946 adaptation of Chandler's *Lady in the*

Lake, which is shot entirely from the detective's point of view, exaggerating the film genre's characteristic use of a subjective camera. Paretsky's novels also use a first-person narrative perspective, but, as Priscilla Walton points out, this rendering of the detective involves a self-conscious critique of the conventional self-sufficient hero (206). It also, perhaps contradictorily, allows for the portrayal of the woman as "agent," an investigator in detection narratives that frequently move from personalized moral transgressions or crimes against bourgeois notions of property to the exposure of patriarchal institutions as *systemically* criminal.

However, the conventions of the detective film genre, as they are adapted in the movie *V. I. Warshawski,* seem unable to accommodate a woman detective who is the empowered subject of the investigation. For the private eye as for the voyeur and film audience, visual perception is implicated in desire, knowledge, and power. Instead of being the subject of the cinematic gaze, the woman detective is here most frequently offered *uncritically* as its eroticised object. Indeed, the film's representation of its heroine often unintentionally foregrounds this problem by dramatizing voyeuristic scenarios of looking and being looked at within its story. The film's opening sequence, for example, concludes with V. I.'s ritual morning jog, in which she is shown in shots that fragment her body, framing Kathleen Turner from the waist down. This is virtually an establishing shot of Turner's body as the site of the film's primary visual interest; it parallels the opening establishing shot of Chicago's skyline. A group of male runners call attention to this objectifying look *within* the narrative, calling out *"Babe—look!"* in military fashion and hooting as they pass her. The film then cuts to a rock video-like closeup of V. I.'s feet in high heels on pavement, followed by a closeup of her first client, and an eye-line match cut to a slow camera tilt up her body, following his clearly lascivious look and offering an exaggerated version of the position that the camera routinely takes through the course of the film. This sequence practically parodies the male-identified gaze of the spectator that has become the subject of feminist analysis of Hollywood narrative cinema since Laura Mulvey's well-known essay on that subject. Because of the collision of subject positions that is enacted in *V. I. Warshawski*—i.e., "detective" as subject of the gaze vs "woman" as its visual object—that gaze does not (or cannot) efface itself as it conventionally does in classical Hollywood cinema.

In a later sequence, V. I. reluctantly converses with her philandering lover Murray, a newspaper reporter who in the novels is a platonic friend, and who in this instance barges into her bathroom while she is taking a bath. The camera pans languidly up her body, again following her male admirer's gaze. Though he is not nominally the detective in the story, Murray's off-screen voice appropriates the role of the voice-over narration often used in detective films, or the role of fictional narrator as voyeuristic "private eye." Murray actually describes his own position-ing—as well as his visceral response to V. I.: "He stood gazing as the steam rose gently from the water, knowing that just beneath this fragile blanket of bubbles lay her silken nubile body. He felt the stirring of a warm throbbing passion . . ." In this instance, dialogue paradoxically positions the male character outside the narrative—or at least he speaks as if he occupied such a position in relation to V. I. The female investiga-tor, on the other hand, is, as Kaja Silverman describes the female subject of mainstream cinema in general, excluded from positions of authority both inside and outside the film's telling of the story, restricted "not only to safe places *within* the story (to positions, that is, which come within the eventual range of male vision or audition), but to the safe place *of* the story" (132). Moments later, the bathroom is invaded by a recent acquaintance and his daughter, turning private space into the site of public spectacle for the eye of the audience *in* the film, a scenario that replicates the situation of the audience *of* the film. The notion of male spectatorship and fantasy are ludicrously linked in the film's placement of V. I.'s apartment, which overlooks the playing field of Chicago's Shea Stadium; Murray visits V. I. to take advantage of her armchair view of Cubs' baseball games.

The power dynamics of the film's reorientation of subjectivity are made all the more disturbing in the film's gendered presentation of vio-lence. While violent incidents in which V. I. prevails are shot primarily in neutral medium or long shot, we are offered lingering point-of-view closeups of her when she must passively submit to being slapped by mobster Earl Smysen. V. I. responds to Smysen's blows by complaining, "Do you know how hard it is to get blood out of cashmere?" The film appears to play on an assumed audience pleasure in seeing Smysen get blood out of V. I.'s cashmere-clad detective, in seeing V. I. pay for her "smart mouthed" challenges to men's authority. The visual pleasure of her punishment, in other words, overwhelms V. I.'s wisecracking verbal resistance. This aspect of the film significantly distinguishes it from the feminist private eye novel, in which the "tough talking" first-person nar-rator is the subject of the narrative enunciation. Her voice controls the story's perspective, and is supplemented by wisecracking dialogue in a manner that "transforms the classic private eye genre into a place from which a woman can exercise language as power" (Christianson 128-29). When V. I. is in a position to return Smysen's blows, the camera is posi-tioned to identify with his pain and humiliation. Later in the film, vio-lence against V. I. is overtly associated with both visual and sexual pleasure. When the villainous Trumble Grafalk threatens her in his office with a set of callipers, V. I. casually looks out the window, then down at his crotch (implying that he is sexually aroused), and poses the double-entendre question, "Does everybody get this view?" to which he replies, "Only the females . . . You see, I fuck a lot." The scene stages a connection between sexual violence against the heroine and visual pleasure.

Even if the language of the last quotation seems a little strong for a film originating with the Disney-affiliated Tri-Star Pictures, the underlying morality of *V. I. Warshawski* is firmly within the Disney tradition of family entertainment, fortified by the Reagan-Bush era's conservative conception of "family values." Despite its generic veneer of detection, the central impetus of the film's narrative is not the detective genre's characteristic gathering of clues and exposure of the criminal. The narrative of *V. I. Warshawski*, in fact, jumbles the plots of Paretsky's first two novels, *Indemnity Only* and *Deadlock*, to such a degree that the detective narrative loses its urgency. *V. I. Warshawski* is impelled, rather, by the attempt to re-configure a version of the "traditional" bourgeois family, which American conservatives perceive to be in crisis. While Paretsky's novels offer alternatives to the nuclear family and often document the defects of its patriarchal structure, Kanew's film is based on the implicit imperative of transforming the professional detective into a wife and mother.

The plot of the film is propelled by two signal events. First, prior to its beginning, V. I. discovers the unfaithful Murray in bed with "a red-head." This recounted sexual incident substitutes for the discovery of a *dead* body conventional to the beginning of mystery stories. In response, V. I. goes to a pickup bar and meets Boom Boom Grafalk, a hockey player to whom V. I. is immediately romantically attracted—though in the novel *Deadlock* Boom Boom is V. I.'s cousin, not a love interest. The romantic, even domestic trajectory of the plot is telegraphed in the early bar scene, when V. I. obsesses on her sequined red stiletto-heeled pumps, which she is convinced magically attract men. Right on cue, Boom Boom trips on the shoes, and as he gallantly slips one of them back on her foot, V. I. says, "Cinderella story," perhaps identifying a happily-ever-after salvation-by-marriage plot as a model for the movie as a whole. The shoes may also remind viewers of *The Wizard of Oz,* another film in which ruby slippers work magic . . . when combined with the mantra, "There's no place like home." Dialogue calls attention to the way V. I.'s detective skills are more centrally directed toward a romantic consummation than a detective resolution. When Boom Boom promises to phone her, V. I. says, "If you don't, I'll hunt you down. I'm a private eye, remember?"

Boom Boom is involved in a custody battle with his wife, Paige, placing the fragmentation of family relationships front and center in the plot. Paige was not only unfaithful to her husband during their marriage, but after the divorce further fragmented the family by marrying her husband's brother. Now she claims custody of their child to further her business interests. Paige is the central criminal of the film, and her crime, it suggests, is not merely dishonest business practices or even conspiracy to commit murder; these are aspects of the deflected detective plot of *Deadlock,* a story that focuses much more heavily on the Byzantine operations of the shipping industry, and presents the institutional locus as the true scene of the crime. Paige's abdication of her role as mother constitutes the film's central transgression. As Susan Faludi describes it, the conservative backlash in 1980s' Hollywood is marked by portrayals of women's lives as "moralist tales in which the 'good mother' wins and the independent woman gets punished" (113). Adrian Lyne's 1987 *Fatal Attraction* is the paradigmatic example of this trend. The backlash thesis, Faludi continues, is repeatedly restated and reinforced: "American women were unhappy because they were too free; their liberation had denied them marriage and motherhood" (113).

V. I. Warshawski goes through considerable generic contortions to demonstrate this thesis, to portray V. I., a single professional hard-boiled detective, as the "good mother," as she must be if she is to occupy the prescribed space available for a female protagonist. The thrust of the film's opening credit sequence seems to be that V. I. is no homemaker: her apartment is a mess, and her refrigerator is full of unidentifiable smelly things, perhaps a signifier of her decadence as a single woman. When Boom Boom hires her to babysit his twelve-year-old daughter, Kat, she seems at a total loss. When he is promptly killed in a mysterious explosion, V. I. is left in charge of the youngster, with whom she teams up for the investigation. It should be noted that in Paretsky's novel, while V. I. professionally represents Kat, she leaves the child safe with a male caregiver in order to pursue the case. In contrast, the film insists on a motif of motherhood not unlike that of Charles Shyer's 1987 movie *Baby Boom,* in which, as Faludi argues, a *deus ex machina* is necessary to transform the single professional woman into a mother, in the latter case an independent advertising executive played by Diane Keaton who unexpectedly inherits a baby in a will.

Perhaps the most obvious foregrounding of the motherhood motif in *V. I. Warshawski* is the fact that Kat has been assigned a social science project at school, an experiment in motherhood in which she must look after an egg as if it were her baby. By the time she meets V. I., she has already "killed" several eggs, and while at first it appears that there will be a humorous parallel between these failed attempts at motherhood and V. I.'s lack of maternal skills, it turns out that the film's narrative is dominated by *the detective's* progressive education as an adoptive mother, particularly in the cultivation of her protective instincts and her progressive grooming of Murray to play the role of faithful husband and father. The "hard-boiled" trope of detective novels is thus refigured in the film as a literal (raw) egg, an image of motherhood. At one point, after having been injured in a fight and sedated by her doctor friend Lotty, V. I. spontaneously asks Murray, "Do you think I'd be a good mother?" to which Murray replies, "Whoa Lotty! Right drug, wrong dose!" a comment that unobtrusively connects maternal feelings with the healing process. Indeed, the film consistently associates healing with the traditional family. For instance, a poster with eggs and baby chicks on it decorates Lotty's health clinic, and V. I., after being injured in a fight, is attentively ministered to by Lotty and a police officer friend of V. I.'s late father (who are visually presented as V. I.'s concerned parents) as well as Murray.

At the beginning of the film, Murray had perversely pretended to be V. I.'s husband in order to thwart Boom Boom's interest in her, leaving the apartment with the line, "Don't forget couples therapy tomorrow." "Therapeutic" role playing, an adult version of playing house, and a kind of "play-within-a-film" device, becomes an important means of reinforcing the mother-daughter relationship between V. I. and Kat in *V. I. Warshawski*. These two characters frequently pretend to be or are mistaken for mother and daughter—the casting of Angela Goethals as Kat encourages the audience's identification of physical similarities between the two fair-haired actors. In one sequence, they use role playing to establish Murray's projected part as husband and father. V. I. and Kat discover Murray in bed with yet another woman, this time "a blonde." Joining forces in order to protect the integrity of the Murray-V. I.-Kat conventional nuclear family, they are in the process of constructing against the "other woman." V. I. and Kat pretend to be Murray's neglected wife and daughter, and shame the interloper into a quick exit.

The climax of *V. I. Warshawski,* which is set on a ship at Chicago's docks, involves the ultimate custody battle: a symbolic shootout between Paige the "bad mother" and V. I. the "good mother" that takes place over Kat's unconscious body, which is suspended in a lifeboat that suspiciously resembles a cradle. After having killed her second husband, Trumble, ostensibly to save Kat, Paige's final dramatic gesture is becoming (to cite yet another backlash film) "the hand that rocks the cradle" in the sinister sense that she presses the button that drops the damaged lifeboat in order, not to protect, but to kill her daughter. For this, according to the logic of the film, she must not only die, but die violently and spectacularly. Nancy Paul, the actor who plays Paige, is costumed in this scene in a shawl-collared coat with very large padded shoulders, an outfit in which 1940s' film *femmes fatales* like Barbara Stanwick or Joan Crawford would have been quite comfortable. As Jon Tuska writes, in the *films noirs* of the 1940s and '50s, the *femme fatale,* a powerful woman in possession of her own sexuality, "behaves as if she is independent of the patriarchal order. In the course of the film therefore, or at least by the end of it, the *femme fatale* must be punished for this attempt at independence, usually by her death, thus restoring the balance of the patriarchal system" (199). In the closing scenes of *V. I. Warshawski,* scenes that are shot in a distinctly *film noir* style, V. I. acts both as a protective mother and as the enforcing, retributive agent of the patriarchal system. In one of the few violent acts identified with V. I.'s point of view, she shoots Paige right between the eyes.

But we cannot read V. I. as simply a representative of the patriarchal order, since the film also seems to be responding to the challenge posed to that order by the role of the contemporary female hard-boiled detective as action hero. One form this response takes, oddly enough, is the "coding" of the detective herself according to the conventions of the cinematic *femme fatale.* As reviewer Manohia Dargis put it, Warshawski is "femmed up to box-office specs" (64)—and this is true both in the sense that she is painstakingly feminized as heterosexual and in the sense that she is *femme fatale*-d up too. The problematic conflation of *femme fatale* and detective is perhaps most absurdly developed in terms of costume when V. I. conducts the preliminary part of her investigation at the shipyard, clad in an elegant black evening dress, a dressing gown, and slippers: "I'm going to a formal slumber party," she tells curious onlookers. The outfit may be a symptom of the film's confusion about just how one dresses a woman detective for work at night within the limited iconography of the detective film genre.

Kathleen Turner is a particularly interesting casting choice for the role of V. I. Warshawski in light of the tradition of the *film noir:* she made a remarkable film debut as a 1940s' style *femme fatale* in Lawrence Kasdan's 1981 *film noir Body Heat,* and subsequently parodied such roles in the Disney cartoon *Who Framed Roger Rabbit?* as the sultry voice of *lapin fatale* Jessica Rabbit.[4] Sally Munt points out that the choice of Turner for the role "was a contentious one, deeply unsatisfactory to those readers of the novels who saw this as a 'sell out' to the screen imperative of glamourous femininity" (32). In *Murder by the Book?* Munt analyzes the ways Turner was represented in British advertisements that publicized her role in the radio adaptation of Paretsky's *Killing Orders.* Munt describes a photograph in a promotional article in the BBC *Radio Times,* and her assessment might well be extended to the representation of Turner in the American film:[5]

Face to camera, Turner sports a low-cut black dress, and highly decorative dark glasses, pulled down from her eyes. Rather than conceal the active gaze of the detective, the glasses have the effect of alluring the (masculine) viewer into a sexualized spectatorship, which is re-inforced by the direct linguistic address 'LOOK GUYS, I'VE NEVER DONE THIS BEFORE.' The role of the female investigator is located as new, naive, transgressive and *sexualized* (the virgin/whore binary is implicated and then collapsed within the same image). The symbolism of the dark glasses she wears shifts from impenetrability to availability, further suggesting impersonation, disguise, and artifice where before there was moral authenticity. (32)

Visual and verbal conventions associated with the *femme fatale* are one way of understanding the representation of violence against the woman detective as it has already been described here, though V. I. escapes the ultimate fate associated with the role because she is more or less "cured" of its most disruptive features by the end of the film, where the family relationship between V. I., Murray, and Kat has been cemented, with V. I. hovering behind an ambulance, apparently poised to nurse the other two back to health after their ordeal. Indeed, this conclusion solves the "female detective plot" by dis-solving the role of the female detective altogether. During the course of the story, V. I. has been teaching Kat the "rules of detection," and as Kat is ushered into the ambulance V. I. tells her the "*last* rule of detection," "never lose a friend," a line which seems to anticipate her outright abdication of the detective's role in favor of a personal relationship with Kat.

The classic *femme fatale* has often been analysed as a manifestation of anxieties about the masculine roles and social and financial power that accrued to women on the "home front" during World War II; in *V. I. Warshawski* the woman private eye embodies similar anxieties about the power of the independent, working woman produced by post-1970s' feminism. The visual representation of the *femme fatale* is also quite consistent with the conspicuous portrayal of V. I. as object of the erotic gaze, particularly the "*directed* glance" that focuses on spiked heels and silk stockings, as Janey Place has noted (45). *V. I. Warshawski* is littered with such shots of its heroine—the "foot fetish" of which Kat accuses V. I. (because of the latter's obsession with shoes) is, in fact, the camera's. Advertisements for *V. I. Warshawski* were accompanied by a caption that read, "Killer eyes. Killer legs. Killer instincts," embodying the deadly eroticism characteristic of the classic *femme fatale*. Mary Ann Doane interprets this threat in her assertion that the figure of the fatal woman "is not the subject of feminism, but a symptom of male fears about feminism" (2-3). Doane's distinction neatly articulates the difference between the V. I. Warshawski of Paretsky's novels (the subject of feminism) and the character as she is transformed by the film (a symptom of male fears about feminism).

Indeed, several reviewers noted an atmosphere of sexual anxiety around the character's portrayal. For example, the *New York Post* reviewer commented "There are saccharine moments that don't really match Vic's character, as if the director or the screenwriters (one of them credited, none of whom include author Paretsky) were too frightened of their material" (Bernard 31). *The Village Voice* also perceived its manifestation of fear (Dargis 64), as did Paretsky herself. Asked what she thought of the film adaptation, Paretsky responded,

They [Disney studios] were scared: having bought the character they were then scared to put her on screen and so they did a lot of silly things like . . . they don't want people to think she's a dyke, so she's in a bar picking up guys. They don't want people to think she's a tough unfeeling broad, so she picks up a thirteen year old kid that she can nurture . . . and the story was kind of silly. (Gzowski interview)

The sexual nature of the threat Paretsky's character posed in the eyes of *V. I. Warshawski*'s producers is epitomized in the film by V. I.'s use of a pornographic nutcracker in the shape of a woman's body as an instrument of torture with which she extracts information from a suspect. Her character literally becomes a "ball breaker." In the final line of the film, the device is turned to less menacing and more socially integrative ends: she threatens to use it to enforce Murray's fidelity, joking, "Have you ever seen what I can do with a nutcracker?" If the nutcracker or the *femme fatale*'s appropriation of the phallic gun weren't obvious enough images of the castrating woman, V. I. foils her pursuers at one point with a borrowed fire hose, whose impressed owner comments, "She can handle my hose anytime." As *The Village Voice*'s film critic remarked, "You don't need to know Paretsky has a lesbian following to smell nervous compensation here—just follow the string of limp gags about sausages, hoses, dicks and nuts" (Dargis 64). The conflation of female detective and *femme fatale* configures a sexual energy that threatens to exceed patriarchal control and containment within the heterosexual economy.

One way of containing the potentially destructive sexual energy of the *femme fatale* is to represent it as a commodity in an economy controlled by male desire: in this case, to see the professional woman as a form of prostitute. One review, in fact, compared *V. I. Warshawski* to another recent hit, Gary Marshall's prostitution fable, *Pretty Woman* (James H7). At the same time as Kanew's film markets motherhood, it offers a counter-motif of prostitution, conveying the point that women's work outside the home is akin to sexual immorality. The pattern is first developed when the bar in which V. I. meets Boom Boom is referred to by Murray as a "meat/meet market." It is no coincidence, then, that V. I.'s first client in the film is a meat packer, and we later learn that she turns down the case because he offered her "$5,000 a week to look after his sausage." When V. I. must make a quick change of clothes in the back of a taxi, the audience is shown a closeup of the cabbie's fascinated eyes in the rear view mirror. Noticing his gaze, V. I. responds by saying, "Consider that your tip." Once again, the male gaze is not only fore-grounded, but thematized, and its object is seen as a consumer product. V. I.'s promised trade of information about the Grafalk family with Murray is likened to an exchange of sexual favors, and when V. I. doesn't "come across" with her half of the bargain, she gloats to Murray that "You always did suffer from premature articulation." This kind of humor is a sexualization of the hard-boiled private eye's wisecracking style, one that, as Dargis intimates, symptomizes a profound uneasiness with representing women's sexuality, and, further, conflates agency with sexual threat. At a metafictional level, such remarks are also a (perhaps unconscious) way of representing the film actress as another kind of prostituted working woman, whose performance allows her to benefit economically from, but ensures that she be subordinate to a mode of production and reception governed by male desire.

The working woman most notably absent from the production of *V. I. Warshawski* is, of course, the novelist herself, Sara Paretsky. The film was written by an all male script committee (Edward Taylor, David Aaron Cohen, Nick Thiel). Lizzie Francke documents the degree to which women writers were and continue to be under-represented in Hollywood. Mainstream film's conventional wisdom, she argues, dictates that the popular action-adventure genre is the indisputable domain of male scriptwriters—a notion that was disproven the same year as *V. I. Warshawski* was released by Callie Khouri's Academy Award-winning script for the highly successful female action-buddy film *Thelma and Louise*.[6] It is interesting to note that Sue Grafton, another highly success-ful woman detective novelist who began her career as a Hollywood screen writer has commented that she will sell the rights to her character Kinsey Millhone, "the day I sell my children into white slavery" (quoted in Max, "Warshawki's Mysterious Journey" 71), but the economic bene-fits of a Hollywood career had afforded Grafton the luxury of that choice. Paretsky's explanation of her decision to sell the rights to her character is, notably, an economic one: she has argued that the initial sale allowed her quit her day job in order to pursue a career as a full time professional writer (Gzowski interview). She has, however, been notably circumspect about her response to the film, and it appears she was given little opportunity to participate in its production. According to press reports, Kathleen Turner attempted by onset agitation, to sustain the political trajectory of Paretsky's project during the film's production.[7] Her work on *V. I. Warshawski* might be seen as one point of resistance, both because her star status allowed her some measure of control and prestige, and because the energy of her performance seems to exceed the limitations of the script. As entertainment journalist Daniel Max recounts, "Paretsky says she is 'tempted to get more involved next time.' Then, recalling that Disney only remembered to invite her to LA for the opening two weeks before the event, she has second thoughts about whether a heroine tough enough for the Windy City could hold her own in Marlowe's backyard" ("Warshawski's Mysterious Journey" 71). Obviously, the transition from Chicago to Hollywood is a matter of institutional and ideological turf that involves differences between the publishing and film industries. There is, given the film's reception, unlikely to be a "next time," though the studio's original plan seems to have been to take advantage of the success of the phenomenon of the serial novel and make a series of V. I. Warshawski films. Kanew's *V. I. Warshawski* is an object lesson in the problematic translation of a feminist "private eye" from novel to the Hollywood screen, in the difficulty of attracting a female audience while constructing a normative, eroticised, male-identified spectatorship, and in the contradictions involved in creating a women's "action film" without inscribing a position for female agency.[8]

Notes

1. See also *Newsweek* magazine's pronouncement in 1990 that "In the booming mystery market, books by and about women are hot—with men readers as well as women" (Ames 66), or B. Ruby Rich's statement in an article titled "The Lady Dicks" in *The Village Voice Literary Supplement:*

The news is that a serious reinvention of the detective genre is under way, with a publishing boom to match.
And women know it. Women's and gay bookstores, from Old Wives' Tales in San Francisco to the new Judith's Room in Greenwich Village, report that woman-detective novels are walking out the door as fast as they arrive on the shelves. In Queens, Jackson Heights Discount Book Store has even set aside a separate room for them. (24)

Dutton editor Carole Di Santi remarks of the publishing industry's role as a proving ground, "You can try a lot more things in publishing. . . . And it's not necessarily because we are nice people or we're progressive or we're feminists or we're gay friendly, not at all. It's not about that. It's about our, you know, weak or fairly modest outlay of capital can explore new areas. That's why we are sort of the seeding ground of the entertainment industry and a lot of things spin off from our forays into it. And, you know, we're like a talent scout, really" (Walton interview).

2. Kanew had directed such features as *Black Rodeo* (1972), *Natural Enemies* (1979), *Eddie Macon's Run* (1983), *Revenge of the Nerds* (1984), *Gotcha!* (1985), *Tough Guys* (1986), and *Troop Beverly Hills* (1989).

3. The figure, from a Quigley poll of U.S. theatre owners, is quoted in Francke (98). Francke also cites a 1990 Screen Actors Guild report that stated that men had nearly 71 per cent of all feature film acting roles, and a statement by Meryl Streep, who responded "If the trend continues . . . by the year 2010 we may be eliminated from the movies altogether" (98).

4. Turner has played other roles that re-interpret gender roles too: In 1985 she portrayed a Mafia "hit-woman" in John Huston's *Prizzi's Honor*, and in 1988 she appeared in *Switching Channels*, reproducing the strong-minded "newspaper man" role played by Rosalind Russell in *His Girl Friday* (1940), which was itself a gender-reversed re-interpretation of the male reporter in *The Front Page* (1931).

5. Munt offers an insightful analysis, but she is nominally engaged in a discussion of Paretsky's fiction, and her argument makes the fundamental error of conflating the BBC promotional article's presentation of Turner with Paretsky's presentation of Warshawski in her novels, a conflation which elides the very differences in medium, authorship, production, and audience that are of interest to me here.

6. Lizzie Francke cites Los Angeles literary agent Bettye McCartt's comment: "When we get a call [from a producer] for a writer, they'll say, 'Who do you have who can write an action adventure piece?' If I suggest a woman, well, they laugh at me. There are certain genres where a woman won't even be considered" (103).

7. Paretsky says of Turner's role, "Kathleen brought a lot of energy to the role and she was very committed to the character and I'm very grateful to her for that" (Gzowski interview).

8. There is, however, some wisdom in the notion that even bad publicity is publicity. Paretsky's publisher comments that "*Warshawski* may have been a bomb, but the effect was that we have 800,000 copies in print of Sara Paretsky's new paperback, as against 400,000 of the last one. The movie made Warshawski a name people knew" (Max, "La Plante" 79).

Acknowledgments

I would like to acknowledge the financial support of the Social Sciences and Humanities Research Council of Canada. This paper began as a guest lecture for an undergraduate seminar led by Dr. Priscilla Walton at Carleton University. Since then, Professor Walton and I have further shared our enthusiasm for women's detective fiction in a forthcoming collaborative book, *Detective Agency: Women Rewriting the Hard-Boiled Tradition.* I am deeply indebted to Priscilla Walton for her friendship and intellectual generosity. The paper that resulted from my original lecture for her class is part of *Detective Agency's* final chapter; this article is an extended version of the argument offered in that study. I would also like to thank my graduate research assistants on the project, Jason Kuzminsky and Andrew Fieldsend.

Works Cited

Ames, Katrine, and Ray Sawhill. "Murder Most Foul and Fair." *Newsweek* 14 May 1990: 66-67.

Anthony, Carolyn. "Mystery Books: Crime Marches On." *Publishers Weekly* 237.15 (13 Apr. 1990): 24-29.

Christianson, Scott. "Talkin' Trash and Kickin' Butt: Sue Grafton's Hard-boiled Feminism." *Feminism in Women's Detective Fiction.* Ed. Glenwood Irons. Toronto: University of Toronto Press, 1995. 127-47.

Corliss, Richard. Review of *V. I. Warshawski. Time* 8 May 1991: 66.

Dargis, Manohia. Review of *V. I. Warshawski. The Village Voice* 36 (6 Aug. 1991): 64.

Doane, Mary Ann. *Femmes Fatales: Feminism, Film Theory, Psychoanalysis.* New York: Routledge, 1991.

Faludi, Susan. *Backlash: The Undeclared War Against American Women.* New York: Doubleday, 1991.

Francke, Lizzie. *Script Girls: Women Screenwriters in Hollywood.* London: British Film Institute, 1994.

Gzowski, Peter. Interview with Sara Paretsky. *CBC Radio: Morningside.* 27 Mar. 1992.

Irons, Glenwood. "Introduction: Gender and Genre: The Woman Detective and the Diffusion of Generic Voices." *Feminism in Women's Detective Fiction.* Ed. Glenwood Irons. Toronto: University of Toronto Press, 1995. ix-xxiv.

James, Caryn. "These Heels Aren't Made for Stompin.'" *New York Times* 4 Aug. 1991: H7.

Klein, Kathleen Gregory. *The Woman Detective: Gender & Genre.* Urbana and Chicago: University of Illinois Press, 1988.

Maio, Kathi. *Popcorn and Sexual Politics: Movie Reviews by Kathi Maio*. Freedom, CA: Crossing P, 1991.

Max, Daniel. "La Plante in Her 'Prime:' The Creator of TV's 'Prime Suspect' Mysteries Is on a Roll." *Variety* 8 Mar. 1993: 79.

——. "'Warshawski's' Mysterious Journey: How the Tough-gal Private Eye Got the Shakers Moving in Hollywood." *Variety* 22 June 1991: 71.

Mulvey, Laura. "Visual Pleasure and Narrative Cinema." *Screen* 16.3 (1975): 6-18.

Munt, Sally. *Murder by the Book? Feminism and the Crime Novel*. New York: Routledge, 1994.

Place, Janey. "Women in Film Noir." *Women in Film Noir*. Ed. E. Ann Kaplan. London: British Film Institute, 1978. 35-67.

Reddy, Maureen T. "The Feminist Counter-Tradition in Crime: Cross, Grafton, Paretsky, and Wilson." *The Cunning Craft: Original Essays on Detective Fiction and Contemporary Literary Theory*. Ed. Ronald G. Walker and June M. Frazer. Macomb, IL: Western Illinois University, 1990. 174-87.

Rich, B. Ruby. "The Lady Dicks: Genre Benders Take the Case." *The Village Voice Literary Supplement* June 1989: 24-27.

Silverman, Kaja. "Dis-Embodying the Female Voice." *Re-Vision: Essays in Feminist Film Criticism*. Ed. Mary Ann Doane, Patricia Mellencamp, and Linda Williams. Los Angeles: American Film Institute, 1984. 131-49.

Turan, Kenneth. Review of *V. I. Warshawski*. *Los Angeles Times* 26 July 1991: Calendar, 1.

Tuska, Jon. *Dark Cinema: American Film Noir in Cultural Perspective*. Westport, CT: Greenwood Press, 1984.

V. I. Warshawski. Dir. Jeff Kanew. With Kathleen Turner. A Buena Vista release of a Hollywood Pictures presentation in association with Silver Screen Partners IV of a Jeffrey Lurie and Chestnut Hill production, 1991.

Walton, Priscilla L. Telephone interview with Carole Di Santi. 15 Apr. 1996.

——. "Paretsky's V. I. as PI: Revising the Script and Recasting the Dick." *LIT* 4 (1993): 203-13.

Wolf, William. "USA." *Variety International Film Guide 1992*. Ed. Peter Corvie. London: Andre Deutsch; Hollywood: Samuel French, 1992. 358-76.

RACISM, SEXISM, AND ANTISEMITISM
IN MYSTERIES FEATURING WOMEN SLEUTHS

Frances A. Della Cava and Madeline H. Engel

As more and more women achieve prominence in mystery fiction, both as writers and main characters,[1] a growing concern about social issues has begun to permeate the literature; "humanistic crime fiction" has come to the fore. This subgenre "incorporates in-depth characterization with plot realism and social commentary with detection." While not limited to books by women, Marcia Muller argues that "this type of novel has become more visible because of the large influx of women into the field" ("In the Tradition" 157). Jon Breen also sees contemporary mystery writers as freer to deal with a variety of themes than were their predecessors. He notes:

[T]oday's writers, aside from the somewhat exaggerated specter of "political correctness," can deal with just about any subject matter and any point of view in a mystery novel and can seriously explore social issues and subcultures that a writer of the thirties would never have dreamed of addressing. (5)

However, Breen does not view this freedom in an entirely positive light. He goes on to say:

[Some] writers who have been associated with the crime and mystery genre from the beginning of their careers have tended to downplay [the mystery] elements in their works, *stinting* on plot while using the mystery as an *excuse* for social observation. . . . (5, emphasis added)

Regardless of whether or not one agrees with Breen's interpretation, a detailed analysis of the novels featuring women as amateur or professional detectives makes clear that the authors have moved beyond the narrow "whodunit" questions of past fiction to become social commentators and social critics. Although several of the social problems touched upon might be defined as "women's issues"—i.e., child abuse,[2] domestic violence,[3] prostitution,[4] abortion[5]—others affect a broad spectrum of the United States' population. These include alcoholism and the abuse of other substances,[6] driving while intoxicated,[7] homelessness,[8] AIDS,[9] homophobia,[10] as well as conservation and other environmental concerns.[11]

Research Method

To assess the extent to which such issues have become important elements in mysteries featuring American women as professional or amateur sleuths, we have reviewed over 800 mystery novels in more than 205 series. Although a few date back to the late 1800s, 80 percent of these series have been created since 1980. This essay is based upon a content analysis of relevant books among those reviewed. No claim is made concerning the randomness of the sample.

Antiminority Sentiment

Among the seemingly endless litany of social problems encountered in contemporary mystery fiction, one set of issues stands out because of its prevalence. Antiminority sentiments, including racism, sexism, and antiSemitism, recur in books featuring female sleuths. Evidence of these sentiments is found in: (1) stereotypical descriptions of non-whites, women and Jews; (2) expressions of prejudice towards these groups; and/or (3) discriminatory behavior directed against them, especially in employment. An analysis of series published in the past 20 years reveals three patterns in the way these themes are depicted.

In some the issues are no more than the subject of incidental commentary, while in others the themes are more pronounced in that they affect the racial, religious, or gender group with which the sleuth identifies. In a third set of novels antiminority sentiment is a major plot element crucial to the mystery.

Incidental Commentary

Throughout the dialogue in mysteries, slurs against minorities are common. In several novels antiminority sentiment is alluded to or commented on, but receives minimal attention and plays no role in the development of the plot. In Julie Smith's Skip Langdon series, antiSemitic remarks are made in her family's New Orleans home. In one of Michael Kahn's novels, the heroine's Jewish colleague is blocked in his bid to become a partner in the Chicago law firm that employs them. In her role as narrator, the heroine comments that the men in the firm would "shudder at the prospect of introducing [him] to a client as 'my partner, Ben Goldberg.'" Mr. Goldberg describes the situation more graphically: "[They'd] rather be proctoscoped with an electric cattle prod than have me as a partner" (45). Jews fare no better in the staid New England community which provides the setting for Charlotte MacLeod's Kelling and

Bittersohn series. In an early novel her amateur detective's fiancé is referred to as "that Jew-boy," his uncle is termed "a shyster," and when one of the townspeople discovers that the fiancé is staying at the detective's boarding house, he calls the guests a "bunch of God-knows-whats all over the place" (189, 27).

Racial minorities are met with similar antagonism. In a book by Robert Nordan one of the characters chooses to "pass" as white rather than continue to suffer the indignities she has met when her black heritage is known. Despite the 1960s' civil rights movement and her own accomplishments—graduating from a northern college with honors—she feels she has to lie to further her career and so she checks "white" whenever a potential employer asks about her race (146-47). Both the lies and the fear of their discovery weigh heavily on the woman's psyche, but she sees them as necessary if she is to succeed socio-economically.

Racism is also apparent in Wendy Hornsby's mystery involving a federal housing project about which her character is making a film documentary, and in P. M. Carlson's *Gravestone* in which the activities of the Ku Klux Klan are described (189).

Reactions to the Group with Which the Sleuth Identifies

The past two decades reveal an increasing focus on minorities in the mystery genre. A small but growing percentage of the new female sleuths are members of ethno-racial minority groups—African Americans or black Americans, Hispanic Americans or Latinas, Native Americans, and Asian Americans. In part this new trend reflects the emergence within the mainstream press of minority authors, such as Eleanor Taylor Bland, Barbara Neely, Nikki Baker, Soledad Santiago, and Carolina Garcia-Aguilera. This new focus also is reflected in the attention paid to minority issues and characters by white authors. This may be merely an effort to be politically correct. But one should not discount the rising affluence of minorities and the likelihood that they may become a significant element among potential readers as a factor in this trend. Since people often enjoy reading about characters with whom they can identify, the rise of the minority sleuth is to be expected.

In both Jean Hager's Molly Bearpaw and Dana Stabenow's Kate Shugak series, racist slurs aimed at Native Americans and discrimination against tribal peoples are common occurrences. In neither series is the protagonist herself a target, but her tribe certainly is. The authors suggest that discrimination results in poverty, unemployment, crime, suicide, mental illness, substance abuse, fetal alcohol syndrome, and a variety of other social ills among Native Americans. A parallel theme is the depiction of white characters as money-hungry racists seeking to cheat the tribes out of their lands in order to profit from natural resources or sacred artifacts.

Even when a sleuth's biological connection with a minority group is minimal, she may identify with it. At first the reader's only clue to the ethnic identity of Muller's sleuth, Sharon McCone, is her objection when her lover calls her "papoose" (*Edwin* 180, 184). Many years and several books later, McCone becomes angered when a Latina colleague declares that McCone could not possibly understand the hardships she and her family have faced. The P.I.'s reply suggests that she now not only identifies with her Shoshone ancestry rather than her European roots, but the former also has taken on greater meaning for her:

"How do you know I've had it so easy? You don't know anything about me— haven't even bothered to ask. I haven't experienced as much hardship as you, but my life hasn't been so wonderful, either. Especially not when it comes to prejudice. You may have noticed, although you've never remarked on it, that I have Indian blood—I'm one-eighth Shoshone. Bigots don't like half-breeds—or eighth breeds." (*Wolf* 67)

In this later work not only has McCone's self-concept changed, but so have the characteristics of her colleagues. For many years the staff had been all white and presumably straight; now it includes new characters—a Latino, an Asian American, and a black American. In addition, one continuing character is now openly gay. The redefinition of self by the sleuth and the changing composition of the office staff lend support to the idea that authors of mystery fiction are paying increasing attention to minority status.

While racism still affects only a few of the featured characters under study, many of the employed fictional sleuths find gender stereotyping and discrimination by colleagues, supervisors at work, and the general public an almost daily occurrence. Hess's protagonist in the Maggody series is initially treated by a coworker as "a silly girl playing police officer;" it is not until he recognizes her as a "functional professional" that they can work together (92). In Kahn's series the attorney sleuth is referred to frequently as a girl, albeit a beautiful one, which presumably is more flattering than being called a silly one:

I was twenty-nine years old, a member of the Illinois bar, and the veteran of more than a dozen federal and state jury trials and appellate arguments. To [the partners in the firm I worked for], I was still a *girl*. (16, emphasis added)

Other fictional characters face more serious discrimination. The deputy sheriff who is the heroine of one of P. M. Carlson's series labors under the protection of her superior because she is his old friend's "little girl." He assigns her only to cases that seem simple and safe: "Five years in this department and here came another kindergarten job. The token woman. The lady cop. She sighed. Get serious, . . . , you know what the world's like" (7). The deputy does not get her chance to deal with a major case until the sheriff is hospitalized unexpectedly.

The motives of other commanding officers are less pure. Susan Dunlap's Jill Smith only gets assigned to assistant field commander's work when it means tedious work and possibly bad publicity (109). The glass ceiling is clearly operant and she is "kept in her place" even in as liberal a community as Berkeley, California. One result of this sexism is that Smith will not admit to women's intuition, fearing criticism. So she is left to ponder: "Should I square my shoulders, adopt a manly voice, and call it playing a hunch?" (31).

Barbara Paul's protagonist, a police sergeant, finds both her commander and partner patronizing and unwilling to accept her professionally. She considers resigning from the New York Police Department when she is skipped over for promotion largely because her captain— whose own work is shoddy—refuses to recommend her for the position of lieutenant. She is warned by a friend, a former CIA agent, who is trying to get her to become his partner in a private detective agency, that the New York Police Department (NYPD) is not an affirmative action agency:

"Walk away or you'll spend the rest of your life watching men who are less able and less intelligent than you being promoted over you. The NYPD doesn't want you in a lieutenant's office—not someone who had the effrontery to get herself born a woman. . . ."

That struck home. Getting passed over had not been an easy pill to swallow; despite her high score on the rarely given lieutenant's exam, [she] had watched the only opening go to a man with an equivalent score but fewer years served on the force. It was an inequity that rankled all the more because she was powerless to do anything about it. (68)

In the first novel in L. V. Sims' series, the female police sergeant faces a sexist boss and colleagues who do not believe that she is capable of handling her job. But she, the daughter and grand-daughter of Irish policemen, is determined to prove herself the equal of the men she works with on the San Jose, California, police force. Her partner quickly comes to recognize her competence; other colleagues are slower to do so, but their harassment of her slowly subsides.

New York City homicide detective Norah Mulcahaney, created by Lillian O'Donnell, is also familiar with resentment toward women on the force. She often sensed it when she "walked into a strange squad room and introduced herself to a police officer" (*Pushover* 100). Almost all of her first year on the force was spent doing routine chores such as matron duty and the clerical work usually associated with women's roles. More than a decade later Mulcahaney says, "it still wasn't easy [for a woman] to be accepted on the basis of ability" (*Pushover* 106). And she is one of the more fortunate women on the force as her late husband's friend, her commanding officer, continues to foster her career. He consistently "got her the good assignments and covered her rear in case of a foul-up" (44). In essence he provides her with the mentoring, friendship, and networking that most women lack. But the reader is never sure whether he does so out of respect for her husband who died in the line of duty or out of respect for her competence.

One of O'Donnell's books specifically focuses on women police officers. *No Business Being a Cop* describes rampant stereotyping and discrimination against policewomen, and the toll these take on their psyches, self-esteem, morale, and job performance. For example, when Mulcahaney tries to enter the scene of the murder of a policewoman, the sergeant, "responding to his inbred instinct that a woman should be protected . . . , stepped into her way" (8). Though she realizes he is trying to spare her the particularly gruesome sight, Mulcahaney pushes forward and says to him: "It's part of the job." In acting this way, she senses:

He didn't like her answer and, [Mulcahaney] suddenly realized, he didn't like her either .... Policewomen had not gained the acceptance in the department that the public thought they had. Discrimination was still practiced subtly and sometimes not so subtly. (9)

In trying to figure out how the victim had gotten to the spot where she died, an interview with the deceased officer's partner reminds Mulcahaney once again of the plight of policewomen:

[He] grimaced. The whole two hundred pounds of him quivered. "I sent . . . [her] to check the dressing rooms. I figured if there were any ladies still in there. . . ." *Matron duty,* [Mulcahaney] thought, that's what it amounted to. Would the women ever shake loose of it? (11)

O'Donnell's series began in 1972 and in *No Business Being a Cop,* published in 1979, Mulcahaney reflects the views of real women who had already "come of age" in the 1970s. They had made their way as individuals in the work place, achieving as a result of their own diligence and ability. Mulcahaney pondered the continued conflict between men's and women's attitudes about women who had "made it" on the police force:

> She thought that the women in the police department had definitely come a long way. [The captain's] . . . attitude clearly indicated that the rights the women thought they'd won on merit and hard work, standing there beside the men, working the same hours, taking the same risks, were rights not earned but conferred. Conferred by the grace and favor of the men. (71)

Despite having risen to the rank of lieutenant after ten years on the force, Mulcahaney still faced sexism on the job, and though less blatant it was no less problematic. As recently as 1994, prejudicial attitudes remained common at the station house and she received harassing telephone calls at home. In one the caller used a muffled, disguised voice to warn her: "You're not wanted. You don't belong. Resign while you still can" (*Lockout* 54).

Several other professionally employed female law enforcement agents also face sexism on the job. Eleanor Taylor Bland's police detective in Lincoln Prairie, Illinois, J. J. Jance's Cochise County Arizona sheriff, Ruby Horansky's police detective in Brooklyn, New York, Charlene Weir's police chief in Hampstead, Kansas, and Nancy Herndon's police officer in the Crimes Against Person Department of Los Santos, Texas, come to mind as illustrations of the fact that women in the rest of the country fare no better than Mulcahaney does in New York City.

Situations in which women professional sleuths come into contact with people other than supervisors and colleagues are no less fraught with stereotypes. When Muller's P.I. chases a thug in her first case, he says to her: "I don't like being badgered by little girls playing detective" (*Edwin* 109). When Trocheck's sleuth is interviewing a man about a murder she is investigating, he questions her about her work: "Then he wanted to know how a nice girl like me got into something as seedy as private investigation" (*To Live* 142). A potential client reacts to Dain's heroine being a private eye: "Really? A girl like you? I mean, you're a big girl, and you look like you could take care of yourself, but . . ." (13). The male client is extremely reluctant to acknowledge that she might be a competent investigator and bodyguard. The idea of a woman protecting a man is initially too much of a role reversal for him to deal with.

People also stereotype women by casting them in traditional roles. Hess's police chief is mistaken by a "baby faced" doctor for a juvenile suspect's mother when she comes to question the youth in the hospital

(170). Similarly, Martin's police officer is mistaken for a secretary by a victim's wife who exclaims, "I don't want to talk to a secretary, I want to talk to a *cop*" (25). This incident suggests women are not necessarily less sexist than men in their preconceptions. The point is made again when Maron's leading character is addressed as "Judge honey" by the elderly aunt of a defendant (*Southern* 40).

In other situations townspeople clearly object to a woman holding a position of authority on the police force. The chiefs of police in both the Hess and Weir series find themselves criticized and ridiculed by towns-people and city officials. In one case the critics include the town's mayor (Hess 92).

Major Plot Element

As is obvious from the preceding pages, the trend of incorporating current social issues into the genre of women detective fiction has been observed for at least 20 years. In the past these social issues were periph-eral to the mystery; more recently they have become the major plot ele-ment. This occurs because fiction often draws on the real world for its characterizations and situations. Issues of care of the elderly, homeless-ness, addiction, child abuse, racism, sexism, and antiSemitism are major crises in modern society. Thus contemporary writers are paying consid-erable attention to these themes. What follows is an analysis of two works in which current social problems take center stage, one dealing with racism and the other with antiSemitism.[12]

Gillian Roberts, herself a former English teacher in Philadelphia, has created the protagonist Amanda Pepper in her own image: Pepper teaches English in Philly Prep, an exclusive private high school in the "City of Brotherly Love." In a recent volume in this series, racism rears its ugly head. The following major events unfold: the death of a young Vietnamese boy, the harassment of an extremely competent black faculty member, and the near-death attack on a young white student because of his involvement with a female Vietnamese student. These acts are com-mitted by members of a clandestine association called WAPA—White Alliance to Preserve America—to which Philly Prep students have been recruited by a white male instructor hired to teach in a special summer program.

Roberts masterfully builds to these major events. Initially, subtle comments and situations reveal the racist undertones of the plot. In a verbal confrontation, a white teacher attacks a black teacher for her use of the term "handicapped" rather than "physically challenged" to describe a student who has cerebral palsy. The dialogue unfolds:

"Oh you!" [the white teacher] said. "You'd think you of all people would show a little sensitivity to the power of language. If we stopped stigmatizing exceptional people through the violence of our syntax. . . ."

"[W]hy me of all people? Were you trying to say that I'm black? Well, hey, I'm aware of that," [the black teacher said]. (21)

That life in the City of Brotherly Love is not so loving is also conveyed by the musing of the heroine after viewing a park scene on a beautiful summer day: there are slow-moving elderly women, young students sitting on the fountain's edge—chattering and dipping their feet in the cool water, three children—one white, one olive-complexioned, and one "the color of smoke" with dreadlocks—playing frisbee together, and a nanny caring for a little Asian boy. Pepper thinks: "*Reader's Digest* would make a cunning anecdote out of this sliver of Americana. Except the reason the sight had so impressed me was because it was rare. It was how it was supposed to be, more or less, but not how it was" (35).

The illusionary nature of the moment is soon very clear—shortly after the heroine returns to her classroom, one of the most violent incidents depicted in the book occurs when a young Vietnamese boy is killed outside of Philly Prep. It is not immediately tied to the school since he is not a student there and the killing is thought to be a random act, a drive-by shooting (38).

At the school racism increases in intensity from words to action. Flora Jones, the black computer science teacher, reveals to Pepper that she has been the target of racial harassment. The first attack is only one of words: one of the milder hate messages on her answering machine tells the Cincinnati-born woman to return to Africa (35).

As in real life, the acts of violence against Jones escalate from threats to physical attack. It is not her person that is attacked, but her space—her office is desecrated, her equipment dirtied, and *M-U-D!* is written on her blackboard. The word, she says, is used by "the crazies [who] call people like me and Asians and anybody who doesn't have their gray skin—they call us the mud people" (71).

Not only are members of the minority communities themselves the targets of attack but, in the book as in American society today, persons who associate with the minorities are also attacked. The heroine finds a note in her faculty mail box warning her against her friendship with Jones:

STOP LOVING MUD PEOPLE OR ARE YOU ONE TOO, A JEW? YOUR KIND HAS TO GO, NO MORE NIGGERS AND GOOKS. NO MORE WARNINGS. (106)

Such guilt by association does not stop at warnings. One of the most violent attacks is perpetrated against the young white male student, Woody, who was recruited into WAPA. Because of his friendship with the Vietnamese student, April, he reconsiders his membership and tries to drop out. But no one is allowed to leave. As an example to others, Woody is literally crucified—nailed to the basketball backboard in the school gym. Fortunately, Pepper and her policeman friend come upon the scene and cut Woody down in time to save his life. The hideousness of the action overwhelms the paramedics who have been called to the scene. One of them, a Latino, recognizes the letters that have been carved into Woody's skin—WAPA. "Vicious lunatic white supremacists. But what in God's name do they want with him? The boy looks to be or have been, at least, precisely what they so horribly want to preserve" (150). And what justification do such racists give? The teacher/organizer of WAPA at Philly Prep makes clear their rationale:

"[W]e're nothing more than patriots, good solid Americans trying to make this a better place. . . . Like it or not this country was founded by revolutionaries, and revolutionaries will save it. . . . [Save it] from pollution—disintegration—mongrelization. A complete loss of identity." (194)

The racism in this book highlights the way in which prejudice—negative *attitudes*—gets translated into discrimination—*actions* against the minority. But prejudice has other consequences for the minority. It sometimes results in minority group members turning against their own people or rejecting the ethnic, racial, or religious status that makes them the target of such negativism.

A second novel, *Angel of Death* by Rochelle Majer Krich, has anti-Semitism as its main focus. It is a very complicated plot, depicting malicious acts and interweaving these with reactions from Jews which either harm them personally or others of their group. Another response to anti-Semitism on the part of Jews is their rejection of their own ethnic heritage.

The mystery begins with a common hate crime—a Star of David painted in red, along with a note pinned on the door of a prominent Jewish attorney. The note said: "The Angel of Death spared your forefathers—will he spare you?" (5).

The reason for this message is that the lawyer, Barry Lewis, is defending the right of the white supremacist group, White Alliance, to parade through Jewish neighborhoods on Hitler's birthday. His rationale: "[T]he First Amendment guarantees my client a right to conduct that parade . . . and I'm committed to seeing that those rights aren't violated.

Sometimes you have to defend your enemy to ultimately protect your-self" (9). Lewis is interested in protecting the rights of all, even those who are antiSemitic, in order to ensure his own right to speak out against the bigotry and hatred directed at him and other Jews.

AntiSemitism is often subtle. Immediately one wonders what other pressures operate on Lewis to take this case. It is unclear whether the American Civil Liberties Union (ACLU) asked him to take the parade case or he insisted that it be assigned to him. Later, when a member of the Alliance is charged with an assault on an elderly Jewish woman during the parade, Lewis's firm is approached by the Alliance to take the case and to assign Lewis to it. How likely is it that the firm would have pressured a nonJew to take a case in which the defendant is accused of attacking a member of the attorney's own ethnic, racial, or religious group? Is this another form of antiSemitism? When Lewis argues he cannot "zealously defend . . . and do his case justice," the partner inti-mates that he is to do so or risk his future with the firm: "I wouldn't ask you to do anything that you found morally abhorrent. But I think that after . . . evaluating all the factors, you'll be able to make the right choice" (145-46).

The widespread hostile attitude toward Jews also is evident in this work. Jessica Drake, the homicide lieutenant assigned to the case, becomes more aware of it when several of her colleagues question the veracity of the Holocaust. In fact, her love affair with a fellow police officer begins to unravel when he expresses his agreement with these colleagues: "How do we know there really *was* a Holocaust? . . . [T]here was a war, and Jews died. So did lots of other people. That's what hap-pens in wars. But six million Jews? . . . Sounds exaggerated to me" (154).

But the essence of this work is the way in which antiSemitism neg-atively affects the behavior of Jews themselves. Not all Jews believe it is their *personal* obligation to protect the rights of those who would harm them. Lewis becomes the target of retribution in the form of telephone calls and letters from many Jewish groups and individuals. Then the most violent of all acts occurs: Barry Lewis is murdered. Since many Jewish groups have been involved in the harassment of Lewis, some of their organizers become possible suspects. The police find the killer, a Jew. He is an ordinary man who became unhinged after his mother, the assault victim at the parade, died. Without the hatred and prejudice against Jews fueled by antiSemitic groups, this murder of one Jew by another would not have been committed.

Another element of the Jewish response to antiSemitism is woven into the plot: the issue of the denial of one's Jewish identity. Here the focus is the detective herself. The crisis is Drake's need to come to grips with her newly discovered Jewishness in the face of her mother's denial of her heritage. The mother is unwilling to acknowledge that she has Jewish relatives and is negative toward things Jewish. Drake exclaims:

"You have this look of distaste whenever you see someone wearing a skullcap or Hasidic clothing. . . . You say things like 'This is America' or 'Why can't they look like everybody else?' You don't say the same thing when you see Sikhs or Hare Krishnas or other people who dress differently." (218)

Her mother reveals to her that Drake is Jewish; that her mother's family perished in the Holocaust, having left their youngest daughter in the care of a Christian family in Poland. Drake's comment that she would have liked to have known that she was half-Jewish elicits this response from her mother: "You are what you choose to be, Jessica. I'm perfectly happy with the life I've chosen. I have no regrets, no guilt" (227).

This issue is complicated by the fact that Drake's former husband, with whom she is re-establishing a relationship, is Jewish. She reflects back on why her mother was so relieved when his family had not insisted that the couple be married by a rabbi. These revelations leave her confused. All of a sudden, she is Jewish, not Episcopalian.

"Is being Jewish genetic or spiritual . . . ? There's something about Judaism that appeals to me. I want to explore that feeling. My mom wants to go on as if nothing's changed. So does [my sister]. But everything *has* changed." (319)

Krich attacks the issue of antiSemitism on many levels. The bigotry of others toward Jews, the "issue of liberty versus license,"[13] and, perhaps most interesting, the degree to which antiSemitism engenders attacks on Jews by Jews. Also explored is the crisis of identity that many face when confronted with their Jewish heritage.[14] All are crucial to the plot, even though the last is not relevant to the mystery *per se* or its solution.

The Sleuths' Viewpoints

No matter how prominent or insignificant antiminority sentiment is as a theme, the stands taken by female sleuths are almost universally liberal and politically correct. Nowhere are the views more explicit than in Nevada Barr's third novel when the mice that have invaded the park ranger's summer quarters are termed "politically correct pets" (241) or when Maron's protagonist eagerly participates in an informal trapshooting contest and muses:

I know it's not politically correct to enjoy shooting, and given the option I'd certainly vote for much stricter gun control; but we all know it's not a constitutional issue no matter what the NRA [National Rifle Association] says. Why else would so many men use gun images to describe sex? "Hotter'n a two-dollar pistol." "Shoot my wad." "Firing blanks." All that power, all that force and all you have to do is pull a trigger. (*Shooting* 93)

But what are more revealing than mere words are the sleuths' actions, particularly their surprising number of interracial and interreligious personal and professional associations,[15] close friendships,[16] love interests,[17] and marriages.[18] One especially liberal view is found in Judith Van Gieson's works. The narrator and heroine of the series awakens one night and looks at her young Mexican lover:

I looked at his skinny body stretched out naked in my bed and thought how familiar it was . . . I thought about the alien population to the south that sneaks across our borders increasing the heterozygosity of our breeding population, expanding the gene pool, adding to our diversity. I woke him with a kiss. (179)

Sometimes the female sleuth's political position on race issues is apparent from a casual remark. Sara Paretsky's private eye, V. I. Warshawski, notes at one point that she had spent many years fighting the "prowar, anti-abortion, racist world" (*Killing* 88). In other series the sleuth's ideological position is more frequently called into play, but not necessarily as a plot element. Isabelle Holland's character is an assistant rector in a Protestant church, who views combating racism as a significant part of her vocation as an urban minister, not as part of her avocation as an amateur detective. Mary Daheim's newspaper editor, the main character in her Alpine series, remarks about a young African American nurse who has taken a job in her community: "She'll offer Alpine a positive image of African-Americans. . . . I'm glad she's here. With so many commuters from Everett and even Seattle, it's about time we get some racial mix" (11).

Other sleuths reveal their liberal leanings in the groups they join, the causes they support, and the illegalities they ignore. In the first book in her new series, Carolyn Hart's amateur sleuth, Henrie O., solves the mystery and discovers that an apparent murder is actually a suicide. But she decides not to notify the authorities so that the man's heir can collect the insurance money, and use it to fund a media empire through which he will continue his fight for various social causes. An amateur sleuth created by Virginia Rich, and later developed by Nancy Pickard, tacitly approves of her ranch hands helping illegal aliens. She and her late husband "had always viewed it as humanitarian aid":

"like the underground railroad that sheltered runaway slaves during the Civil War. And so [they] had never interfered with what was obviously a moral imperative for their ranch manager and their hired hand." (*The 27** 55)

Similarly, Susan Wittig Albert's protagonist is an attorney who worked to help illegal aliens during the U.S. government's declared amnesty in the 1980s.

Furthermore, whenever anything racist or antiSemitic occurs in the books reviewed, more likely than not the criminal did it. For example, Nancy Baker Jacobs' sleuth finds herself involved in a case that brings her into contact with the Aryan Supremacy Party (ASP), a mid-western group that staunchly supports the NRA and seeks political power, hoping to take back the cities from the minorities. Its slogan is "Hitler was right;" its members are described as "people whose lives've been ruined by the moneymen—the Jews." One of ASP's officers describes the organization this way:

"We were a helluva team until that asshole Jew of yours poisoned [our treasurer], like the slimy, sneaky bastards all his race are. . . . ASP wants the country the way it was before the kikes, the niggers and the slant-eyed illegals started takin' over and we're gonna get it back." (140)

White supremacist criminals are featured also in Bridgit McKenna's *Dead Ahead*. Similarly, in one of Linda Barnes' books the murderer is an extreme bigot whose only regret in killing an African American nurse was that she was not an African American doctor! (356). The victim had stumbled onto his plan to sell worthless, dangerous chemotherapy substitutes in third-world countries.

If anyone makes a prejudiced or biased remark, it is rarely the heroine. Early in the novels by Dana Stabenow, the protagonist's Aleut grandmother exhibits extreme prejudice against whites; the sleuth herself is highly assimilated in the larger society and has had both a white and an African American lover. In Mary Bowen Hall's series the bigot is one of the heroine's suitors, who consistently refers to Asians as "Jap bastards" or "Jap clowns" (45). Similarly, there is a sheriff, an antiAsian bigot, whose remarks offend Louise Hendricksen's character. "Slant eyes" and "gook" are among the epithets he uses to describe Asian Americans, especially the Vietnamese and Cambodians living in the state of Washington (145, 148). And in Marissa Piesman's series, Nina

Fischman admonishes fellow Jews, including her mother, for making disparaging remarks about Gentiles or portraying Jews as superior to other people. In one scene, the mother comments about the disappearance of a suspect: "Leaving your wife and child, your business partners, your mother, without any idea of where you've gone. Characteristically, it's not very . . .um . . ." (22). Fishman retorts:

"Jewish. It's not very Jewish, is that what you're trying to say? . . . Haven't you ever read that stuff about the abandonment rate on the Lower East Side at the turn of the century? . . . Apparently all those Jewish husbands took off like shots. [This one] was just a throwback, I guess." (22)

But even Fischman nearly gets caught up in what she terms "shiksaphobia," noting that when "you had four Jewish women in a room discussing a thin, blond Gentile woman who had married a rich Jewish man, it was easy to get carried away" (210).

There are a few exceptions—that is, books in which it is the woman sleuth who is prejudiced and does the stereotyping. Stephanie Matteson's leading character describes one young Chinese woman whom she has come to know:

Even in pigtails and the ubiquitous blue drill Mao suit, she was lovely, with a grace and dignity that was lacking in most Chinese women. The homeliness of the Chinese women was a mystery to [me]. (54-55)

But even in this instance, a qualification or disclaimer is made which attempts to soften the impact of the remark. Matteson's character continues: "The Taiwanese women she'd seen had been beautiful, *so it wasn't a racial thing* . . . It was as if the constrictions on their freedom had somehow been imprinted on their features" (54-55, emphasis added). In the same way, B. J. Oliphant's heroine supports the English-only referendum in her state, but still has friends in the ACLU and gets along well with her Hispanic neighbors. Nonetheless her plan for solving the urban crisis is:

Compulsory schooling for all illiterates and quasi-literates—sex segregated work camps until they could read, write and speak standard English. . . . "I'm all for all *human* rights to every unfeathered thing that walks about on two legs. . . . But *civil* rights can only apply to civilized people, and children aren't born civilized. They're born barbarians. And if parents can't and the state won't [civilize them], you end up with barbarian tribes warring through the streets of your cities!" (3)

What is a more interesting exception to the pattern of female sleuths being unbiased, is the tendency of some to rail against the dominant group. Are those views prejudiced? Are the characterizations of whites, especially Gentile white men, stereotypical? Apparently not! In liberal, politically correct circles it seems socially acceptable to be antiwhite Anglo-Saxon Protestants, and to refer to the group's members as WASPs, even though similar remarks about a minority group would be considered epithets and ethno-racial slurs. Consider a remark by Carolina Garcia-Aguilera's sleuth about her current lover: "for a WASP, Charlie was unusually passionate" (129).

Michael Kahn's Jewish heroine derides her Gentile colleagues:

Benny Goldberg was an anomaly at Abbott & Windsor, a chubby Jew among tall, athletic Wasps. . . . Benny also had a first name that sounded like a first name and a last name that sounded like a last name. This, too, put him in the minority at Abbott & Windsor, where most of the lawyers had interchangeable first and last names. The firm's letterhead included Sterling Grant, Hamilton Frederick, Porter Edwards, Hayden James. . . (47-48)

In a review of a recent book by Piesman, Marilyn Stasio of *The New York Times* states:

Alternate Sides finds this die-hard Jewish liberal in a crisis of indecision because her new boyfriend . . . has asked her to move in with him—in an architecturally insipid high-rise on the *WASP-infested* East Side. It's bad enough that the tenants of this "low I.Q. building" wear toupees and live to play tennis; but the mailman is running a prostitution ring and somebody just killed the doorman. Is this the proper environment for a socially conscious West Sider like [Fischman]? (21, emphasis added)

Carolyn Hart's senior citizen sleuth is extremely distressed by the fact that an employee of her former lover beats his Latina wife. The amateur detective confronts her former lover:

"[Y]ou know how that man treats Rosalia, and you haven't done a damn thing about it." He shrugged. "All right, sometimes I'm a bastard. I never said I was perfect. But why the hell does she put up with it?" It didn't surprise me. He had the arrogant confidence of a rich white man who had never been dependent, never in his whole life. No one had ever physically hurt him or threatened him. The world belonged to him and men like him. They had a trigger-quick disdain for anyone who wouldn't fight back. They didn't believe in a victim's resigned acceptance of abuse, the victim's pitiful sense of punishment deserved. "She puts up with it . . ." I began. Then I shook my head. "She's scared and she's cowed and emotionally crippled. But you aren't, and you've got the chips. You'll remedy it?" (115)

Nowhere in the literature reviewed is the sleuth's remark more pointed than when Barbara Neely's protagonist exclaims about rich white men:

Being in possession of that particular set of characteristics meant a person could do pretty much anything he wanted to do, to pretty much anybody he chose— like an untrained dog chewing and shitting all over the place. (125)

These references make clear the trend: the series incorporate dialogue and issues that reflect prejudice and discrimination. Most do so from the politically correct position of the female authors. But some remarks, which if directed against a minority would be considered offensive, inappropriate or prejudicial, when leveled at the dominant group are perfectly acceptable.

Conclusion

Although the central core of today's mystery fiction still revolves around traditional motives of greed, jealousy, and revenge, novels featuring serialized female sleuths often include broader social, economic, or political issues. Among the most frequently cited issues are prejudice and discrimination against minorities. The issues may or may not be important to the solution of the mystery, but they provide a level of insight into the problems of the society in which the stories take place that was absent in earlier mysteries.

The question now arises as to whether the tendency to use the mystery novel as a platform for social commentary is as common to male sleuths and their authors as it appears to be for their female counterparts. Is the content of the literature reviewed here typical of all mystery fiction written since 1980 or does it reflect gender differences among the authors and the perceptions of how female sleuths should be portrayed given that most of their fans are women? A preliminary look at the broader genre suggests male dominated mystery fiction focuses far less on broader social issues and contexts. The literature analyzed here is typical only of that featuring women as amateur or professional detectives.

Notes

1. In 1988 only about one quarter of all mystery titles first published in the United States in any format (26%) or titles published in paperback whether original or reprints (25%) were written by women. By 1991, the figure for first mysteries with female authors was up to 29% and for paperbacks it was 36%. Preliminary figures for 1995 showed a dramatic leap to 42% and 48.5% respectively. Overall the number of titles by women has risen substantially; paperback mystery publishing is almost evenly divided between men and women authors. Data taken from *Drood Review of Mystery*, as reprinted in Sisters in Crime *Newsletter,* 3.2 (June 1996): 8. Also see *The New York Times*, 17 Mar. 1997: D1, with respect to the book market becoming "increasingly a woman's market."

2. Abigail Padgett's series features a childcare worker concerned about abuse while the lead characters of both Elaine Raco Chase and Carol O'Connell were severely abused as children.

3. See for example, Nancy Pickard, *Marriage Is Murder* (New York: Scribner's 1987); Carolyn G. Hart, *Dead Man's Island* (New York: Bantam, 1993); Lillian O'Donnell, *Used to Kill* (New York: G. P. Putnam's Sons, 1993); and Janet Dawson, *Take a Number* (New York: Fawcett, 1993).

4. Julie Smith's attorney-sleuth joins a group in support of legalizing prostitution. Prostitution is also a theme in Barbara D'Amato, *Hard Women* (New York: Macmillan, 1996), and a social issue sympathetically portrayed in a series by Isabelle Holland featuring an assistant rector whose ministry involves as much social work as it does pastoral care.

5. Sara Paretsky, *Burn Marks* (New York: Delacorte, 1990); Pat Welch, *Smoke and Mirrors* (Tallahassee, FL: Naiad, 1996).

6. For example, Linda Barnes's heroine was married to a coke addict and the father of the little girl to whom she is a "Big Sister" is a Colombian drug lord. The Edwina Crusoe series by Mary Kittredge focuses on the sleuthing of a nurse and makes repeated reference to addiction, especially of people in the medical profession. The sleuth or a member of her family is an alcoholic or in recovery in the following: Susan Wittig Albert, *Witches' Bane* (New York: Scribner's, 1993); Nevada Barr, *Ill Wind* (New York: Putnam, 1995); Patricia Cornwell, *The Body Farm* (New York: Scribner's, 1994), Jean Femling, *Hush Money* (New York: St. Martin's, 1989); Marcia Muller's novels featuring Joanna Stark; and the series by Pele Plante, Elaine Raco Chase, Kerry Tucker, Jean Hager, Catherine Dain, Meg O'Brien, Karen Saum, Sharon Zukowski, and Sarah Shankman.

7. For example, the sleuths in the series by Sarah Shankman, Annette Meyers, and Nancy Baker Jacobs all have loved ones who were killed by drunken drivers; in Kathy Hogan Trocheck, *Heart Problems* (New York: Harper

Collins, 1996), a white female offender gets off lightly in a racially charged DWI killing.

8. Richard Barth's character is a volunteer in homeless shelters and a number of her cronies are threatened with the prospect of becoming homeless. Also see, Lee Harris, *The Yom Kippur Murders* (New York: Fawcett, 1992), Sara Paretsky, *Burn Marks, op. cit.* and her *Tunnel Vision* (New York: Delacorte, 1994).

9. See, for example, the series by Jaye Maiman or Mary Wings; Julie Smith, *Jazz Funeral* (New York: Fawcett Columbine, 1993); Marcia Muller, *Wolf in the Shadows* (New York: Mysterious Press, 1993); and Paretsky, *Burn Marks, op. cit.*

10. Homophobia is an issue for several characters. See for example the series by Dorothy Tell and Pele Plante. It also arises in Annette Meyers, *Murder: The Musical* (New York: Doubleday, 1993) and in the later works in Julie Smith's Skip Langdon series.

11. The environment is a particular concern in the writings of Nevada Barr, Jean Hager, B. J. Oliphant, Dana Stabenow, and Judith Van Gieson.

12. Several other books could be used to illustrate these issues: Edna Buchanan, *Contents Under Pressure* (New York: Hyperion, 1992) deals with an attack by racist police on an African American man who is a retired football player and current inner city youth worker in Miami, FL; Elizabeth Atwood Taylor, *The Northwest Murders* (New York: St. Martin's, 1994) in which historical prejudice in California against Native Americans and Chinese is integral to the plot; Penny Mickelbury, *Keeping Secrets* (Tallahassee, FL: Naiad, 1993), and *Night Songs* (Tallahassee, FL: Naiad, 1994). The latter two books are in a series featuring a woman detective who heads the recently formed Hate Crimes Unit in Washington, DC. They deal with antigay crimes, but the Unit is intended to deal with all types of hate crimes.

13. Quotation from a reviewer reprinted at the beginning of the book.

14. This issue has recently received a lot of attention in the media because of the discovery by Secretary of State Madeleine Albright that her parents were Christian converts from Judaism.

15. See the series by Catherine Dain, Linda Grant, Nancy Baker Jacobs, and Kathy Hogan Trocheck.

16. See the recent books in the series by Catherine Dain, in which the sleuth is dating a Filipino; in Lee Harris's series the sleuth, a former Roman Catholic nun, has as best friends her Jewish employer, a Jewish neighbor, and the Mother Superior of the convent she has left; in Abigail Padgett's series the sleuth's best friend is a Latina.

17. Among the series in which interreligious or interracial love affairs occur are those by Judith Van Gieson, Sara Paretsky, Nevada Barr, Dana Stabenow, and Margaret Maron (the Deborah Knotts series).

18. Sara Paretsky's and Linda Barnes's heroines are the offspring of inter-religious marriages and Katherine Lasky Knight's sleuth herself was married to someone of another faith.

Works Cited

Albert, Susan Wittig. *Witches' Bane.* New York: Scribner's, 1993.

Barnes, Linda. *Snapshot.* New York: Dell, 1993.

Barr, Nevada. *Ill Wind.* New York: Putnam, 1995.

Breen, Jon L. Introduction. *The Fine Art of Murder.* Ed. Ed Gorman et al. New York: Carroll & Graf, 1993. 3-6.

Buchanan, Edna. *Contents Under Pressure.* New York: Hyperion, 1992.

Carlson, P. M. *Gravestone.* New York: Pocket Books, 1993.

Cornwell, Patricia. *The Body Farm.* New York: Scribner's, 1994.

Daheim, Mary. *Alpine Decoy.* New York: Ballantine, 1994.

Dain, Catherine. *Sing a Song of Death.* New York: Berkley, 1993.

D'Amato, Barbara. *Hard Women.* New York: Macmillan, 1996.

Dawson, Janet. *Take a Number.* New York: Fawcett, 1993.

Dunlap, Susan. *Time Expired.* New York: Delacorte, 1993.

Femling, Jean. *Hush Money.* New York: St. Martin's, 1989.

Garcia-Aguilera, Carolina. *Bloody Waters.* New York: Putnam, 1996.

Hall, Mary Bowen. *Emma Chizzit and the Napa Nemesis.* New York: Walker & Co., 1992.

Harris, Lee. *The Yom Kippur Murders.* New York: Fawcett, 1992.

Hart, Carolyn G. *Dead Man's Island.* New York: Bantam, 1993.

Hendricksen, Louise. *Lethal Legacy.* New York: Putnam, 1995.

Hess, Joan. *Madness in Maggody.* New York: St. Martin's, 1991.

Hornsby, Wendy. *Bad Intent.* New York: Dutton, 1994.

Jacobs, Nancy Baker. *The Turquoise Tattoo.* New York: Pocket Books, 1991.

Kahn, Michael. *Grave Designs.* New York: Signet, 1992.

Krich, Rochelle Majer. *Angel of Death.* New York: Mysterious Press, 1994.

MacLeod, Charlotte. *The Bilbao Looking Glass.* New York: Avon, 1983.

Maron, Margaret. *Shooting at Loons.* New York: Mysterious Press, 1994.

——. *Southern Discomfort.* New York: Mysterious Press, 1993.

Martin, Lee. *Deficit Ending.* New York: St. Martin's, 1990.

Matteson, Stephanie. *Murder on the Silk Road.* New York: Diamond Books, 1992.

McKenna, Bridgit. *Dead Ahead.* New York: Berkley, 1994.

Meyers, Annette. *Murder: The Musical.* New York: Doubleday, 1993.

Mickelbury, Penny. *Keeping Secrets.* Tallahassee, FL: Naiad, 1993.

——. *Night Songs.* Tallahassee, FL: Naiad, 1994.

Muller, Marcia. *Edwin of the Iron Shoes.* New York: David McKay-Washburn, 1977.

——. "In the Tradition of . . . Herself." *The Fine Art of Murder.* Ed. Ed Gorman et al. New York: Carroll & Graf. 156-57.

——. *Wolf in the Shadows.* New York: Mysterious Press, 1993.

Neely, Barbara. *Blanche on the Lam.* New York: St. Martin's, 1992.

New York Times, 17 March 1997: D1.

Nordan, Robert. *Death Beneath the Christmas Tree.* New York: Fawcett, 1991.

O'Donnell, Lillian. *Lockout.* New York: Putnam, 1994.

——. *No Business Being a Cop.* New York: Putnam, 1979.

——. *Pushover.* New York: Putnam, 1992.

——. *Used to Kill.* New York: Putnam, 1993.

Oliphant, B. J. *Deservedly Dead.* New York: Fawcett, 1992.

Paretsky, Sara. *Burn Marks.* New York: Delacorte, 1990.

——. *Killing Orders.* New York: Ballantine, 1985.

——. *Tunnel Vision.* New York: Delacorte, 1994.

Paul, Barbara. *The Apostrophe Thief.* New York: Macmillan, 1993.

Pickard, Nancy. *Marriage Is Murder.* New York: Scribner's, 1987.

——. *The 27* Ingredient Chile Con Carne Murders.* New York: Delacorte, 1993.

Piesman, Marissa. *Heading Uptown.* New York: Delacorte, 1993.

Roberts, Gillian. *In the Dead of Summer.* New York: Ballantine, 1995.

Sims, L.V. *Murder Is Only Skin Deep.* New York: Charter, 1987.

"Sisters in Crime." *Newsletter* 3.2 (June 1996): 8.

Smith, Julie. *Jazz Funeral.* New York; Fawcett, 1993.

Stabenow, Dana. *A Cold Day for Murder.* New York: Berkley, 1992.

Stasio, Marilyn. Review of Marissa Piesman. *Alternate Sides* in *The New York Times, Book Review* 20 Aug. 1995: 21.

Taylor, Elizabeth Atwood. *The Northwest Murders.* New York: St. Martin's, 1994.

Trocheck, Kathy Hogan. *Heart Problems.* New York: Harper Collins, 1996.

——. *To Live and Die in Dixie.* New York: Harper Collins, 1993.

Van Gieson, Judith. *The Wolf Path.* New York: Harper Paperbacks, 1992.

Welch, Pat. *Smoke and Mirrors.* Tallahassee, FL: Naiad, 1996.

First Volumes in Series Cited

Baker, Nikki. *In the Game.* Tallahassee, FL: Naiad, 1991.

Barth, Richard. *The Rag Bag Clan.* New York: Dial, 1978.

Bland, Eleanor Taylor. *Dead Time.* New York: Signet, 1992.

Chase, Elaine Raco. *Dangerous Places.* New York: Bantam, 1987.

Grant, Linda. *Random Access Murder.* New York: Avon, 1988.

Hager, Jean. *Ravenmocker.* New York: Mysterious Press, 1992.

Herndon, Nancy. *Acid Bath.* New York: Berkley, 1995.

Holland, Isabelle. *Flight of the Archangel.* New York: Doubleday, 1985.

Horansky, Ruby. *Dead Ahead.* New York: Avon, 1990.

Jance, J. J. *Desert Heat,* New York: Avon, 1993.

Kittredge, Mary. *Fatal Diagnosis.* New York: St. Martin's, 1990.

Knight, Kathryn Lasky. *Trace Elements.* New York: Pocket Books, 1987.

Maiman, Jaye. *I Left My Heart.* Tallahassee, FL: Naiad, 1991.

Muller, Marcia. *The Cavalier in White.* New York: St. Martin's, 1986.

Neely, Barbara. *Blanche on the Lam.* New York: St. Martin's, 1992.

O'Brien, Meg. *The Daphne Decisions.* New York: Bantam, 1988.

O'Connell, Carol. *Mallory's Oracle.* New York: Putnam, 1994.

Padgett, Abigail. *Child of Silence.* New York: Mysterious Press, 1993.

Plante, Pele. *Dirty Money.* Los Angeles, CA: Clothespin Fever Press, 1991.

Santiago, Soledad. *Nightside.* New York: Doubleday, 1994.

Saum, Karen. *Murder Is Relative.* Tallahassee, FL: Naiad, 1990.

Shankman, Sarah. (Originally issued as Alice Storey.) *First Kill All the Lawyers.* New York: Pocket Books, 1988.

Smith, Julie. *Dead in the Water.* New York: Ballantine, 1992.

Tell, Dorothy. *Murder at Red Rock Ranch.* Tallahassee, FL: Naiad, 1990.

Tucker, Kerry. *Still Waters.* New York: Harper Collins, 1991.

Weir, Charlene. *The Winter Widow.* New York: St. Martin's, 1992.

Wings, Mary. *She Came Too Late.* Freedom, CA: The Crossing Press, 1987.

Zukowski, Sharon. *The Hour of the Knife.* New York: St. Martin's, 1991.

ETHNIC DETECTIVES IN POPULAR FICTION:
NEW DIRECTIONS FOR AN AMERICAN GENRE

Gina Macdonald and Andrew Macdonald

Cross-Cultural Detective Fiction

Popular culture's concern with the ethnic is clearly established by the recent explosion of cross-cultural detectives. These non-mainstream detectives explore cultural differences—in perception, in way of life, in visions of the world—and act as links between cultures, interpreting each to each, mainstream to minority and minority to mainstream. Their function as emissaries between different groups is a natural outgrowth of the intermediary function of many traditional American hardboiled detectives, figures who moved easily between their upper-class employers and the shadowy criminal underworld, or perhaps between the lower-middle-class police and aristocratic crime victims or criminals. Ethnicity has replaced class barriers, but the need for linking problem-solvers remains the same.

Early American Multicultural Detectives: Faux Ethnicity

A handful of cross-cultural detectives have existed in the past, of course, but they have leaned toward the stereotyped exploitation of the exotic rather than being serious explorations of the experience of the Other. For example, one of the earliest cross-cultural detectives was Earl Derr Biggers's Charlie Chan, a middle-aged Chinese detective on the police force in Honolulu, Hawaii. Based on an actual Honolulu police detective, Chan was noted for his flowery, Confucian aphorisms, his lapses into pidgin English, his patience, attention to detail, character analysis, and discourses on justice, tradition, and cultural identity. Chan is an American popular culture folk hero, known more as an allusion than as a literary or movie character, but nevertheless perhaps the original inspiration for numerous other cross-cultural detectives. Another early stereotype is John P. Marquand's multitalented Mr. Moto. A special agent of the pre-World War II Japanese government, Mr. Moto was educated in the United States, spoke flawless English, and acquired a good understanding of Western ways. The Western belief that Asians look alike aided him in his disguises. However, Mr. Moto was retired with Pearl Harbor and did not reappear until the Cold War, helping Americans defeat Russian agents in Japan in *Stopover: Tokyo*.

In the 1960s Elizabeth Linnington writing as Del Shannon produced the Lieutenant Luis Mendoza series, traditional police procedurals but with a Mexican-American police detective, the independently wealthy head of Homicide in the Los Angeles Police Department. When the series first appeared (*Case Pending*), Mendoza was the only ethnic minority hero in a series of this kind in the U.S. Mendoza, a dapper cynical bachelor who later marries and raises a family, uses Spanish words and phrases in conversation but has little else to distinguish him from mainstream America except his taste in food and architecture. Shannon's other detectives with their Italian, Irish, and Jewish ethnic heritages are as assimilated as Mendoza. Another interesting Hispanic detective who ultimately went nowhere was Elmore Leonard's Raymond Cruz in *City Primeval—High Noon in Detroit*. A *chicano* from McAllen, Texas, Cruz was a curious figure in frigid Detroit, a potential challenger to big-industrial-city policing methods when set up against a racist, redneck killer. The subtitle suggests the collision of values brought to Detroit by outsiders from varied geographical regions. Cruz was not distinctively ethnic in culture since he seemed fairly well assimilated, but he was an appealing detective, significant because such a respected writer as Leonard purposely chose an ethnic hero. However, the character ended with the novel as Leonard moved on to other out-of-place characters in locations from Miami to Los Angeles.

Michael Delving's 1960s' Dave Cannon novels featured Oklahoma Cherokee amateur detective Bob Eddison, partner and sidekick of Cannon, an amiable young dealer in rare books and manuscripts. Eddison's "Indian" ethnicity was irrelevant to the stories except as a lecture platform about general injustices imposed on Indians, the difference in perspective between traditional views of American history and the views of Indians, and the cultural insensitivity of even genuinely nice people:

"Are you really a Red Indian?" Jill asked.

"Yep. One of the old original Americans, at least on my father's side," Bob said. "He was a rarity, one of the Cherokee who managed to get an education and become an important man in the paleface world. He was a lawyer, and finally he was made a judge. But he remained an Indian, a member of the Ani-waya clan, the Wolf people, and he never let me forget it either."

"How marvelous!" she said.

Out of the corner of my eye I saw Bob's mouth twist.

"That's right," he said. "Marvelous. I wish I could tell you about the great buffalo hunts, the war dances, the gallops over the wild prairie in feathers and beads. Trouble is, the nearest I ever came to a prairie was a vacant lot on Wilson Street. As for the warpath, the closest I ever came to that was when I beat up a

kid in the neighborhood because he said my father was a dirty nigger. He was kind of dark, my father, darker than I am."
I could feel a silence settle over Jill. (*The Devil Finds Work* 66 and 67)

In point of fact, the rest of *The Devil Finds Work* is a conventional British village mystery told from an American perspective.

Inspirational Foreign Models: True Ethnicity
Current practitioners of ethnic detective fiction have moved toward greater complexity of character, details to reveal character as reflective of culture, and a sympathetic exploration of the cross-cultural experience and of movements toward assimilation. Their inspiration and models have been some nonAmerican writers who first published in English in this country from the fifties through the early eighties and who drew on other cultures for their settings and detectives. These writers laid the foundation for and stirred popular interest in explorations of bicultural and multicultural interaction in detective fiction and in the complexities created by very different psychologies, perspectives, and cultural patterns. They sensitized Americans to the cultural differences explored by such anthropologists as Benjamin Whorf, Edward T. Hall, and Robert Kaplan. By doing so, they paved the way for the uniquely American types of multicultural detection. Without these precursors of the American ethnic detective, the home-grown use of the genre would be less rich and less effective. In addition to the important impact these writers have had on American ethnic detective fiction, they are worth looking at briefly because, where the American ethnic detective patterns are muddled by degrees of assimilation, these foreign works usually treat totally distinct cultures and provide clear-cut patterns for integrating them into a detective fiction mode. These models make it easier to distinguish the similar patterns that occur in varying degrees in American ethnic detective fiction. Because of the multicultural context within a single nation, the model provided by James McClure is a particularly good one for evaluating what produces effective multicultural or ethnic detective fiction. These international works have generally taken three key directions depending on whether the writers have seen their relationship to another culture as that of enthusiastic promoter, crossroads interpreter, or sociologist.
The first type of cross-cultural explorers are the enthusiasts who capture an alien world, its mentality, mindset, and values. Enthusiasts take readers into the world of the Other with such care for detail and for capturing attitudes and behavior patterns that, by the end of a story, what seemed foreign and inexplicable has become familiar, understandable,

and universally human. Their interest is less in exploring and evaluating differences than in pulling back the curtain to show an unknown world. Beginning in 1950 Dutch author Robert van Gulik, who was struck by the number of third-rate Western mysteries popular in China and Japan, decided to demonstrate how rich the ancient Asian literature was in crime stories. He laid his "Judge Dee" series in seventh-century Canton, a port city where the Chinese and Arab worlds met for trade; then, as he says, he drew on original ancient Chinese plots and mingled history and fiction to create an Asian sensibility and detection based on Confucian thought, Eastern authoritarianism, consultation with ghosts, and other methods foreign to Western detection. Gulik takes readers into the heart of Chinese culture—the judicial system—where all classes meet and where values and sensibilities collide. His central figure is a Chinese magistrate (based on a real judge) for whom floggings, public strangulation, and beheadings are standard punishments for convicted felons. Westerners, of course, have difficulty with the sometimes superficial nature of the evidence on which a conviction is based and with the cruelty of punishments inflicted for crimes, for example, the lingering death (a slicing and cutting process said to last for several hours) for parricide, high treason, and a wife killing her husband.

Another precursor to the American ethnic detective tale is the Bonaparte series (29 stories) of Arthur Upfield, which features half-aborigine crime investigator Detective Inspector Napoleon Bonaparte of the Queensland Police; like Gulik's Dee, the series reflects the enthusiast's fascination with the Other. Upfield's Inspector "Bony" series grew out of his friendship with an educated half-caste police tracker and his fascination with Australia and its diverse peoples. Upfield communicates this enthusiasm through his descriptions of survival in the desolate, treeless expanse of sand and saltbush that comprises Southern Australia's Nullarbor Plain (*The Man of Two Tribes*), of the silent, maddeningly motionless West Australian forest (*Bony and the Mouse*), and of *mauia*, a very powerful magic aborigines use against enemies (*The Bone Is Pointed*, 1958). A unique feature of Upfield's novels is his examination of intercultural relationships and the various stages of aboriginal assimilation into the dominant white culture, and his vision of what civilized white culture can learn from the older, primitive, communal, aboriginal outback culture and its people's instinctual understanding of the land. As with all enthusiasts, the emphasis is on the disclosure of a previously obscure culture to show its rich variety of exotic ways.

The second type of cross-cultural explorer is the crossroads interpreter. Interpreters are like the enthusiasts in their deep-rooted interest in a strange culture, but they examine two or more cultures at a point of crossing in order to sensitize readers to clashes of values and perspectives. Interpreters interpret other worlds for readers and guide them to a deeper understanding. Starting in 1979 and continuing through the 1980s, British diplomat James Melville sought to bridge the cultural gap between East and West through Western ratiocination carried out in part by the son of a Japanese diplomat, a U.S. trained, Japanese-born-and-bred detective, Jiro Kimura. Kimura's strong English-language skills, his affinity for Western lifestyles, and his personal predilection for foreign women land him in the role of police force liaison with Kobe's foreign community. Kimura exemplifies a pattern that has become a cliché in the cross-cultural detective story, the men or women of two worlds, whose birth and ethnic or cultural heritage place them in one world, but whose education and adult experiences place them in another; such figures act like Dante's Beatrice to guide readers through the pitfalls and confusions of cultural differences. Melville plays Kimura off against his insular and self-contained senior detective, Tetsuo Otani, the superintendent of the Hyogo Prefectural Police, a grandfatherly figure, firm, traditional, and home-centered. Yet Otani reads *haado-boirudo misteri* or hard-boiled detective stories avidly, and has rejected the authoritarian, thought-police mentality of his pre-war police predecessors. As crossroads interpretations, Melville's novels center on meeting points of East and West, for example, the murder of an Irish Catholic priest at a Zen Buddhist temple (*The Wages of Zen*), the murder of a British resident with ties to the Japanese homosexual underworld (*The Chrysanthemum Chain*), a "love hotel" murder of a Filipino pleasure girl that leads to the recovery of a national treasure from an art museum (*The Ninth Netsuke*), the murder of a British madrigal singer at a posh embassy party (*Sayonara, Sweet Amaryllis*), and the murder of a tea-ceremony master performing the rite for prominent British, American, and Japanese dignitaries (*The Death Ceremony*). In *Death of a Daimyo* a wealthy Japanese philanthropist killed at a ceremony at Cambridge University plunges Otani into culture shock as he must deal with both Scotland Yard and the Japanese mafia, the *Yakusa*. Melville's crossroads' detection opens up the world of modern Japan to Western readers and calls attention to the major psychological, cultural, and ethnic differences that separate, but beneath these seemingly insurmountable differences there are suggestions of the common humanity that unites. The Inspector Ghote series of H. R. F. Keating do for India what Melville does for Japan—capture a unique sense of place, culture, and point of view, with Keating exploring an alien culture not so much to interpret its alien features as to discover the common humanity beneath the superficial differences. Thus, although Keating explores crossroads questions of caste and class, and differences in race, religion, diction, and region in the cases of Bombay Crime Branch Inspector Ganesh Ghote, he concentrates on demonstrating the arrogance, corruption, and imperfectability of human nature.

A third group is the sociologists, insiders who analyze, dissect, and examine the racial, social, class, and cultural encounters that occur within a society that may be their own or that may be the focus of their academic, scholarly, or personal interest—whichever, they know the culture as an insider does but can view it dispassionately. They are often apparently neutral in their stance, avoiding enthusiasms in favor of objective detachment. Of these, James McClure is a prime example of the distanced yet humanizing understanding a good detective fiction writer can provide of a troubled society. His prime law enforcement character is South African policeman Tromp Kramer, an Afrikanner paired with his Bantu assistant Mickey Zondi. McClure, a South African himself, claims that the "neutrality" of the police genre constituted much of its appeal for him, yet his works, though studiously careful to avoid preachiness about apartheid, show the bitter emotional and moral consequences of the separatist policy. Kramer and Zondi must play elaborate roles to avoid politically inappropriate sympathy on the part of the white for his black partner, or "cheekiness" on the part of Zondi when he acts normally toward his friend and colleague. Everything is distorted, shaded, or touched by race; all of Kramer's cases are either race-driven or racially tinged. Character and plot thus arise out of milieu. McClure's books are unthinkable in any other locale, even though overt discussion of apartheid as a theme is avoided. His works are possibly the best examples of multiethnic, multicultural detective novels in English, for they are primers on purely South African psychological states, emotional responses, and even crimes involving black Africans, Afrikanners, the English, and "Colored" or mixed race peoples; critics, in fact, have compared them in sociological and humanistic importance to the works of Alan Paton, Nadine Gordimer, and André Brink. All of the Kramer/Zondi series hinge on racial matters, with Kramer's appreciation of Zondi never in doubt, but with McClure leaving no doubt that the other policemen don't know that Zondi and Kramer work together. In *The Gooseberry Fool,* for example, angry crowds of Africans being evicted from their homes by the white Security Forces riot in the streets, hospitalizing Zondi, but Kramer must keep his fears for his friend's recovery hidden if he is to function effectively as a superior officer. A black-white criminal partnership in *Snake* thrives because investigators are blind to the possibility of a cross-racial alliance, and cross-racial sexual obsessions lead to murder, as does jealousy about passing for white in *The Steam Pig.*

McClure's South African novels are gritty, realistic social commentaries on South African apartheid and on the conflicts inherent in a large frontier country newly empowered by economic and technological development, its indigenous people cowed but restive, its more recent settlers (the Colored) a servant-class, its white power structure divided between ultra-conservative reactionaries (the Afrikanners) and more liberal reformers (English speakers). McClure's South Africa is nightmarish, with its police investigators keeping the masses down by fair means and foul, "fixing" problems by extra-legal means never evident to the public, thus protecting a racial and ethnic system. The self-righteous Boer vigilantes who take the law into their own hands in *The Sunday Hangman* to punish offenders who escape legal conviction are all the more disturbing because they act against the very system that perpetuates their prejudices.

Today we can see parallels between early U.S. hardboiled fiction, McClure's South African version, and more recent ethnic detective fiction. In earlier times it may have been harder to see the mote in our own eye: the myths of American well-being in the 1950s and 1960s and the claim that the Melting Pot assimilated all citizens made admissions that ethnic groups were truly separate, let alone that they might need the services of detectives, impossible. Foreign models of ethnic detectives provided the matrices of character and plot that American writers could use when the nation was ready for them. The three possible approaches represented by Gulik, Melville/Upfield, and McClure—enthusiastic promoter, interpreter, and sociologist—lie behind the multicultural detective in our own continent.

The Multicultural Detective: Problems in Definition

An initial problem when studying the multicultural detective is deciding exactly what "ethnic" means. As with one's dialect, one usually perceives ethnic difference in others while tacitly assuming one's own way as the norm, as natural. Just as we typically undergo a range of reactions to varying accents, so we have modulated responses to perceived differences in cultural behavior, from so-usual-as-to-be-transparent to different-but-understandable to exotic-and-incomprehensible. Ethnocentrism has a bad name, but it is often the firm rule in human behavior, not the shameful exception. Tony Hillerman points out that the Navajo word for white people is also used for other Native Americans in distant regions; the Navajo borrowed Indian words to name their Zuñi, Hopi, and Apache neighbors, but generalized about all others, red or white, as *Belacani*. Inevitably, we judge cultural behavior against what we know as a norm, relegating all else to the category of "exotic," and, unless we are privileged by extensive travel or education, what we know will lie close at hand. Thus, except for the fairly sophisticated, the cultural difference of ethnicity could be represented as a bull's eye, with "normal" lying in the middle and exoticism increasing in direct relation to the psychological distance from the center. Ethnicity is a shifting value, in other words, representing not just minority status in a cultural mainstream but, more importantly, the distance from what the evaluator perceives as the "normal" mainstream itself.

In the United States, historically a grab bag of ethnicities, the colonial and early U.S. mainstream culture tolerated a number of different strains; however, after 1865, the theory of the melting pot reigned and ethnicity was pushed to a temporary status on the road to full Americanism, a condition to be acknowledged, frequently despised, occasionally celebrated, but still one non-permanent in nature. Native Americans, for example, have been denigrated or idealized, sometimes both at the same time; other ethnic groups, from the Irish to Jews to Arabs have made the difficult trek from loathed outsider to varying degrees of acceptance. The federal designations of minority categories in the 1960s have simply confused the issue, with the identification as a "minority" in no way speaking to ethnicity. African Americans, for example, are a numerical minority when categorized by racial origin (itself a problematic category), but they may or may not be ethnically "different" depending on the level of assimilation to mainstream culture. Also, for all the perceived differences between mainstream and black culture, almost all African-American ways (except for the Afro-centric culture practiced by a minority of African Americans) are variations on the American rather than the African. Should African Americans who share the Christian religion, the southern cuisine, western clothing, and North American "mentality" and attitudes be included as "ethnic" in the same category as practitioners of nonChristian religions, speakers of other languages, and the like? As with the term "minority," "ethnic" breaks down when applied to real cases.

In this discussion of the ethnic detective we will focus most heavily on the "most ethnic" of cultures in the American mainstream, that of the Native American. The continuing fascination with the American Indian, as demonstrated in the large number of mysteries with Indian sleuths, is revealing of the attempt to confront and understand the most exotic and legitimate Other Way practiced on the American landscape, a Way indigenous rather than transplanted from afar. Exploring these and other ethnic detectives raises the question of the adequacy of the term "ethnic" as a meaningful category. Perhaps a better descriptive phrase is that used by Jerome Beaty and J. Paul Hunter, in their excellent *New Worlds of Lit-*

erature reader/anthology. In their struggle to find an accurate label for new, multiculturally oriented writers, Beaty and Hunter have coined a useful phrase: "voices not previously heard." The label is also helpful in the detective genre. Some detectives represent true cultures in the traditional sense of the word, ranging from the Native American and Hungarian Gypsy to nisei, Mexican American, and even Vietnamese American, but also the "cultures" of religion (Orthodox Jews, Moslems, sunworshippers, etc.), gender and race. Thus, even while we inevitably use "ethnic" and "culture," we acknowledge that "voices" or "viewpoints" may be more accurate terms.

Representative examples of these new voices in detective fiction are listed at the end of this essay. Because the number of detective "voices not previously heard" is so large, we can make no pretense of our list being comprehensive (it includes only a sampling), and no doubt the reader can provide many others. We have most probably overlooked a number of regional favorites, and we might also multiply their number by including cross-cultural film detectives and characters "crossing" between cultural groups. Clearly, the interest in the multicultural detective is a broad one, representing the yearnings of American culture for a lost unity, for a dialogue with new and strange citizens, and with old citizens newly found. The movement is also a healthy one, in the venerable American tradition of accepting the new and exotic and making it our own.

In general, reader and critical response to multicultural diversity in the detective hero has been positive-to-exuberant, so much so that an ethnic title, multicultural setting, or ethnic detective is almost a guarantee of good reviews. For example, reviewers greeted Jean Hager's books with enthusiastic comparisons to Hillerman ("This is Hillerman with an Oklahoma accent"; "Jean Hager's novels do for the Cherokee culture what Tony Hillerman has done for the Navajo"), praise of her detectives ("thoughtful, emotionally vulnerable, and determined . . . a definite original"; "a delightful addition to the genre") and of her depiction of ethnicity ("a clear-eyed evocation of the Cherokee culture"; "interesting information about the Cherokee culture"; "Among the best mysteries featuring Native American characters and milieu"; "She treats the Indian culture with respect"; "Hager explores the Cherokee culture with trenchant compassion"; "Hager takes readers on a fascinating journey into the world of Cherokee tradition in her superbly written mystery"). J. F. Trainor's novels are called "rich in ethnic lore and custom" and "not for the politically correct," and Trainor is praised for a "keen eye" for understanding "the interplay" between communities. Camillla Crespi gives "a triple whammy of reading pleasure: a neatly plotted mystery . . . and a loving evocation of an affectionate—if volatile—extended Italian family. *Bravissima!*" Sandra West Prowell captures "the stark beauty of Montana and the mystical world of its Native Americans" through her "sassy, tough, and independent," "regional," "feminine" voice. Regardless of the degree of ethnicity or the depth of perception about cross-cultural differences, across the board, authors with ethnic detectives tend to receive rave reviews.

Are All Multicultural Detectives Truly Representative of Other Cultures?
An obvious first question is whether the multicultural detective is truly representative of another culture or whether we simply have a modernized, *fin-de-siecle* version of Charlie Chan, all decorative up-to-date gingerbread but little different in substance. Clearly, the fad for diversity has generated some detective stories that are little more than costume pieces. The range of possibilities here is great, and a definition of when the detective is truly multicultural is worth the attempt. Suspense writer Dean Koontz makes fun of the plethora of multicultural detectives who are basically traditional detectives in an ethnic trenchcoat with his spoof *TickTock*. Therein Southern-Californian, Vietnamese-American detective novelist Tommy Phan finds himself caught up in nightmare when his mother, resentful of his enthusiastic assimilation to California culture and his rejection of Vietnamese language, culture, and values, draws on Vietnamese folklore remedies to frighten him back into the family fold. Phan has totally accepted American popular culture, and his detective-fiction creation Chip Nguyen is a fantasy projection—a James-Bond-style hero, with a fast car, fast blondes, and a ready solution to every problem. As Phan faces real mysteries, he wonders how his detective Nguyen would respond:

Chip was tough, smart, and relentless. He was a master of tae kwon do, able to drink hard all night without losing his edge or suffering a hangover, a chess master who once defeated Bobby Fischer when they encountered each other in a hurricane-hammered resort hotel in Barbados, a lover of such prowess that a beautiful blond socialite had killed another woman over him in a fit of jealousy, a collector of vintage Corvettes who was able to rebuild them from the ground up, and a brooding philosopher who knew that humanity was doomed but who gamely fought the good fight anyway. (37)

Here, Koontz spoofs the idea that ethnic names and a few references to special food, language, or customs really make a detective "multicultural" when the basic concept of the mystery genre depends on Western ratiocination tempered by intuition. The differences between the

Native American novels of Chelsea O. Yarbro, J. F. Trainor, Jean Hager, Tony Hillerman, and Abigail Padgett illustrate the varying degrees to which such novels are "multicultural."

C. O. Yarbro's series detective, Charlie Spotted Moon, was raised on the Ojibwa Iron River Reservation on the Alberta-Saskatchewan border but has a law degree and works for a San Francisco law firm. In emotional moments his accent takes on "a Canadian twinge, slightly Australian with a faint overlay of Scots" (*False Notes*). As a result of childhood influences, Moon loves malamutes (his two are named Caesar and Pompei), is offended by comments about being delighted to meet a real live Indian, and follows the Ojibwa shaman's way to justice when ratiocination fails. The shaman's way in *Ogilore, Tallant and Moon* means that Moon uses special incantations to solve the mystery and, in *Music When Sweet Voices Die,* other forms of traditional magic. Sometimes Moon's shaman magic comes from sweat baths, special blends of herbs and oils, and a sacred medicine finger—a carved stick of wood painted with the symbols of his name and worn against his chest. The medicine finger gives off vibrations that make Moon supersensitive to his environment and sharpen his perceptions to fit him for investigative tasks.

In *Cat's Claw,* Moon takes on a client he initially believes innocent, but later he discovers his client is the "Gold Chain" serial killer who has murdered twenty-eight women. Moon lights up the fires of his modern home's basement heaters, slaps the walls of his Finnish-style sauna with birch and pine boughs, puts a carved wood pendant on a leather thong around his girlfriend Morgan's neck and a small cloth bag filled with dried plants in her hand, and uses a small vial of oil to open the way for what Morgan calls "psychic trash" (151) but Moon confirms as a "frightening" reality (152). This psychic preparation helps Moon receive vibrations given off by his client's gold Rolex. Moon believes that the gold has absorbed the frenzy of death its owner engaged in: "The hideous joy of killing enveloped it, an unsatiated satisfaction that was increasing in ferocity and rapture with each new victim . . . and the malign hunger grew for twenty-nine [victims] . . . insistent as a black hole" (202). Moon regrets not having guarded himself more carefully "with rituals his grandfather had taught him all those years ago at the Iron River Ojibwa reservation in Saskatchewan" to avoid "the rapacity contained in the gold" (202). Later, in a special sweat bath ritual, he calls forth memories of murderous deeds from within the gold and experiences both the psychic dislocation of the victims and the troubled relationships that plunged the murderer into this pattern of death. These mystic experiences lead him to confront his client with his knowledge of the truth, to convince him to accept other legal counsel, and to walk a narrow line between betraying client confidentiality and encouraging the police in their search for conclusive evidence.

This Objibwa magic is disturbing because it is totally dependent on psychic and extrasensory knowledge that comes through mystic experiences and remains unknowable by ratiocination. However, it takes up only a small part of most of the Moon novels. These, in general, follow traditional patterns—a group of suspects, all of whom had reason to hate the deceased, a trail of clues, and a murderer whom no one else suspects—the format could be an Agatha Christie country-house mystery. In fact, except for Moon's occasional forays to his reservation origins and to his shaman arts, these novels are not about Native American cultures at all. They exploit a popular trend—curiosity about other points of view—but, in fact, do not explore that point of view in any depth. Except for his mystical incantations and trust in Objibwa magic, Moon is no different from any other American fictional amateur detective pursuing clues to killers who murder for greed, revenge, love, and sadistic pleasure. *False Notes* is typical: the murder of a famous French tenor on stage during a performance at the San Francisco Opera House, and Moon ferreting out a killer among members of the international opera company of Italians, French, Japanese, and Danes as well as Filipino doormen and suspicious albino blacks! In the terms discussed above, Yarbro may be an enthusiast, but one who makes little effort to understand a particular ethnic group in depth, relying instead on amulets and ritual incantations rather than on psychology and ways of thought. She neither interprets Objibwa culture for readers, nor provides a sociological understanding of it.

The Native American elements in J. F. Trainor's Angela Biwaban mysteries are equally superficial. Biwaban is supposedly an *"Ah-nish-ih-nay-bay"* or "original people" princess, and calls the white man's name for her tribe, "Chippewa," "the C-word," comparing it to calling a Czech "a hunkie" or Italians "wops" (*Corona Blue* 20). She uses *Ainishinabe* words (without translation) throughout the novels, particularly when she wishes to insult those around her, and is an Indian with an attitude. She occasionally dances at powwows, gives relatives mackinaw shirts, and resents being given code-names like "Pocahontas" but gets revenge by calling her parole officer "Kemo Sabe" (*High Country Murder*). She has been in jail on an embezzlement charge, unjustly of course, and, in hiding out from her parole officer and in assisting investigations, has employed a number of aliases. She regularly runs afoul of South Dakota's racist "hick" police who call her "feisty little Injun," "Injun gal," and "squaw," threaten her with physical abuse, and say things like

"You let Injuns off the reservation, and the first thing they're doin' is shakin' hands with John Barleycorn" (*Corona 18*). Except for her use as a sounding post for political correctness and a way to mock the ignorance of South Dakota officialdom, Biwaban is not much different from any other amateur detective who befriends farmers over bankers, who exposes small-town scandals and shady land deals, and who regularly challenges officers of the law. She proves herself a tough survivor, with exceptional tracking skills, but she could be any modern feminist heroine; her ethnic background is irrelevant to the mystery or the detection.

Jean Hager, who is one-eighth Cherokee, sets her stories in Oklahoma and includes in every novel some Cherokee, Osage, or Choctaw tradition that figures peripherally in a criminal case. Her characters have names like Rabbit, Kingfisher, Redeagle, Hummingbird, and Pigeon but, except for the really old-timers like seventy-year-old medicine man Crying Wolf, they seem highly assimilated. References to powwows, moccasins, secret tribal organizations, ancient legends, and special Cherokee skills like fingerweaving provide local color, and Hager includes a smattering of Cherokee words for gods and spirits, descriptions of the power of sacred tobacco, some ritual poems chanted by Crying Wolf (whose reasonableness, tolerance, and insightfulness impress the local sheriff), and several mixed marriages or relationships that, for basic human rather than cultural reasons, go awry. Through Crying Wolf and police assistant Virgil Rabbit, a member of the Cherokee secret organization of Nighthawk Keetoowahs, Hager suggests that truth can be reached through different means: Crying Wolf's dreams, for instance, contain within them symbolic clues that help the sheriff unravel realities, and his rituals for exorcising evil spirits awakened by intruders on an ancient Indian burial ground quieten the fears of local tribe members. Hager counters Cherokee traditions, however, with the cynicism of various locals. For instance, a college student learns in an anthropology class that many of the Cherokee secret traditions were invented by a nineteenth-century lawyer who had his own motives for convincing tribe members to return to the so-called rituals of their ancestors. Hager notes that the Cherokees never held powwows until they became fashionable in the twentieth century, that most powwows are set up to correspond to mainstream national holidays, that parents use mythological villains to frighten youngsters into obedience, and that no matter how diluted the Cherokee blood is, anyone who can trace his or her bloodline back to an ancestor on the Dawes Commission Rolls of 1899-1906 ("a census of the Five Civilized Tribes taken as a prelude to Oklahoma statehood"), is "entitled to all the privileges of tribal membership, including free use of Indian health care facilities" (*Ghostland* 32).

Thus, Hager makes a more serious attempt at showing cultures at the crossroads but still limits her characters to assimilated ways of behaving and thinking. She is an enthusiast but tempers enthusiasm with skepticism; she has little to interpret, due to the assimilation of the group she concentrates on, though she does bring in traditional legends and stories and particulars about arts and crafts; she does try to include some sense of the sociological ramifications of assimilation and to balance raw enthusiasm with, as in the case of powwows, glimpses at cultural complexity and "impurity."

Nonetheless, despite the Cherokees and occasional Choctaw and Apache in the novels, these stories could, in fact, be moved to different settings and ethnic groups (a Mexican-American community in Texas, for example) with only minor changes. That is, the Indian overlay provides local color but in fact makes up only about ten percent of the stories. The reactions of local Cherokees provide misleading possible interpretations of the crime, but the crimes are always mainstream modern ones, or are reducible to basic human motives like greed or jealousy. One of Hager's detectives, Police Chief Mitch Bushyhead, is half-Cherokee but he knows almost nothing about his Cherokee ancestors and is as American as apple pie. His beloved Anglo wife has died of cancer and his main worries are dealing with a teenage daughter who is growing up too fast to suit him, coming to terms with a new love relationship of his own with a local high school teacher, and dealing with local politicians and an overzealous defense lawyer who get in the way of his investigation. The crimes that he investigates could have occurred in any small community: murder that results from drug smuggling (*The Grandfather Medicine*), murder of a bully and wife beater (*Night Walker*), and murder of a child by a sexual pervert (*Ghostland*). Bushyhead's investigations occasionally teach him (and the reader) some few facts about Cherokee ways, but these lessons tend to be surface level. For example, in *The Fire Carrier* readers learn the tradition of the evil spirit, Fire Carrier, because tribal members fear that spirit is responsible for the strange lights that have been recently sighted; however, investigation proves them to have far more modern origins. Ethnic culture is merely a stage backdrop for the thoroughly modern and mainstream action on the front apron.

Hager's second and perhaps less convincing detective, Molly Bearpaw, as an investigator for the Native American Advocacy League and later as the Major Crimes Investigator for the Cherokee Nation Marshal Service in Tahlequah, Oklahoma, knows more about Cherokee traditions than Bushyhead. However, she too is highly assimilated (she is only part Cherokee) and more concerned with carrying out a competent investigation in front of far less motivated males than with the Indian nature of her position. Because she has special knowledge of Indian medicine, she can recognize that an old man's ravings about the angry vengeance of the Cherokee Appropriater make some sense and that seven black stones that seem to indicate Cherokee medicine have really been placed at the scene of the crime by an outsider, and she can convince Cherokees that a local killer is not a witch that sucks the life force from the enfeebled. However, as in the Bushyhead books, the Bearpaw series focuses on crimes that could occur in any community, murder by botulism in a nursing home as part of a conspiracy involving land grabs and the illegal dumping of toxic wastes (*Ravenmocker*), theft and nicotine poisoning to finance medical care for a schizophrenic relative (*The Redbird's Cry*), and construction fraud that leads to double murder (*Seven Black Stones*). Furthermore, the novels' narrative patterns follow whodunit conventions with a list of suspects, misleading clues, and a final unraveling that reduces the mysterious to the almost pedestrian. Even the New Age shaman who attempts to contact a Cherokee ghost at the local Native American Research Library in *The Spirit Caller* could just as easily be an Agatha Christie spiritualist. In other words, Native American culture in these novels is skin deep and contributes little to the readers' understanding of the psychology of the crime, the uniqueness of Cherokee perceptions, or the social interactions of a community or family unit different from that of mainstream America. Perhaps the fact that the Cherokee, traditionally, have assimilated easily and quickly into mainstream culture makes a depiction of them as outsiders difficult. Hager, then, is more honest than Yarbro and Trainor in her use of a Cherokee background to her mysteries, but the very assimilation of her characters means that the Cherokee elements seem superficially applied rather than at the heart of her plots.

In contrast, Tony Hillerman has mastered the art of capturing the perspective and mentality of a relatively unassimilated group, in this case the Navajos, whose ways are clearly different from those of most readers and whose unique psychology affects the nature and solution of the crime. Hillerman is clearly the standard for Native American mysteries, with critics, for example, describing Margaret Coel's first novel as inspiring "comparisons to the work of Tony Hillerman," Peter Bowen's first novel as "the best of Tony Hillerman meets Zane Grey," and Abigail Padgett's first novel as "Quick-paced, packed with good descriptions of Indian lore that would make Tony Hillerman proud," or judging the quality of other regional works by that of Hillerman: "Philip Craig is to Martha's Vineyard what Tony Hillerman is to New Mexico." The use of Hillerman as benchmark is well deserved. *Washington Post Book World* critic Robin Winks notes that Hillerman gets his Zuñi rituals right and knows the Navajo like the back of his hand, so he can make "the vast sunny open spaces of the Southwest as fully threatening . . . as the dark canyons of our corroding cities" (27 May 1990: 12). Hillerman, in an interview with Patricia Holt for *Publishers Weekly,* confirms his role as both interpreter and sociologist, noting that it has always troubled him that "the American people are so ignorant of these rich Indian cultures" and that his personal study of them has determined him "to show aspects of ancient Indian ways [that] are still very much alive and are highly germane even to our ways" (6-7). Hillerman guides readers into the Indian world and makes it to some degree understandable and accessible while stressing its alien perceptions and its very different rules for personal, social, political, and environmental interaction. His plots explore the conflict between modern society and the traditional Native American way of life, mores, values, and customs. Hillerman's high-quality research also makes him a sociologist, who is able to go far beyond tourist perceptions and enthusiasms. Like a social scientist, he recognizes and explores cultural strengths and weaknesses while maintaining a studied objectivity toward his subjects.

His two series detectives bridge two worlds: Joe Leaphorn, a lieutenant of the Navajo Tribal Police and a graduate of the University of Arizona, and the younger, brasher Jim Chee, Sergeant of the Navajo Tribal Police and a graduate of the University of New Mexico. In novels like *The Blessing Way, Dance Hall of the Dead, Listening Woman,* and *A Thief of Time,* Leaphorn's "Navajo Way" of thinking gives him the unique ability to see a pattern in the apparent randomness of violent crime but his cool Western logic helps him see past the Navajo distractions of witchcraft, ghosts, and wolfmen to find rational solutions. His mind is repeatedly described as "orderly," enjoying the "precise application of logic" (*Dance Hall* 53). Pained by the random, the causeless, and the patternless, Leaphorn brings order out of chaos, paralleling the function of Navajo religious myth in making the world understandable. Chee, in turn, is deeply committed to the traditions of his people, and to studying to be a Navajo Singer or Shaman. In novels like *People of Darkness, Dark Wind, The Ghostway,* and *Skinwalkers,* Chee is torn between his love for an Anglo school teacher and his deep-seated need to help restore harmony to his beleaguered people through practicing the old ways. Both detectives must thread their path between cultures, retaining their psychological and spiritual balance as they move between the hurried, sometimes frenzied, complexities of urban white society and the slower-paced, mythic world of the Navajo people (Leaphorn and Chee hardly ever hurry). In *Listening Woman* ritual sand paintings and in *The Ghostway* a death ceremony are clues to murder, while *A Thief of Time*

involves artifact trafficking and *Talking God* kachina spirits and
Yeibichai masks.

Hillerman, like McClure, appreciates the complexity of true multiculturalism and avoids the superficial preachiness of the newly con-
verted. The Navajo perception of reality is vital to Leaphorn and Chee's
investigation, and the pleasure of the novels comes as much from the
insights into a world different from that of most readers as from the mystery itself. Hillerman has the rare ability to avoid tendentious comparisons between opposed cultural practices. He can stand aside and see
both Navajo and Western cultures whole, each having virtues and vices
but each with a valid adaptation to different geographical and historical
circumstances. Hillerman is also no cheerleader, for he is willing to
reject the simplistic relativism that insists all cultures are equal. His
crossroads heroes thus pick and choose among the best of each culture,
but even here Hillerman sees no easy answers. Culture is more than costume and setting; it is ways of thought and action and mixing two diver-
gent ways can bring disaster.

Somewhere in between Yarbro and Hillerman lie the intriguing
novels of Abigail Padgett. Padgett relies on Anglo detectives with
Native American victims or assistants or with the key clues to a crime
located on a reservation. Although she seems the sociologist studying
the cultural mix and clash of values and perspectives in Southern California, she uses her novels to sell readers an idea. Her basic argument is
that the special sensitivities and perceptions created by being manic-
depressive, gay, Native American, or impoverished African American
have their place and make valuable contributions to the whole. To prove
this, she draws on an eclectic mix: (1) a manic-depressive San Diego
child abuse investigator and amateur sleuth, Bo Bradley, who occasionally shares her Celtic grandmother's second sight and who draws on
Irish mythology to understand parallels in her own life; (2) her Mexican-
American co-worker and friend, Estrella Benedict; (3) her Iroquois
friend and occasional psychiatrist, Eva Blindhawk Broussard; (4) her
Cajun lover, Dr. Andrew LeMarche (Lagneaux) from Lafayette,
Louisiana; (5) two gay friends, Rombo and Martin; (6) an arthritic sev-
enteen-year-old terrier; (7) and a changing group of people on the fringe,
including Paiutes, Iroquois, California desert Neji Indians, and Mayan
Indians from Guatemala, rural African Americans, and schizophrenics.
Amateur detective Bradley has studied Indian lore, worked among the
Iroquois in upstate New York, and bases her own therapeutic paintings
on ancient Native American rock drawings. Clearly, Padgett pulls out all
the stops to explore outsiders in American society. In her *Child of
Silence* a Paiute grandmother and mystic finds a young deaf Anglo boy

abandoned on a local Indian reservation, and becomes a family legend through a courageous final act. Once Bradley unravels the boy's tangled ancestry and exposes the evil force behind his would-be killers, she and the child are free to join in the Paiute "Cry-dance" to release the dead grandmother's spirit. In *Strawgirl* an Iroquois mystic helps Bradley protect an eight-year-old and find the rapist-killer of a dead three-year-old, while in *Turtle Baby* a Guatemalan mother of Mayan heritage has fled persecution as a *ladino* and the narrow prejudices of the traditional Mayan clans to find an American life for her son, Acito, or Little Turtle, and Bradley must see time and relationships from a Mayan perspective to understand the clues to double murder. *Moonbird Boy*, in turn, weaves together Neji Indian ritual with neurophysiological research, medical manipulation for megabucks, and World War II atrocities as Bradley recovers from extreme depression at a rehabilitation facility run by desert Indians.

Part of the interest of Padgett's stories is grounded in the concept of perception, with Bradley's manic-depression making her sensitive to voices outside the Establishment. She is sensitive to the inadequacy of a term like "neighborhood" to describe a transient Paiute community, to the abruptness of her questions in the face of Native American indirection, and to the Paiute way of going "behind the blanket" of the mind to shut out disturbing realities. Padgett takes ethnicity in multiple and sometimes contradictory directions: (1) to capture the interesting variety produced by the American patchwork of racial and cultural mixes; (2) to argue the need to reject the prejudices and narrow limitations of cultures that immigrants like Guatemalans Chac and Acito flee; (3) to suggest the unique contributions those with alien, but viable, perspectives can make; (4) but to also recognize the human tendency to label a different perspective or lifestyle "crazy." Her shotgun approach to ethnicity means that no particular voice or view is explored in any depth; instead, there is a chaotic mix of peoples, values, and perspectives that fits neatly with her main character's manic-depressive sense of perceptual overload—too many sensory perceptions bombarding the mind from second to second for there to be a sense of direction or meaning beyond the impulses of the moment. Despite their good writing and unique conception of the amateur detective, Padgett's novels are not truly multicultural: instead, they are somewhat like a tourist picking up souvenirs from a trip across cultures—a dazzling array of colors and styles but a touristic survey in nature rather than a Hillerman-like immersion in the practices of particular cultures.

In each of these five examples of Native-American detectives and advisors, the writers themselves are not Native Americans, but they have chosen to interpret Native-American culture for the audience. Yarbro's Moon and Trainor's Biwaban are not even as culturally distanced as was Charlie Chan, nor in fact are Hager's Bushyhead and Bearpaw. Hillerman's Leaphorn and Chee come closer to representing another culture, but they are, perforce, torn between two worlds, and not wholly of one or the other. Padgett's Native Americans are clearly separate from the mainstream, and find in this separation a cultural uniqueness but also limitations and restrictions. Her Dr. Eva Blindhawk Broussard bridges Western logic and Iroquois mysticism with both medical and psychiatric degrees and an intuitive understanding of the psychological value of Native American mythology.

For multicultural detectives to perform their functions as detectives they must have a Western sense of ratiocination and of police procedures, of the deductive and inductive logic necessary to "detect," or the detective becomes something else—a shaman, a seer, a truth-teller, but not a detective. However, an understanding of another culture allows ethnic detectives insights into the psychology and sociology of those involved in their cases and engages the readers in the exciting experience of discovering a new point of view. The emphasis on intuition and heightened powers of perception fits with the Holmesian tradition of detection being the combination of close observation, logic, and intuition. Nonetheless, when that intuition is reduced to a shaman's medicine finger and its powers remain incomprehensible to Western readers, the ethnicity works against the genre and the result is muddled and unsatisfactory.

Literary Consequences of the Multicultural Detective Movement

If the examples of Yabro, Trainor, Hager, Hillerman, and Padgett are signposts to the future, the ultimate literary consequences of the multicultural detective become clearer. When such stories are read simply for their cultural value, the role of the detective tradition becomes moot. What aesthetic is at work when a good deal of the pleasure of the story involves culture rather than the traditional elements of the story itself? Different readership communities interested in different ethnic groups may become hermetic, shutting out the mainstream elements that made the genre popular in the first place. For example, can the hard-boiled survive in a feminist or gay environment without transforming either the hard-boiled conventions or the cultural values of women or gays? What role does police procedure play in a cultural milieu (such as that of some Native Americans) that is indifferent to such procedure?

Function is an effective measure of the significance, value, and truthfulness of ethnicity in detective fiction. Traditionally, detectives serve at least one of three key functions: (1) champions of class interests;

(2) intermediaries between a world of violence and the world of most readers; (3) distanced, uncommitted commentators on the foibles of mankind. Just as the traditional detective is often the champion or defender of class values and traditions, so the ethnic detective functions effectively as the champion/defender of particular cultural values. Just as the traditional hard-boiled detective mediates between the haves and the have-nots, interpreting each for each, so the ethnic detective mediates between the culturally assimilated and the culturally unassimilated, interpreting each for each. Finally, the commentator detective stands aloof, studying a culture, commenting on it, but intellectually and emotionally distanced from it—taking its measure in the comparative scheme of things. A measure of falsity is when the ethnicity does not serve one of these functions. A novel can be a perfectly good story but contain nothing real in a cultural sense.

A related question about the multicultural detective story is whether the interest comes from the detective story itself, from the exploration of culture, or from an attempt at balance between the two. Does the ethnicity simply provide interesting local color or is it essential to the nature of the detective or to the social milieu in which s/he works? In general, the less cultural interest the greater the reliance on genre conventions, and the more cultural milieu provided the greater the departure from genre conventions. In many modern ethnic detective stories the ethnicity is totally irrelevant to the story; in others, the ethnicity creates a dramatic tension that allows the writer to explore two worlds at the crossroads and to enhance the mystery through providing an alien set of characters to be understood if the mystery is to be solved; in still others, the ethnicity serves a political or social function that the writer values more highly than the detection. In the latter instances, the story often begins to depart decidedly from the genre patterns.

Works in Which Ethnicity Is Irrelevant or Local Color

As we have seen, at one end of the ethnic scale are writers whose characters have ethnic names but whose origins are irrelevant because they are totally assimilated Americans and any association with the culture of their roots is handed down only from grandparents or great-grandparents. Many such characters are traditional European "ethnics" —Irish, Italian, French or German, with names like Irene Kelly, Meg Halloran, Jocelyn O'Roarke, Maggie Ryan, Devon MacDonald, Kojak, Columbo, and so forth. A glance through the mystery section of any library will turn up hundreds of these, but cultural differences and ethnicity will have almost no place in their novels. Other writers, like Camilla Crespi, Marilyn Wallace, Sara Paretsky, Michael Collins, and

Carolina Garcia-Aguilera use ethnicity as a backdrop, for local color or to capture an urban milieu. Crespi's Italian-American detective Simona Griffo tosses out Italian words and talks about Italian food and fashion, for example, sharing a lasagna recipe with readers, but is basically as American as baseball, and the mysteries she solves have nothing to do with her family origins. The Wallace's Oakland detective team, Sergeant Carlos Cruz and Sergeant Jay Goldstein, don't even bother with Spanish or Yiddish words or ethnic markers of any sort. Cruz is a generic Hispanic with no special culture designated, and neither he nor Goldstein have any ethnic distinctions; nor do the seemingly international assortment of gang members, criminals, and local personalities they deal with, despite names like Ali Khamir, Buwande Mumbabe, Nguyen Tho Doc, Angela Martinez, Lisa Wong, and Ian McPherson. Basically, despite skin-deep physical differences, they are all culturally assimilated Californians, and their ethnicity has little or nothing to do with the detection. Thus, the melting pot is still alive and well in some precincts; the ethnic names are a tip of the hat to the convention established in old war movies, but little more.

Sara Paretsky's V. I. Warshawski is equally assimilated. A Chicago private investigator of Polish descent (actually her mother was an Italian immigrant who married a Polish Jew), she is a tough professional with a wry sense of humor and a feminist "attitude." She specializes in financial crime and only rarely gets involved in the ethnic concerns of the Polish community. Her closest friend, Dr. Lotty Herschel, is a Viennese immigrant who fled the Nazis and who is now a renowned perinatalogist at Beth Israel Hospital. Attention to racial issues is an integral part of *Bitter Medicine,* which includes a black detective, the murder of a black doctor, a Hispanic gang, and Warshawski's Hispanic friend as a victim of racist dealings in suburban hospitals. However, cultural differences take second place to detection and the ethnicity realistically represents the cultural mix of Chicago rather than being an attempt to express other voices.

Michael Collins (Dennis Lynds) takes his interest in the urban cultural mix a step further than Paretsky. His disabled (one-armed) Polish private investigator, Dan Fortune, resides in the Chelsea district of New York City and plies his investigative trade primarily among its downtrodden inhabitants. His settings shift from cheap hotels and mean streets where brutality and violence are commonplace to luxurious apartments and executive suites. His topic is the American Dream—its many failures and its bright hope. He is a philosopher of the slums, who deals with blacks, Indians, Latinos, and Vietnamese, and the stories focused on him are realistic sociological studies of the immigrant population. His cases range from drug trafficking and white slavery to murder and terrorism; they capture the nightmare of poverty, and the alienation of the down-and-out. *Minnesota Strip* is typical: a search for a missing Vietnamese girl later found brutally murdered leads to a profitable underground network for helping Vietnamese escape to America. Fortune is a jaded Philip Marlowe, but his New York streets are meaner and tougher, a result of a failure of the melting pot to provide a common opportunity. He asserts: "We are a species that preys on itself. We live on our own kind, hunt each other" (*Minnesota Strip* 3). His America is unassimilated and conflicted, and his detection, though tempered with sympathy for the plight of the immigrant and though dependent on understanding the realities of diverse ethnic groups, remains that of hard-boiled ratiocination— the detective as urban guide opening doors on immigrant life, providing brief glimpses and some insights, and moving on. For Michael Collins, ethnicity heightens the hard-boiled quality of the detection, the class conflict, and the sense of urbanity.

Cuban-born Carolina Garcia-Aguilera creates a bright and sassy Cuban-American private investigator, Lupe Solano, based on her own ten years as a Miami P.I. Lupe's family got out of Cuba before the fall of Batista and are wealthy, privileged American immigrants, with multiple cars, mansions, luxury apartments, sailboats, and servants from back home. The daughters think of themselves as "CAP"s—Cuban-American Princesses. Yet they can not give up their dream of a lost island home even though common sense and daily news reports confirm Cuba's transformation into something very different from the homeland the parents once knew but which their offspring have never seen. Despite this Cuban heritage (the baggage of a mythic land that no longer exists as it once was), Lupe is a sexually liberated, guntoting American feminist, who particularly enjoys trapping dead-beat dads and who complains about the hypocrisy of forgiving wandering males their sexual peccadilloes, mistresses, and womanizing while expecting Cuban-American women to remain seemingly virginal, at least in appearance, manners and speech, long after marriage. Lupe has multiple lovers (often with sex the reward for male assistance on cases), and in *Bloody Waters* several of her villains are finished off by a machete-wielding, pregnant earth-mother, who acts violently to protect the child she carries and her numerous offspring by various partners. In other words, despite a plot involving Cuban nuns assisting the illegal trafficking of Cuban babies to rich, childless, Cuban Americans, the most "ethnic" qualities of Lupe are her preference for thick, rich Cuban coffee over the watered-down American version, her "Cuban" sense of time as an excuse for being late, and the occasional use of *querida, chica, salud,* and *mojocita* to remind readers the central characters are Cuban-American rather than simply American. Otherwise, the conflicts Garcia-Aguilera describes, despite the Miami trappings, are the typical generational differences between liberal youngsters and conservative parents, and between traditional male attitudes and feminist ones.

Works in Which Ethnicity Is a Discovery of Commonalities

In contrast are writers for whom ethnicity not only adds local color but becomes a way for the detective to make the mystery seem initially more mysterious and the crime more impenetrable. In such stories, the detective takes readers into new and alien territory where the familiar patterns of communication and understanding break down. The result is that the detective either becomes a cultural traveler discovering commonalities amid differences or reflects the tensions and frustrations that contact with a different mindset can produce. In other words, just as Raymond Chandler's Phillip Marlowe exposed the hidden life of Los Angeles' communities, so the modern ethnic detective lays bare the hidden world of an ethnic colony. Once that world is revealed, the writer can either make it comprehensible to readers through the detective's dawning recognition of commonalities or use the tensions produced by contrasting visions of reality to heighten the drama. Thus, the detective may become a crossroads interpreter of ethnic differences or a participant in a drama heretofore unknown to the reader.

While there are numerous examples of detectives who find commonalities with an alien culture, a representative example can be found in Walter Satterthwait. His approach to the conflict between detection and ethnicity is to employ a sympathetic crossroads encounter with one group, the Navajos. As we have seen with Hillerman and other writers who use Native American characters and settings, the built-in exoticism of cultures that use different languages, follow arcane religions, and practice folkways unknown to mainstream Westerners allows greater depth of study and more possibilities for interpretation. In *At Ease with the Dead,* Satterthwait sets up a story line that requires both an Anglo and Navajo perspective in order to understand events, centers the crime at the crossroads of two cultures, with the actions of one requiring the response of the other, and has his series detective, Southwesterner Joshua Croft, firmly within the genre guidelines for solving a mystery. Before the mystery part of the story begins, Satterthwait shows his crossroads characters meeting and interacting; their ways of communicating knowledge are clearly different but their first encounter marks a beginning that the rest of the novel exploits as detective Joshua Croft and Navajo Daniel Begay respond to each other on a nonverbal level. Begay hires Croft to bring back the remains of a tribal leader dead since 1866, his body stolen by a geologist as a gift for a daughter with a budding interest in archeology. Doing so involves not only uncovering an unsolved murder but exploring ethnic differences and conflicts. Begay's decision to recover this ancestor is driven by the nightmares of one of the dead man's descendants, dreams that the Navajo take seriously. Satterthwait provides interesting details about Navajo history relevant to the case, for instance, "The Long Walk." When Kit Carson rounded up over 6,000 Navajos and herded them over 300 miles back to Santa Fe, the Navajo dreamer's ancestor hid in the mountains and was eventually buried in Cañon del Muerte.

However, Satterthwait's main focus is on the differences that Croft encounters as he works with Begay, seeking the missing body and then trying to explain the deaths associated with it. Satterthwait explores the Navajo's understated, distanced form of social interaction through Croft's encounters with and developing respect for Begay, and his growing understanding of the man's competence, insights, and importance within his own culture. Satterthwait shows us the human side to ethnic encounters: the closeness and closedness of the Navajo family and community, their suspicion of outsiders, their respect for ancestors and their obligations to them, their internal politics and rivalries, their close ties to the land, the differences in ideas about distance and hardship, the acceptance of violence as inevitable when dealing with violent people, their very different concepts of time and of the ties between past and present, and so on. We experience the differences through Croft rather than simply being told there are differences. The theft of the body ties in with a grab for oil contracts and land leases on Navajo land and involves dirty dealings Croft is used to, but the process of discovery, pursuit, and justice depends on Begay and his Navajo associates. The cultural interest, then, lies in the nature of the crime, the reservation landscape, and the confrontations between individuals who practice different forms of communication. In sum, Satterthwait does not let his interest in Navajos dominate his detection but instead selects those ethnic differences which will add interest and uniqueness to his story and will make Croft's puzzling out of the mystery seem even more ingenious. However, ultimately, the crime is not simply one of cultural insensitivity but of exploitation and greed, and its solution depends on piecing together the clues in the puzzle and combining Western logic with a crafty detective's intuitive leaps. Through Croft and Begay Satterthwait acts as somewhat of a crossroads interpreter, with his detective finding commonalities with the Navajo that help him get to the heart of the crime. Nonetheless, overall, detection, not culture, guides his tale.

Works in Which Ethnicity Produces Conflict

Where Satterthwait shows shared interests (fishing), a shared respect for the land, and a shared expertise bringing together representatives of two cultures, Martin Cruz Smith and Sandra West Prowell concentrate on the tensions between cultures, the differences that divide and that produce misunderstandings. Smith's plots are driven by the suspicion and distrust that separate his ethnically different protagonists. In his *Nightwing,* for example, Hopi Youngblood Duran, a deputy investigating the death of an Indian medicine man apparently killed by a wild animal, initially clashes with Hayden Paine, an expert on bats hired by the Navajo tribal leaders to identify the source of an outbreak of the plague. Cruz shows the Hopi clashing with Navajo and Indians clashing with whites, as Duran and Hayden confront each other antagonistically in the middle of the Painted Desert and as other Indians warn Duran that his Anglo lover, Anne Dillon, is only interested in sex with a savage. Smith also uses this mix of ethnic and racial tensions to drive his gypsy novels (*Gypsy in Amber, Canto for a Gypsy*). Necessity compels partnership between opposites. Smith's Gypsy antique dealer and amateur sleuth, Roman Grey, walks the line between Gypsy and *gaja* (non-Gypsy). Dating a *gaja* woman and trusted by a *gaja* police officer—both relationships condemned by other Gypsies, who accuse him of betraying his heritage—he works on criminal cases involving Gypsy honor. Yet, he has a mystical Gypsy connection with other Gypsies and with animals that markedly sets him apart from people like Harry Isadore, the New York Police Department's expert on Gypsies Grey deals with. Smith acknowledges what some enthusiasts refuse to confront, that ethnic differences can create mutually exclusive ways of behaving, with the necessity of deciding which is "right." What Hillerman's Native American characters call their "Way" (the Navajo Way, the Zuñi Way) may be a harmless or easily tolerated departure from the mainstream norm but also can be an irreconcilable opposite struggling for primacy or survival.

Sandra West Prowell also sees in ethnicity a potential tension that produces a meaningful exploration of contrastive values and perceptions. Her thirties-something, single, Irish-Jewish, Montanan detective, Phoebe Siegel, has a nose for trouble, a phobia about March (it springs with "the ferocity of a lion"—*By Evil Means* 105), and an attraction for Kyle Old Wolf, a Crow Indian police detective whose cases intersect with hers and who eventually becomes her lover. The ethnic tensions begin in her own family (convinced and sentimental Irish Catholics versus Jewish cynics and atheists) and extend to her cases and personal relationships. In *The Killing of Monday Brown,* Kyle Old Wolf involves Siegel in a murder charge against a cousin, Matthew Wolf, and her first meeting with the twenty-year-old, hot-blooded radical and his taciturn extended family is confrontational: their way of checking her out is not her way; their way of communicating leaves her with more questions than answers. Unlike Satterthwait's Croft, who respects the Indian way, she is not sure she even likes Kyle Old Wolf's relatives, much less trusts them; and she only tolerates them because of Kyle. The young males in the family, in turn, are contemptuous of her and delight in making her feel uncomfortable. Matthew Wolf plays on her squeamishness with stories of scalp taking, with warnings about wild animals, and with angry epithets in Crow. Through the tensions between Siegel and Kyle and between Siegel and her Crow clients, Prowell shows differences that alienate and differences that teach lessons about culture, values, expectations, preconceptions, and perceptions; differences that seem insurmountable and differences that are simply other ways of coping with reality. Kyle continually advises her to deal with Crows the Crow way if she is to have any success: "you're going to be entering a third world country compared to down here [Billings]. Their ways are different. Most of which is going to be way outside your reality" (*Monday Brown* 63). However, when he explains what this means, she tells the readers, "I couldn't quite get that look of disbelief off my face" (63). His advice leads to unnerving confrontations with an old woman who communicates with "the Little People . . . a race of dwarfs, with great spiritual powers " (63) and with large family groups that invade her domain, have no sense of private property or private space, and even take her beloved cat off with them for a few days—without even considering asking permission. It also leads to a claustrophobic experience in a sweat lodge purification ceremony and a terrifying, nighttime encounter on a mountaintop with a ceremonially painted murderer. The murder victim, a trader in Indian artifacts, desecrated graves to find valuable merchandise, like a fingerbone necklace and a scalp-lock bag (possibly from the head of the infamous General Custer); one of Kyle's friends makes Siegel (and readers) understand the Crow attitude to the theft of graveyard artifacts through an analogy with the grave sites of her beloved and much mourned brother and father: "Picture this. The rosary is gone, the [police] shields, rings, everything, except for the torso, and that's been pretty ravaged by the elements . . . take what you're feeling right now and multiply it by about three hundred years and several thousand people and you might, just might, come close to what Indian people feel" (38). The perfectly natural Native American outrage at grave desecration is thus made comprehensible to the mainstream reader. However, at the end, with the mystery solved in conventional detective genre fashion, Siegel and the readers are left with a sense of the Crow as still impenetrably alien, as they attend the white-man's funeral for the victim/desecrator and ritual-istically spit on his coffin but then conduct a fully traditional, ceremonial Crow burial for him themselves.

Works in Which Ethnicity Serves Socio-Political Ends

Ethnicity has also provided the detective genre with more direct opportunities for political and social commentary. Just as Dashiell Hammett's Continental Op stories were inseparable from the politics of their day, so many of the modern ethnic detectives are inseparable from the socio-political concerns of modern America. E. V. Cunningham (Howard Fast) was among the first to use an ethnic detective for political reasons, to play off Western materialism (in an area famous for its rich, corrupt lifestyles) against Asian spirituality. His Beverly Hills Police Department detective, nisei Masao Masuto, cultivates the Yin and the Yang, and finds in the meditative philosophy of Zen Buddhism the introspective calm and the self-assured insights that guide his detection. Yet, with twelve years experience in karate, he can explode in violence when rich criminals threaten friends or family. A traditionalist, Masuto takes pride in his Japanese American wife's observance of traditional Japanese customs and rituals like the tea ceremony, hot family baths, massage, and Japanese cuisine. His obedient and respectful son and daughter seem like stereotypical Asian children, but his wife sometimes demonstrates the American part of her heritage by asserting her independence in small matters and by demanding his attention and respect. Readers see Masuto stung by callous taunts about his nisei status (he and his family had been interned during World War II) and by the acid tongues of Southern Californians as he intrudes on their crass, empty life-styles. In the face of racial bigotry, he plays an inscrutable and self-effacing Charlie Chan, polite and accommodating. However, this serene demeanor cannot always hide his American maverick streak: his independent thinking and his contempt for overbearing authority that leads him to ignore political pressure and to unexpectedly subvert the coverups his superiors intend. Through Masuto's Eastern cultural practices, Cunningham exposes the corruption of too much power and wealth and extols the virtues of family life and of liberal and humanitarian values; in other words, here ethnicity brings a social conscience to the detective genre, combining political statement with clever detection.

Paula L. Woods' *Spooks, Spies, and Private Eyes: Black Mystery, Crime, and Suspense of the 20th Century* provides a compact history, with short, illustrative samples, to demonstrate the compelling political and sociological use African American writers have made of the detective and mystery genre to explore questions of "black identity, racism,

crimes against women, infidelity, color consciousness, and sexuality"
(xviii). She views the African American detective story as debunking
stereotypes, providing "unusual and powerful accounts of the impact of
crime" on victims and on the families of the criminal, dealing with murders of victims often ignored by law enforcement "in fact as well as fiction," and, in general, seeking to raise the consciousness of its readers
(xviii). Hughes Allison, the African American author of the 1937 play,
The Trial of Dr. Beck, about a black physician on trial for murdering his
wife, asks, in a letter to his editors, "Could tough, hard-boiled Sam
Spade or suave, gentlemanly Ellery Queen enter that dark, costly
museum room [of Negro culture] and single out the culprits? While it's
possible they could, it's improbable they really would. For neither . . . is
equipped to think with his skin. Moreover, merely apprehending the
room's culprits is not the most important factor involved" (Woods 70).
Authors like John Ball, Chester Himes, and Ed Lacy laid the foundation
for the African-American detective story as social commentary. John
Ball's Virgil Tibbs, a black detective on the Pasadena, California, police
force, has risen above his deprived boyhood in the segregated South of
the 1940s, yet in his job he must repeatedly confront the effects of discrimination.

Chester Himes's Harlem detectives Coffin Ed Johnson and Grave
Digger Jones have their own personal interpretation of law enforcement
when protecting the "good colored people of Harlem." This series
focuses on the social, cultural, racial, political and economic dynamics
of Harlem and makes a trenchant commentary on the nature of American
society as viewed through the joys and fears of African Americans. Ed
Lacy (Leonard Zinberg) has two series, with Toussaint Moore a black
private investigator reared in Harlem and Lee Hayes a black police
detective in New York City. Moore is torn between security and possible
wealth, between the pain of racial discrimination in the South and the
American Dream of success for all. More recently, Eleanor Taylor Bland
has explored the plight of the African-American woman through her
detective, Marti MacAlister, a black female detective with two children
to raise on her own and with female clients with hard-luck stories;
Valerie Wilson Wesley's ex-cop-turned-P.I. Tamara Hayle is another
working mother trying hard not to be trapped into a one-sided relationship with charming but irresponsible African American males.

In addition to these home-grown political voices, conflicts from
other nations have spilled over into the American ethnic detective scene.
For example, Cleveland's Slovenic P.I. Milan Jacovich, in Les Roberts'
The Cleveland Connection, deals with the ethnic hatreds played out in
Cleveland's Serbian and Croate communities, a painfully current theme,

while David Lindsay in *A Requiem for a Glass Heart* shows the Russian Mafia moving into American cities like Houston, Texas, and driving up the crime rate. The tradition of linking detectives to headline stories and concerns has promoted the cause of the ethnic detective as the world grows smaller and more interconnected.

Like Fast, New Yorker Soledad Santiago has a political message to push about power and corruption. Her detective, Irish Puerto Rican Jesus O'Shaugnessy, is in the background; what dominates the foreground and most of the novels is the message. In *Nightside,* for example, Santiago uses an ex-nun, Anna Eltern, the founder of a half-way house, shelter, and counseling center for runaway youngsters caught up in the night-mare world of New York's Minnesota Strip, as her mouthpiece to tie the upwardly mobile to the underground world of addiction and child prosti-tution. As Eltern addresses a United Nations Committee on Children about abused and endangered children in Guatemala (where she worked at a Covenant House) and in New York, as she takes the new special council to the Senate Select Committee on Children on a shocking walk-ing tour of her working neighborhood, and as she speaks to potential halfway-house patrons, Santiago aims to upset readers and win their sympathy and support for causes that are her own:

In the thirty-six seconds it took me to walk up here, an American child was injured or killed by a gun. Every sixty-seven seconds a teenager gives birth. Every eight seconds a child drops out of school. Every forty-seven seconds a child is seriously abused by a parent. Every twenty-six seconds a child runs away from home. These children are not really runaways, they are *throwaways.* Isn't it time we begin to ask some questions about the adults who are running the show? (*Nightside* 104)

Other characters confirm the message. A nurse speaks out, "To many of you the AIDS epidemic is old news. For us at Harlem Hospital, the crisis is just beginning. If the current trend continues, within the next few years fifty percent of the children we see will be HIV positive" (49). O'Shaugnessy, who began his job as an idealist who thought he could single-handedly change the world, now wears a medallion for the patron saint of lost causes, St. Jude, pragmatically recognizes the limits of his power, but continues, like Sisyphus, to struggle against seemingly impossible odds. Santiago's ethnically diverse microcosm provides a vision of a common humanity gone awry, with adult perversions and a lust for wealth and power destroying the futures of urban youths and making them old or dead before their time. This trend of having the detective act out headline issues is likely to continue in the future.

However, not all recent ethnic detectives reflect new immigrants and new concerns. Harry Kemelman's long running Rabbi David Small series employs a mild-mannered, scholarly, and shy Jewish detective, the rabbi of the Barnard's Crossing Conservative Temple, to provide a series of lessons in ancient Judaic tradition and modern Jewish sociology. A devout man of inflexible principles regarding Judaic tradition and ethics, Rabbi Small solves crimes involving temple members by using *pilpul,* the traditional, hairsplitting analysis employed in rabbinical schools to study the Talmud. Following in his footsteps are the mysteries of Faye Kellerman. Kellerman's goal is more ethnically centered: to teach readers about Orthodox Judaism. This goal justifies a deeper immersion into an ethnic community but, as with the other writers exploring heavily ethnic subcultures, she recognizes the need for a guide to bridge cultures. Thus, she has her LAPD Detective Sergeant Peter Decker, a Jew raised by Gentiles, not only assigned as a liaison between the Orthodox Jewish community and the police force, but also fall in love with a committed Orthodox Jew, Rina Lazarus. They first meet in *The Ritual Bath.* Rina Lazarus believes that Decker's assimilation is a betrayal of his genetic heritage and takes on the task of educating him (and the readers) about the values, customs, and secrets of the Orthodox community. Her goal is to move Decker away from his mainstream culture and to guide him back to what she considers the practices of the true faith and of his religious and genetic tradition. Decker's studies with an old rabbi force him to confront the conflict between the sacred world of ancient tradition and the profane world of a homicide cop. With time, Decker and Rina marry. Through this conflicted pair, Kellerman interprets the mysteries of Judaism for nonJews in books like *Sacred and Profane, Day of Atonement,* and *Milk and Honey.*

Reviewers emphasize Kellerman's skill in combining "a depth of Jewish lore and an intuitive grasp of personality" or "a superb mystery plot" with "valid insights into Jewish life" or "juxtaposing orthodox Judaism against a brutal and brilliantly drawn homicide investigation." One secret of her success in combining ethnic concerns with detection is that her crimes and their solutions grow directly out of the conflicts between Orthodox perceptions, values, and traditions and those of the culture around them. However, her confrontations are weighted on the side of Orthodoxy, difference, and refusal to assimilate. Decker's assimilation into mainstream culture is attacked as a cop-out, a result of personal loss and male rootlessness. The female must bring him back to the fold and teach him the security of a protective bubble of ethnicity and of isolation from the mainstream. In other words, Kellerman is less interested in the detection than in teaching readers to appreciate the social, religious, and cultural values of Orthodox Jews, and in demonstrating what she sees as their superiority to mainstream practices. As with Santiago, detection yields to message and much time is spent on clarifying religious practices whose value nevertheless remains mysterious to non-Orthodox, let alone nonJewish readers.

In *The Tree People,* set in the Pacific Northwest's Olympic Peninsula, Naomi Stokes takes this cultural difference one step further so that what begins as detection turns into supernatural horror, with logic and rationality yielding to Salish myth, the Indian equivalent of witchcraft, ancient, mystical and hallucinogenic inspired rituals, ceremonies to bring back souls that evil shamans have separated from their bodies, and natural destructive forces powered by sentient spirits—plant, animal, and once human. As such, the book is a fine example of the hazards of straddling cultures. The bicultural conflict is all the more telling because of the high quality of the fiction: *The Tree People* is interesting, highly evocative of its setting, intelligent, learned, and even poetic at times. Yet ultimately it suffers from a schizophrenic vision about the place of Native American culture in U.S. mainstream life, a vision no doubt reflecting an ambivalence in Stokes herself, who though part Cherokee and clearly well-informed about the environmental consequences of timber exploitation, nevertheless edited a logging newspaper and owned a logging company on the Olympic Peninsula, just as one of her heroines does.

The Tree People's two heroines reflect Stokes' double background perfectly. Jordan Tidewater is acting tribal sheriff for the Quinault Nation, great-granddaughter of Old Man Ahcleet, the last of the old-time shamans who himself is a direct descendant of a great preColumbian shaman named Musqueem. Yet Jordan has turned her back on her family and tribal heritage, and, after a failed marriage, plans to study at the FBI Academy in Quantico. She sees the future for herself and her small son Tleyuk in the material world of the white man, a universe of scientific rationalism, of clear cause-and-effect relationships among visible material things, and of evolving progress measured by ease of living and increasing choice among products and actions. Great-grandfather Ahcleet fulminates at Jordan's rejection of her heritage, but can offer no motive powerful enough for her to embrace it. Her twin brother Paul Prefontaine, like Jordan a police officer and a modern rationalist, suffers doubts about how well events are explained by mainstream Western philosophies but generally goes along with the tide, rejecting the past.

In contrast to Jordan is the other heroine, Hannah McTavish, the owner with husband Michael of Quinault Timber, which has the contract to cut some of the last old-growth timber on the Olympic Peninsula. Initially bored by the timber business and concerned only with the artistic photographic studies the old forests provide, she is forced to become a hands-on manager of the company when her husband is discovered dead. Although she fiercely confronts radical environmentalists who block her operation, threatening to run them over herself, she also suffers increasing doubts about the morality of cutting old-growth timber, and though some of her regrets are about the loss to science and the environment, the heart of her objection is aesthetic and spiritual: the loss of the old trees cannot be reduced to bookkeeping or material measures.

With these two changing heroines (among a host of minor characters and events too numerous and complex to be recounted here), Stokes captures the loss both Native Americans and mainstream whites feel about giving up the past and its aesthetic and spiritual power. However, when her son is possessed by an ancient demon, Jordan accepts her heritage as shaman, the replacement for Old Man Ahcleet; she undergoes the complete training process and visits the Land of the Dead to rescue her son's spirit. At the end of the novel she has been reborn:

Quinault blood. Ancestral blood. The blood of The People. The People who had lived in pride and knowledge and harmony with the other lives on earth since time began. A shaft of moonlight fell upon Jordan. Realization came that she had been granted something wonderful. She, a practical, educated, modern woman, a law enforcement officer, a woman of the almost twenty-first century, had been permitted into the world of her ancestors, the supernatural world of the old shamans. The world of incredible power. Mind power. Spirit power. . . . Pride in her lineage flowed through her . . . (374)

On certain winter evenings like this, the time when the world changes, when one can be transformed, Jordan imagines that the Old Cedar, guardian of the The People, stands upright yet, its crown in the heavens, its roots deep in the earth. But she is a police officer, a woman of the almost twenty-first century, and she plays with fantasy, because the Old Cedar lies prostrate behind her . . . (409-10)

Hannah too is changed, in her case by her direct responsibility for the loss of the old timber:

She stopped every now and then and gazed upward into the lofty branches that seemed like loving arms bending down to welcome her presence. What courteous, benevolent beings trees were! She gave thanks for her new awareness, knowing it was not mere romanticism. Rather, it was a heightened state of consciousness— that enabled her to see what was already there, what was truly real, truly important. This oneness with the earth was what life was all about.

How could she and Michael be in the business of cutting down the ancient forests? (400-01)

At the end of the book Hannah witnesses Ahcleet, Jordan, and Paul burying the evil sorcerer who possessed Jordan's son and brought sickness and malaise to the Peninsula. She is frightened, sensing "a mystery behind their physical facades: a power ancient, wonderful. Something she could never comprehend, never possess. Tears ran down her cheeks. She shook her head and walked slowly away. [Her husband] Michael [along with their timber business] was waiting" (406-07). Just as Jordan returns to her heritage since "what good was a shaman who only half-believed, who was apologetic about the old beliefs?" (374), so Hannah must go back to the timber company, although she will never cut old growth again. Stokes is quite unromantic and realistic here: one may perceive the value of another culture, but one cannot live fully in two cultures at the same time.

There is great literary and philosophic satisfaction in seeing the changes in the two heroines, in Jordan's transformation from an uncritical acceptance of mainstream material culture—in its "just-the-facts" approach that arrogantly denies all reality to spiritual things—to a warm acceptance of her grandfather, her heritage, and her role in her community. Similarly, there is satisfaction in seeing Hannah change from somewhat shallow aesthete, a photographer of ancient beauty her husband is cutting down to finance their luxurious lifestyle and even her photography, into a woman troubled by the morality of lumbering and aware that deeper realities exist, even if she is unable to fully embrace them. However, for all its many virtues, *The Tree People* is not really detective fiction and Jordan Tidewater, at least in her actions in the novel, is no detective: the book serves as a signpost that we have left detective country behind, and that new, magical country lies ahead, a land where normal rules of logic and physics do not apply.

Two facts about culture should be kept clearly in mind when testing whether an ethnic story truly fits the limits of the detective genre. Firstly, all culture depends on context; secondly, lending and borrowing between cultures happens all the time, but is meaningless unless the culture doing the borrowing accommodates its context to the other culture. A Guatemalan shirt in Guatemala City is a work shirt; the same shirt in Chicago becomes a work of ethnic art. A shaman in Native American culture represents a complete and self-sustaining system; in the U.S. mainstream, the practices of shamanism might be anything from a brief entertainment for tourists on a tour of Indian locales to fodder for a master's degree to a supplementary religion.

Context rules, in other words, transforming the meaning of what is borrowed; only if large segments of context are also absorbed does true cultural melding take place. Jordan recognizes that she can't exist in two worlds ("What good is a shaman who only half-believed, who was apologetic about the old beliefs?" [374]). By the end of the book she fully believes. She has solved the "crime" (actually a spirit possession and the unloosing of evil, which are not against the laws of the state of Washington) through her great-grandfather's shamanistic methods. In doing this (and in incidentally finding nothing to charge Aminte—the witch who triggers events—with) she is no longer a ratiocinative detective. She may return to her regular police position, finding culprits the FBI way through forensic evidence and tracing means, motive, and opportunity, but then she will no longer be acting as a shaman.

Stokes also shilly-shallies a bit when she has white characters term the mystical sickness that afflicts the Peninsula a "virulent allergy," a form of "cedar poisoning" called "red lung disease" (320-21). Perhaps she only wishes to show how the white community defines the evil loosed on the Peninsula. However, one suspects juggling of terminology to evoke the comforting notion that all cultures are essentially the same, and that only the words change. In fact, the "allergy" responds very poorly to medication, and we are assured that Jordan's son will surely die without her ritual intervention. Stokes is squarely in the shamanistic context and cannot scramble back out with some scientific-sounding words.

If we are ready to accept detectives who purge themselves and vomit, fast in sweat lodges, mortify their flesh, and chant for days, all in the service of crime-solving (the crime itself having no visible means of commission) then we have indeed entered a new phase of Western culture. Our assertion is that Jordan Tidewater, admirable as she is as a character, is no detective, and her example should serve to mark the boundaries for other "detectives." The problem with *The Tree People* is that for all Jordan's new commitment to her people, shamanism as we see it in the book is simply an alternate crime-solving heuristic, not a complete belief system or a way of life. Like the simple artifact from Guatemalan daily life hung on the wall as an example of folk art, it changs meaning when it changes context. Perhaps for Ahcleet the old ways provide a full context, but Jordan-as-shamanistic-investigator will still drive her Dodge Power Wagon, put out all points bulletins, and use the office computer. Her shamanism ill accords with any conceivable police work except in the special circumstances of the plot.

Overview

Overall then, the writers of mysteries with ethnic detectives best use ethnicity when they depict crossroads encounters between sympathetic or at least understandable characters; despite differences or tension, the characters or the detectives explore cruxes and elucidate them for the reader. In the best works these encounters, differences, and tensions are made integral to the plot and to the detection. When the writer begins to push a political or social message or to overtly teach readers about the designated culture, the plot often gives way to lecture or preaching and the detection becomes less and less central. In addition, such writers face the difficulty of truly representing another cultural perspective and the tendency of reading their own interpretations into others. If the alien culture is given its true voice, readers are likely to have difficulty understanding or relating; thus, a guide or go-between is essential. Yet, by their very nature, such guides or interpreters must translate attitudes, values, and perceptions into terms that make some sense to readers. In other words, the alien must become, to some degree, nonalien and familiar.

Is the Multicultural Detective a Positive Development?

Finally, we should ask if the multicultural detective movement is a positive development for the genre's general readership. Aside from the western and cowboy genre, no other form has enjoyed such success in American popular culture as the detective. One of the few unifying elements in our popular culture, the detective has been recognized as a primarily American figure, at least in more hard-boiled manifestations. Does the multicultural detective signal the end of this tradition? Can a detective who uses a medicine stick to solve a crime be truly a detective in the sense of "detection," that is, a logical process of ratiocination that readers can share and whose conclusions they can confirm by the same process? Genres, like all organically changing things, have their lifetimes, and the detective genre may run its course at some point. A parallel might be to the Western, which dominated television in the fifties and early sixties, became conventionalized and rigid, lost its relevance as women and minorities found new social roles in the sixties, and re-emerged as a more pointed and historically inclusive genre in recent years. The detective genre may be undergoing a similar transformation: breaking with conventional traditions and now experimenting with alternatives. If so, it promises exciting times for readers in the near future.

However, just as a modern Western is still recognizably a Western, and the experiments with the genre have resulted in some failures and some successes, so the present experimentation with ethnicity in detective fiction can be expected to produce both successes and failures, with failures to meet the essential criteria of the genre ultimately producing some new form and with successes modifying and expanding detective fiction to give it new life. Current detective fiction, then, attempts to bridge the developing gap between traditional American culture and the new, much less European and/or nontraditional culture. Ironically, most of the books discussed above have been written by representatives of the older popular culture which is threatened by rising tides of change and immigration—few detective heroes have actually been created by minority writers themselves (though this fact may already be changing). Their sociological function is clear, however, no matter their progenitors: to interpret the newcomers (if they are immigrants) or the "newly discovered" and therefore exotic cultures within the American community (African American, indigenous Native American Indian) to the traditional public for detective fiction, to allow the detective to act as surrogate for the reader in a plunge into an alien, often threatening culture, but one which promises all the excitements of the unknown. When the detective story functions to examine, interpret, or mediate between cultures at the crossroads, the ethnic distinctions often substitute for the class distinctions of the traditional detective story, and the more tightly bound the ethnicity is to plot, character, and solution, the more effective the resultant story.

In summary, the explosion of ethnic detective fiction in the last decade or so has had both positive and negative impacts. The heightened interest has produced a good deal of fringe ethnicity in novels that are like old west theatrical entertainments: very mainstream in style and substance but tarted up with backdrops and costumes that are meant to suggest an exotic locale. The other extreme can be seen in *The Tree People,* where the ethnic context moves so far afield that the defining elements of the genre are lost. Neither extreme does a great deal of damage to detective fiction, but those who love the genre should not be shy about naming names: the best works using ethnicity fall between the extremes and have been created by such writers as Hillerman, Sattenthwaite, and Prowell. Readers offended by *faux* ethnicity should express themselves appropriately and should also resist the encroachment of other types of works into their favorite genre.

Attacking such exploitation is made difficult because of the protection ethnicity and minority status provides. As the rave reviews for works of marginal ethnicity suggest, few wish to seem to be attacking deserving minorities themselves, however cynically such groups may be being used. However, defending the proper use of ethnicity in the detective novel is in fact simply respectful of ethnicity and the genre, a recognition of its importance in a new vision of America.

A Sampling of Ethnic Detectives

African-American Detectives	*Authors*
Virgil Tibbs	John Ball
Pharoah Love	George Baxt
Marti MacAlister	Eleanor Taylor Bland
Sam Kelly	J. F. Burke
Florian Slappey	Octavus Roy Cohen
Max Gold	
Carver Bascomb	Kenn Davis
Madeline Moore	Aya de Leon
Bolivar Manchenil	Donald McNutt Douglas
Harry Holmes	David Farrow
Dr. John Archer & Perry Dart	Rudolph Fisher
(1932: 1st mystery by an African	
American to feature black characters)	
Freeman	Sam Greenlee
C. J. Floyd (bailbondsman)	Robert Greer
Theresa Galloway	Terris McMahan Greer
Ted Washington	Nan Hamilton
Aaron Gunner	Gar Anthony Haywood
Joe & Dottie Loudermilk	
Sam McKibbon	Nat Hentoff
Ezell "Easy" Barnes	Richard Hilary
Coffin Ed Johnson	Chester Himes
Grave Digger Jones	
Cmdr. Larry Cole	Hugh Holton
Webster Flagg	Veronica Parker Johns
Clio Brown	Dolores Komo
Toussaint Moore & Lee Hayes	Ed Lacy
Leonard Pine (gay with straight	Joe Lansdale
white partner)	
Joe Cinquez	Clifford Mason
Arthur (Big Bad LeRoy) Brown	Ed McBain
Easy Rawlins	Walter Mosley
Gianna Maglione & Mimi Patterson	Penny Mickelbury
Blanche White	Barbara Neely
Big Bull Benson	Percy Spurlark Parker
Hawk (Spenser's sidekick)	Robert B. Parker
Alex Cross	James Patterson
Ivan Monk	Gary Phillips

PaPa LaBas (hoo-doo priest &
   reluctant detective)
Lew Griffin
Coffin Ed Johnson

Grave Digger Jones
John Shaft
Tamara Hayle
Miranda Torres
   (Puerto Rican Black from
   Spanish Harlem)

Ishmael Reed

James Sallis
Njami Simon
   (continuing Himes series)

Ernest Tidyman
Valerie Wilson (later Wesley)
Dorothy Uhnak

Armenian-American Detectives
Levon (Lee) Kaprelian (amateur)
Milo Kachigan (19th C. Pittsburgh)

Authors
William Campbell Gault
Karen Rose Cercone

Basque-American Detective
Dominica "Dee" Laguerre

Author
Kirk Mitchel

Cajun Detectives
Dave Robicheaux
J. J. Legendre (sidekick)
Dr. Andrew LeMarche

Authors
James Lee Burke
Dick Lochte
Abigail Padgette

Chinese-American Detectives
Charlie Chan
Kit Chang
Lydia Chan

Authors
Earl Derr Biggers
Charles Goodrum
S. J. Rozain

Cuban-American Detectives
Charlie Morell (a Cuban-American
   whose cases involve Marielitos)
Lt. Cremona (sidekick)
Tico Rico (amateur)
Britt Montero
Lee Valdez of Miami
Lupe Solano

Authors
Alex Abella

Eric Bercovici
Richard Bertematti
Edna Buchanan
William Dantz
Carolina Garcia-Aguilera

French-Canadian Detective
Lt. Valcour (assisting New York police)

Author
Rufus Frederick King

Gypsy Detectives	*Authors*
Michael Vlado (Romanian)	Edward Hoch
Roman Grey	Martin Cruz Smith

Hindu Detective	*Author*
Dr. Motilal Mookerji (sidekick)	Lawrence Blochman

Hispanic Detectives (generic rather than from a particular culture)	*Authors*
Tom Aragon	Margaret Millar
Carlos Cruz	Marilyn Wallace

Irish Detectives	*Authors*
Neil "Hock" Hockaday	Thomas Adcock
Bunny Freedman (half Irish, half Jewish)	Milton Bass
Fergus O'Breen	Anthony Boucher
Jimmy Flannery	Robert Campbell
Father John Aloysius O'Malley	Margaret Coel
Lance O'Leary	Mignon Eberhart
Francis Xavier Flynn	Gregory McDonald
Francis Xavier Killy	Martin Cruz Smith
Neal Rafferty	Chris Wiltz

Irish-Puerto Rican Detective	*Author*
Jesus O'Shaugnessy	Soledad Santiago

Italian-American Detectives	*Authors*
Mike Tozzi	Anthony Bruno
Simona Griffo	Camilla Crespi
Tony Tulio	Nick Gaitano
Joe Puma	William Campbell Gault
Lt. Minardi	Leonard Holton
Vic Varallo	Elizabeth Linington
Joe Carella	Ed McBain
Nick Delvecchio (and many more, mainly assimiliated)	Robert Randisi

Japanese-American (Nisei) Detectives	*Authors*
Bob Nakamura	John Ball
Tina Tamiko	Paul Bishop
Masao Masuto	E. G. Cunningham (Howard Fast)
Reiko Masada	Ray Gilligan

Sam Ohara	Nan Hamilton
Josef Tanaka (forensic sidekick)	Richard LaPlante
Mark Shigata	Anne Wingate

Jewish Detectives	*Authors*
Harvey Krim	E. G. Cunningham (Howard Fast)
Slots Resnick (half Jewish, half Irish)	Michael Geller
Max Guttman	Arthur David Goldstein
Simon Ark	Edward Hoch
Lt. Levy	Elisabeth Sanxay Holding
Sargeant Rosenman	Leonard Holton
Abe Lieberman	Stuart Kaminsky
Rabbi David Small	Harry Kemelman
Peter Decker & Rina Lazarus	Faye Kellerman
Noah Green	Nat Hentoff
Zachery Klein	Matt Jacob
Lt. Shomri Shomar (Israeli detective assisting New York police)	Henry Klinger
Deena Vogler (accused acting as detective)	Rochelle Majer Krich
Nate Rosen (investigates among Cheyenne and Sioux)	Ronald Levitsky
Jesse Falkenstein	Elizabeth Linington
Meyer Meyer	Ed McBain
Attorney Joshua Rabb	Richard Parish
Nina Fishman	Marissa Piesman
Phoebe Siegel	Sandra West Prowell
Alexander Gold	Herbert Resnikow
Norma Gold	
Ed Baer & son Warren	
Avram Cohen	Robert Rosenberg
Dr. Roy Basch (psychiatrist)	Samuel Shem
Moses Wine (hippie)	Roger Simon
Jay Goldstein	Marilyn Wallace
Sammy Golden	Jack Webb
Mom (a Jewish mother) & son Dave (a NY police investigator) (most highly assimilated)	James Yaffe

Mexican-American Detectives	*Authors*
Sonny Baca	Rudolfo Anaya
Gabriel Villanueva Wager	Rex Burns

Antonio (Chico) Cervantes
Jose Manuel Madero
Chief Vince Gutierrez
  (sidekick of Meg Halloran)
David Cruz
Raymond Cruz
Tom Aragon (amateur)
Elena Oliverez
Elena Oliverez
Gimiendo Hernandez Quinto
Luis Mendoza
Henry Rios (gay lawyer)
Luis Montez (lawyer)

Bruce Cook
Geoffrey Homes
Janet La Pierre

John Lantigua
Elmore Leonard
Margaret Millar
Marcia Muller
Muller with Bill Pronzini
James Norman
Del Shannon
Michael Nava
Manuel Ramos

Mexican-Indian Anglo Detective
Johnny Ortiz

Authors
Richard Martin Stern

Native American Detectives

Tribes	*Detectives*	*Authors*
Seminole	Chief Moses of the St. John's Detective Agency	William Babula
Nez Percé (and French)	Gabriel Du Pré	Peter Bowen
Apache	Trade Ellis	Sinclair Browning
Arapaho	Vicky Holden (tribal attorney)	Margaret Coel
Sioux (and French)	Ginevra Prettifield	Cecil Dawkins
Pueblo (Santa Ynez)	Tina Martinez	
Cherokee	Bob Eddison	Michael Delving
Ute	Charlie Moon Daisy Perika (shaman who assists)	James D. Doss
Navajo	Sam Watchman	Brian Garfield
La Costa (a fictitious tribe)	Cindy (Morning Tree) Rhodes (police officer who assists FBI investigator)	Ed Gorman
Cherokee	Mitch Bushyhead Molly Bearpaw	J. L. Hager
Navajo	Joe Leaphorn Jim Chee	Tony Hillerman
Cowlitz	Willie Prettybird (assists)	Richard Hoyt
Lakota Sioux	shaman (assists)	Ronald Levitsky

Kiowa	Tay-bodal (19th c.)	Mardi Oakley Medawar
Iroquis	Eva Blindhawk Broussard (assists)	Abigail Padgett
Hopi/Anglo	Connie Barnes (sidekick)	Jake Page
Seneca	Jane Whitefield	Thomas Perry
Crow	Kyle Old Wolf	Sandra West Prowell
Navajo	Daniel Begay (assists)	Walter Satterthwait
Hopi	Youngblood Duran	Martin Cruz Smith
Aleut	Kate Shugak	Dana Stabenow
Apache	Johnny Ortiz	Richard Martin Stern
Salish	Jordan Tidewater (1st female sheriff of the Salish reservation)	Naomi M. Stokes
Navajo	Ella Clah	Aimée and David Thurlo
Ainishinabe (Chippewa)	Angela Babewan	J. F. Trainor
Passamaquoddy	Christine Saksis	Margaret Truman
"Tsichah" (fictitious tribe based on Cheyenne/Pawnee; the first Native American detective, 1946)	David Return	Manly Wade Wellman
Objibwa	Charlie Spotted Moon (legal investigator)	C. O. Yarbro

Norwegian-Japanese Detective	*Author*
Trygve Yamamura	Poul Anderson

Pennsylvania-Dutch Detective	*Author*
Hana Shaner (Amish)	Roma Greth

Polish-American Detectives	*Authors*
Dan Fortune (disabled)	Michael Collins
V. I. Warshawski	Sara Paretsky

Portuguese-Chinese Detective	*Author*
Inspector Emilio Cortez Rodriguez (born in Hong Kong)	George Hunt Atwood

Puerto Rican Detective	*Author*
Angel the Sex Change (transsexual sidekick of "Easy" Barnes)	Richard Hilary

Russian-American Detective	*Authors*
Dmitri K	Camilla Crespi
Father Tibor Kasparian	Jane Haddam
& Gregor Demarkian	

Scottish-American Detectives	*Authors*
Inspector McGregor	Henry Kane
Inspector Christopher McKee	Helen Reilly

Slovenic-American Detective	*Author*
Milan Jacovich	Les Roberts

Tibetan Detectives	*Author*
(practicing in America)	
Chin Kwang Kham	Ken Crossen
Green Lama	

Vietnamese-American Detective	*Author*
Chip Nguyen	Dean Koontz

Bibliography

Note: The name of the detective is given in parentheses at the end of the listing. If no name is given, the community in which the detective works is an ethnic community.

References

Ball, John. *Five Pieces of Jade.* Boston: Little Brown, 1972. (Tibbs)

——. *In the Heat of the Night.* New York: Harper, 1965. (Tibbs)

Beaty, Jerome, and J. Paul Hunter. *New Worlds of Literature.* New York: W. W. Norton, 1989.

Biggers, Earl Derr. *Behind That Curtain.* Indianapolis: Bobbs Merrill, 1928. (Chan)

——. *The Black Camel.* Indianapolis: Bobbs Merrill, 1929. (Chan)

——. *Charlie Chan Carries On.* Indianapolis: Bobbs Merrill, 1930. (Chan)

——. *The Chinese Parrot.* Indianapolis: Bobbs Merrill, 1926. (Chan)

——. *The House without a Key.* Indianapolis: Bobbs Merrill, 1925. (Chan)

——. *Keeper of the Keys.* Indianapolis: Bobbs Merrill, 1932. (Chan)

Bland, Eleanor Taylor. *Dead Time.* New York: St. Martin's, 1992. (MacAlister)

——. *Gone Quiet.* New York: St. Martin's, 1994. (MacAlister)

——. *Slow Burn.* New York: *Signet*, 1993. (MacAlister)

Chastain, Thomas. *Vital Statistics.* New York: Times Books, 1977.

Coel, Margaret. *The Eagle Catcher.* New York: Berkley Prime Crime, 1995. (Holden)

——. *The Ghost Walker.* New York: Berkley Prime Crime, 1996. (Holden)

——. *The Dream Stalker.* New York: Berkley Prime Crime, 1997. (Holden)

Collins, Michael. *An Act of Fear.* New York: Dodd Mead, 1967. (Fortune)

——. *Blue Death.* New York: Dodd Mead, 1975. (Fortune)

——. *The Blood-Red Dream.* New York: Dodd Mead, 1976. (Fortune)

——. *The Brass Rainbow.* New York: Dodd Mead, 1969. (Fortune)

——. *Minnesota Strip.* New York: Donald I. Fine., Inc.,1987. (Fortune)

——. *Night of the Toads.* New York: Dodd Mead, 1970. (Fortune)

——. *The Nightrunners.* New York: Dodd Mead, 1979. (Fortune)

——. *Shadow of a Tiger.* New York: Dodd Mead, 1972. (Fortune)

——. *The Silent Scream.* New York: Dodd Mead, 1973. (Fortune)

——. *Walk a Black Wind.* New York: Dodd Mead, 1971. (Fortune)

Crespi, Camilla. *The Trouble with a Bad Fit.* New York: Harper Collins,1996. (Griffo)

——. *The Trouble with Going Home.* New York: Harper Collins,1995. (Griffo)

Cunningham, E. V. (Howard Fast). *The Case of the Kidnapped Angel.* New York: Delacorte, 1982. (Masuto)

——. *The Case of the Murdered Mackenzie.* New York: Delacorte, 1984. (Masuto)

——. *The Case of the One-Penny Orange.* New York: Holt Rinehart, 1977. (Masuto)

——. *The Case of the Poisoned Eclairs.* New York: Holt Rinehart, 1979. (Masuto)

——. *The Case of the Russian Diplomat.* New York: Holt Rinehart, 1978. (Masuto)

——. *The Case of the Sliding Pool.* New York: Delacorte, 1981. (Masuto)

Delving, Michael. *The Devil Finds Work.* New York: Charles Scribner's Sons, 1960.

——. *Smiling the Boy Fell Dead.* New York: Charles Scribner's Sons, 1968.

Hager, Jean. *The Fire Carrier.* New York: Warner Books, 1996. (Bushyhead)

——. *Ghostland.* New York: Warner Books, 1992. (Bushyhead)

——. *The Grandfather Medicine.* New York: Warner Books, 1989. (Bushyhead)

——. *Night Walker.* New York: Warner Books, 1990. (Bushyhead)

——. *Ravenmocker.* New York: Warner Books, 1994. (Bearpaw)

——. *The Redbird's Cry.* New York: Warner Books, 1994. (Bearpaw)

——. *Seven Black Stones.* New York: Warner Books, 1995. (Bearpaw)

——. *The Spirit Caller.* New York: Warner Books,1997. (Bearpaw)

Hillerman, Tony. *The Blessing Way.* New York: Harper, 1970. (Leaphorn)

——. *Coyote Waits.* New York: Harper, 1990. (Chee)

——. *Dance Hall of the Dead.* New York: Harper, 1973. (Leaphorn)

——. *The Dark Wind..* New York: Harper, 1981. (Chee)

——. *The Ghost Way.* New York: Harper, 1984. (Chee)

——. *Listening Woman.* New York: Harper, 1978. (Leaphorn)

——. *People of Darkness.* New York: Harper, 1980. (Chee)

——. *Sacred Clowns.* New York: Harper, 1993. (Chee & Leaphorn)

——. *Skinwalker.* New York: Harper, 1986. (Chee)

——. *Talking God.* New York: Harper, 1989. (Chee & Leaphorn)

——. *A Thief of Time.* New York: Harper, 1985. (Leaphorn)

Himes, Chester. *All Shot Up.* New York: Avon, 1960. (Johnson & Jones)

——. *The Big Gold Dream.* New York, Avon, 1960. (Johnson & Jones)

——. *Blind Man with a Pistol* (also as *Hot Day, Hot Night.*). New York: Morrow, 1969. (Johnson & Jones)

——. *The Crazy Kill.* New York: Avon, 1959. (Johnson & Jones)

——. *Cotton Comes to Harlem.* New York: Putnam, 1965. (Johnson & Jones)

——. *For Love of Imabelle* (also as *A Rage in Harlem*). New York: Fawcett, 1957. (Johnson & Jones)

——. *The Heat's On* (also as *Come Back Charleston Blue*). New York: Putnam, 1966. (Johnson & Jones)

——. *Plan B.* Mississippi: University Press of Mississippi, 1993. (Johnson & Jones)

——. *The Real Cool Killers.* New York: Avon, 1959. (Johnson & Jones)

Holt, Patricia. "Tony Hillerman." *Publishers Weekly* 218.17 (24 Oct. 1980): 6-7.

Keating, H. R. *Inspector Ghote Breaks an Egg.* London: Collins, 1970. (Ghote)

——. *Inspector Ghote Caught in Meshes.* London: Collins, 1967. (Ghote)

——. *Inspector Ghote Goes by Train.* London: Collins, 1971. (Ghote)

——. *Inspector Ghote Hunts the Peacock.* London: Collins, 1968. (Ghote's preconceptions about Londoners are sorely tested)

——. *The Perfect Murder.* London: Gollancz, 1964. (Ghote)

Kellerman, Faye. *Day of Antonement.* New York: William Morrow, 1991. (Decker/Lazarus)

——. *False Prophet.* New York: William Morrow, 1992. (Decker/ Lazarus)

——. *Grievous Sin.* New York: William Morrow, 1993. (Decker/ Lazarus)

——. *Justice.* New York: William Morrow, 1995. (Decker/Lazarus)

——. *Milk and Honey.* New York: William Morrow, 1990. (Decker/ Lazarus)

——. *The Ritual Bath.* New York: Arbor House, 1986. (Decker/Lazarus)

——. *Sacred and Profane.* New York: Arbor House, 1987. (Decker/ Lazarus)

——. *Sanctuary.* New York: William Morrow, 1994. (Decker/Lazarus)

Kemelman, Harry. *Friday the Rabbi Slept Late.* New York: Crown, 1964. (Small)

——. *Monday the Rabbi Took Off.* New York: Crown, 1972. (Small)

——. *One Fine Day the Rabbi Bought a Cross.* New York: Crown, 1987. (Small)

——. *Saturday the Rabbi Went Hungry.* New York: Crown, 1966. (Small)

——. *Someday the Rabbi Will Leave.* New York: Crown, 1985. (Small)

——. *Sunday the Rabbi Stayed Home.* New York: Crown, 1969. (Small)

——. *Thursday the Rabbi Walked Out.* New York: Crown, 1978. (Small)

——. *Tuesday the Rabbi Saw Red.* New York: Crown, 1973. (Small)

——. *Wednesday the Rabbi Got Wet.* New York: Crown, 1976. (Small)

Koontz, Dean. *TickTock.* New York: Random House, 1996. (Phan/Nguyen)

Lacy, Ed. *Harlem Underground.* New York: Pyramid, 1965. (Hayes)

——. *In Black and Whitey.* New York: Lancer, 1967. (Hayes)

——. *Moment of Untruth.* New York: Lancer, 1964. (Moore)

——. *Room to Swing,* New York: Harper, 1957. (Moore)

Leonard, Elmore. *City Primeval—High Noon in Detroit.* New York. Arbor House Publishing, 1980. (Cruz)

Lindsey, David. *Requiem for a Glass. Heart.* New York Doubleday, 1996.

Marquand, John. *Last Laugh, Mr. Moto.* Boston: Little Brown, 1942. (Moto)

——. *Ming Yellow.* Boston: Little Brown, 1935. (Moto)

——. *Mr. Moto is So Sorry.* Boston: Little Brown, 1938. (Moto)

——. *Stopover: Tokyo.* Boston: Little Brown, 1957. (Moto)

——. *Thank You, Mr. Moto.* Boston: Little Brown, 1936. (Moto)

——. *Think Fast, Mr. Moto.* Boston: Little Brown, 1937. (Moto)

McClure, James. *The Caterpillar Cop.* London: Gollancz, 1972. (Kramer & Zondi)

——. *The Gooseberry Fool.* London: Gollancz, 1974. (Kramer & Zondi)

——. *Rogue Eagle.* London: Gollancz, 1976. (Kramer & Zondi)

——. *Snake.* London: Gollancz, 1976. (Kramer & Zondi)

——. *The Steam Pig.* London: Gollancz, 1971. (Kramer & Zondi)

——. *The Sunday Hangman.* London: Gollancz, 1972. (Kramer & Zondi)

Melville, James. *The Chrysanthemum Chain.* London: Martin Secker & Warburg, 1980. (Otani & Kimura)

——. *The Death Ceremony.* London: Martin Secker & Warburg, 1985. (Otani & Kimura)

——. *Death of a Daimyo.* London: Martin Secker & Warburg, 1984. (Otani & Kimura)

——. *The Ninth Netsuke.* London: Martin Secker & Warburg, 1982. (Otani & Kimura)

——. *Sayonara, Sweet Amaryllis.* London: Martin Secker & Warburg, 1983. (Otani & Kimura)

——. *The Wages of Zen.* London: Martin Secker & Warburg, 1979. (Otani & Kimura)

Mosley, Walter. *Black Betty.* New York: Norton, 1994. (Easy Rawlins)

——. *Devil in a Blue Dress.* New York: Norton, 1990. (Easy Rawlins)

——. *A Red Death*. New York: Norton, 1991. (Easy Rawlins)

——. *White Butterfly*. New York: Norton, 1990. (Easy Rawlins)

Padgett, Abigail. *Child of Silence*. New York: Time Warner, 1993. (Bradley)

——. *The Dollmaker's Daughters*. New York: Time Warner, 1997. (Bradley)

——. *Moonbird Boy*. New York: Time Warner, 1997. (Bradley)

——. *Strawgirl*. New York: Time Warner, 1994. (Bradley)

——. *Turtle Baby*. New York: Time Warner, 1995. (Bradley)

Paretsky, Sara. *Bitter Medicine*. New York: William Morrow, 1987. (Warshawski)

——. *Blood Shot*. New York: Delacorte Press, 1988. (Warshawski)

——. *Burn Marks*. New York: Delacorte Press, 1990. (Warshawski)

——. *Deadlock*. New York: The Dial Press, 1984. (Warshawski)

——. *Indemnity Only*. New York: The Dial Press, 1982. (Warshawski)

——. *Killing Orders*. New York: William Morrow, 1985. (Warshawski)

Pronzini, Bill, and Martin H. Greenberg, ed. *The Ethnic Detectives: Masterpieces of Mystery Fiction*. New York: Dodd, Mead & Co., 1985.

Prowell, Sandra West. *By Evil Means*. New York: Walker and Co., 1993. (Siegel)

——. *The Killing of Monday Brown*. New York: Walker and Co., 1994. (Siegel and Wolf)

——. *When Wallflowers Die*. New York: Walker and Co., 1996. (Siegel and Wolf)

Roberts, Les. *The Cleveland Connection*. 1996.

Santiago, Soledad. *Nightside*. New York: Doubleday, 1994. (O'Shaugnessy)

——. *Room 9*. New York: Doubleday, 1993. (O'Shaugnessy)

——. *Undercover*. New York: Doubleday, 1992. (O'Shaugnessy)

Satterthwait, Walter. *At Ease with the Dead*. New York: St. Martin's Press, 1990.

Shannon, Dell. *The Ace of Spades*. New York: Harper, 1961. (Mendoza)

——. *Case Pending*. New York: Harper, 1960. (Mendoza)

Smith, Martin Cruz. *Canto for a Gypsy*. New York: Random House, 1972. (Grey)

——. *Gypsy in Amber*. New York: Random House, 1971. (Grey)

——. *Nightwing*. New York: Random House, 1977. (Duran)

Stokes, Naomi M. *The Tree People*. New York: A Tom Doughtery Associates Book, 1995. (Tidewater)

Trainor, J. F. *Corona Blue*. New York: Kensington Books, 1994.

——. *Dynamite Pass*. New York: Kensington Books, 1992.

——. *High Country Murder*. New York: Kensington Books, 1995.

——. *Target for Murder* New York: Kensington Books, 1991.

——. *Whiskey Jack*. New York: Kensington Books, 1993.

Upfield, Arthur. *The Bone Is Pointed*. Sydney: Angus and Robertson, 1938.

——. *Bony and the Mouse*. London: Heinemann, 1959. (Bonaparte)

——. *The Man of Two Tribes* . New York: Doubleday, 1956

Van Gulik, Robert. *The Chinese Bell Murders*. New York: Charles Scribner's Sons, 1958. (Dee)

——. *The Chinese Gold Murders*. New York: Harper & Row, 1959. (Dee)

——. *The Chinese Lake Murders*. New York: Harper & Row, 1960. (Dee)

——. *The Chinese Maze Murders*. New York: Harper & Row, 1957. (Dee)

——. *The Chinese Nail Murders*. New York: Harper & Row, 1961. (Dee)

——. *Judge Dee at Work*. New York: Charles Scribner's Sons, 1967. (Dee)

——. *The Monkey and the Tiger*. New York: Charles Scribner's Sons, 1965. (Dee)

——. *Murder in Canton*. New York: Charles Scribner's Sons, 1966. (Dee)

——. *Necklace and Calabash*. New York: Charles Scribner's Sons, 1967. (Dee)

——. *The Phantom of the Temple*. New York: Charles Scribner's Sons, 1966. (Dee)

——. *Poets and Murder*. New York: Charles Scribner's Sons, 1968. (Dee)

Wallace, Marilyn. *A Case of Loyalties*. New York: St. Martin's Press, 1986. (Goldstein & Cruz)

——. *Seduction*. New York: Doubleday, 1993. (Goldstein & Cruz)

——. *A Single Stone*. New York: Doubleday, 1991. (Goldstein &Cruz)

——. *So Shall You Reap*. New York: Doubleday, 1992. (Goldstein & Cruz)

Winks, Robin. "Tony Hillerman." *Washington Post Book World* 27 May 1990: 12.

Woods, Paula L., ed. *Spooks, Spies, and Private Eyes: Black Mystery, Crime, and Suspense of the 20th Century*. New York: Doubleday, 1995.

Yarbro, C(helsea). O. *Bad Medicine*. New York: The Berkley Publishing Co., 1991. (Spotted Moon)

——. *Cat's Claw*. New York: The Berkley Publishing Co., 1992. (Spotted Moon)

——. *False Notes*. New York: G. P. Putnam's Sons, 1979. (Spotted Moon)

——. *Music When Sweet Voices Die*. New York: G. P. Putnam's Sons, 1979. (Spotted Moon)

——. *Ogilore, Tallant and Moon*. New York: G. P. Putnam's Sons, 1976. (Spotted Moon)

Ethnic Detective Novels Not Discussed in This Essay

Abella, Alex. *The Killing of the Saints*. New York: Crown, 1991. (Morell)

Adcock, Thomas. *Dark Maze*. New York: Pocket Books, 1993. (Hockaday)

——. *Devil's Heaven*. New York: Pocket Books, 1995. (Hockaday)

——. *Down All the Dogs*. New York: Pocket Books, 1994. (Hockaday)

——. *Sea of Green*. New York: Mysterious Press, 1989. (Hockaday)

Anaya, Rudolfo. *Albuquerque* New York: Warner, 1992. (Baca)

——. *Bendîcime, Ultima*. New York: Warner, 1994. (Baca)

——. *Bless Me, Ultima.* New York: Warner, 1993. (Baca)

——. *Rio Grande Fall.* New York: Warner, 1996. (Baca)

——. *Zia Summer.* New York: Warner, 1995. (Baca)

Anderson, Poul. *Perish by the Sword.* New York: Macmillan, 1959. (Yamamura)

Atwood, George Hunt. *The Prowler of Mount Hebron.* Bryn Mawr, Pennsylvania: Dorrance and Co., 1986 (Rodriguez)

Bagula, William. *According to St. John.* New York: Carol Communications, 1989. (Chief Moses)

——. *St. John and the Seven Veils.* New York: Carol Publishing, 1991. (Chief Moses)

——. *St. John's Baptism.* New York: Citadel Presss, 1988. (Chief Moses)

——. *St. John's Bestiary.* Colorado: Write Way Publishing, 1994. (Chief Moses)

Ball, John.*The Belfast Connection.* New York: New American Library, 1988. (Freedman)

——. *The Cool Cottontail.* New York: Harper, 1966. (Tibbs)

——. *The Eyes of Buddha.* Boston: Little Brown, 1965. (Tibbs)

——. *Johnnie Get Your Gun* (revised as *Death for a Playmate*). Boston: Little Brown, 1969. (Tibbs)

——. *Mark One—The Dummy.* Boston: Little Brown, 1974. (Tibbs)

——. *Police Chief.* New York: Doubleday, 1977. (Tibbs)

——. *Singapore.* New York: Dodd, Mead, & Co., 1986. (Tibbs)

——. *Then Came Violence.* New York: Dodd, Mead, & Co., 1980. (Tibbs)

Bass, Milton. *The Bandini Affair.* New York: New American Library, 1987. (Freedman)

——. *The Moving Finger.* New York: New American Library, 1988. (Freedman)

Baxt, George. *A Queer Kind of Death.* New York: St. Martin's, 1979. (Love)

——. *A Queer Kind of Love.* New York: Otto Penzler Books, 1994. (Love)

——. *A Queer Kind of Umbrella.* New York: Simon & Schuster, 1967. (Love)

——. *Swing Low, Sweet Harriet.* New York: Simon & Schuster, 1995. (Love)

——. *Tipsy and Evil.* New York: Simon & Schuster, 1968. (Love)

Bercovici, Eric. *So Little Cause for Caroline.* New York: Atheneum, 1981. (Cremona)

Bishop, Paul. *Citadel Run.* New York: Tom Doherty Press, 1989. (Tamiko)

Blaise, Clark. *A North American Education.* New York: Doubleday, 1973.

——. *Tribal Justice.* New York: Doubleday, 1974. (Blaise depicts unassimilated tribes, groups of different ethnic, geographic, religious backgrounds who coexist, skeptical of each other until someone from one group is forced to penetrate an alien group; Blaise confronts how our cultural attitudes shape our lives)

Blochman, Lawrence. *Clues for Dr. Coffee.* New York: J.B. Lippincott, 1950. (Mookerji) (Also has an Inspector Leonidas Prike of Bombay, India series.)

Bowen, Peter. *Coyote Wind.* New York: St. Martin's, 1994. (Du Pré)

——. *Specimen Song.* New York: St. Martin's, 1995. (Du Pré)

——. *Wolf, N Wolf.* New York: St. Martin's, 1996. (Du Pré)

Brandon, Jay. *Predator's Waltz.* New York: St. Martin's, 1989. (a Vietnamese-Texas fishing community)

Brown, Mark. *Game Face.* Woodbridge, CT: Oxbow Press, 1992. (Ben McMillen, Hawaiian detective)

——. *The Puna Kahuna.* Woodbridge, CT: Oxbow Press, 1993. (McMillen)

——. *Yellowfin.* Woodbridge, CT: Oxbow Press, 1992. (McMillen)

Buchanan, Edna. *Act of Betrayal.* New York: Hyperion, 1996. (Montero)

——. *Contents Under Pressure.* New York: Hyperion, 1992. (Montero)

——. *Miami, It's Murder.* New York: Hyperion, 1994. (Montero)

——. *Nobody Lives Forever.* New York: Random House, 1990. (Montero)

——. *Suitable for Framing.* New York: Hyperion, 1995. (Montero)

Burke, J. F. *Crazy Woman Blues.* New York: Dutton, 1978. (Kelly)

——. *Death Trick.* New York: Harper & Row, 1975. (Kelly)

——. *Kelly's among the Nightingales.* New York: Dutton, 1979. (Kelly)

——. *Location Shots* New York: Harper & Row, 1974. (Kelly

Burke, James Lee. *Black Cherry Blues.* New York: Avon, 1990. (Robicheaux)

——. *Burning Angel.* New York: Hyperion, 1995. (Robicheaux)

——. *Dixie City Jam.* New York: Hyperion, 1994. (Robicheaux)

——. *Heaven's Prisoners.* New York: Holt, 1988. (Robicheaux)

——. *In the Electric Mist with Confederate Dead.* New York: Avon, 1993. (Robicheaux)

——. *A Morning for Flamingos.* New York: Avon, 1990. (Robicheaux)

——. *The Neon Rain.* New York: Holt, 1987. (Robicheaux)

——. *A Stained White Radiance.* New York: Avon, 1989. (Robicheaux)

Campbell, Robert. *The Junkyard Dog.* New York: New American Library, 1986. (Flannery)

——. *Nibbled to Death by Ducks.* New York: Pocket Books, 1989. (Flannery)

Cercone, Karen Rose. *Steel Ashes.* New York: Berkley Prime Crime, 1997. (Kachigan)

Cohen, Martin S. *The Truth about Marvin Kalish.* Port Angeles, Washington: Ben-Simon Publications, 1996. (a Jewish mystery full of Jewish mysticism)

Cook, Bruce. *Death as a Career Move.* New York: St. Martin's, 1992.

——. *Mexican Standoff.* New York: Franklin Watts, 1988.

——. *Rough Cut.* New York: St. Martin's, 1990.

Crumley, James. *Bordersnakes.* New York: Warner, 1996.

——. *The Dancing Bear.* New York: Random House, 1983.

——. *The Mexican Tree Duck.* New York: Warner, 1995.

Cunningham, E. V. (Howard Fast). *Margie.* New York: Morrow, 1966. (Cohen and Comaday)

——. *Penelope*. New York: Doubleday, 1965. (Cohen and Comaday)

——. *Samantha*. New York: Morrow, 1967, published as *The Case of the Angry Actress*. New York: Dell, 1985. (Masuto)

——. *Sylvia*. New York: Doubleday, 1960. (Masuto)

Dantz, William. *The Seventh Sleeper*. New York: William Morrow, 1990. (Valdez)

Dawkins, Cecil. *Clay Dancers*. New York: Random House, 1994. (Martinez)

——. *The Santa Fe Rembrandt*. New York: Random House, 1993. (Prettyfield)

Doss, James D. *The Shaman Laughs*. New York: St. Martin's, 1995. (Moon; Perika)

——. *The Shaman Sings*. New York: St. Martin's, 1994. (Perika)

Gaitano, Nick. *Special Victims*. New York: Simon and Schuster, 1994. (Tulio)

Gault, William Campbell. *The Bloody Bokhara*. New York: E. P. Dutton, 1952. (Kaprelian)

Goldstein, Arthur David. *Nobody's Sorry He Got Killed*. New York: Random House, 1976. (Guttman)

——. *A Person Shouldn't Die Like That*. New York: Random House, 1972. (Guttman)

——. *You're Never Too Old to Die*. New York: Random House, 1974. (Guttman)

Gorman, Ed. *Hawk Moon*. London: Headline Book Publishing. 1995. (Rhodes)

Greer, Robert. *The Devil's Hat Band*. New York: Warner, 1996. (Floyd)

Greer, Terris McMahan. *Blood Will Tell*. New York: Signet, 1997. (Galloway)

——. *Somebody Else's Child* New York: Signet, 1996. (Galloway)

Greth, Roma. *Now You Don't*. New York: Pageant Books, 1988. (Shaner)

Haddam, Jane. *Bleeding Hearts*. New York: Bantam, 1994. (Kasparian & Demarkian)

——. *Precious Blood*. New York: Bantam, 1991. (Kasparian & Demarkian)

——. *A Stillness in Bethleham*. New York: Bantam, 1992. (Kasparian & Demarkian)

Haiblum, Isidore. *Murder in Yiddish*. New York: St. Martin's, 1988. (Detective James Shaw)

Hamilton, Nan. *Killer's Rights*. New York: Walker and Co., 1984. (Washington & Ohara)

——. *The Shape of Fear*. New York: Dodd, Mead, and Co., 1986. (Washington & Ohara)

Handler, David. *Kiddo*. New York: Ballantine, 1986. (Jewish community)

Haywood, Gar Anthony. *Fear of the Dark*. New York: St. Martin's, 1988. (Gunner)

——. *Going Nowhere Fast*. New York: G. P. Putnam's Sons, 1994. (Gunner)

——. *Not Long for This World*. New York: St. Martin's, 1990. (Gunner)

Hentoff, Nat. *Blues for Charlie Darwin*. New York: William Morrow, 1982. (Green & McKibbon)

Hilary, Richard. *Pieces of Cream*. New York: Bantam, 1987. (Barnes and Angel)
——. *Pillow of the Community*. New York: Bantam, 1988. (Barnes and Angel)
——. *Snakes in the Greasses*. New York: Bantam, 1987. (Barnes and Angel)
Homes, Geoffrey. *The Street of the Crying Woman*. New York: Morrow, 1942, as *The Case of the Mexican Knife*. New York: Bantam, 1948.
Kaminsky, Stuart. *Lieberman's Choice*. New York: Icy Books, 1993. (Lieberman)
——. *Lieberman's Day*. New York: Icy Books, 1994. (Lieberman)
——. *Lieberman's Folly*. New York: Icy Books, 1991. (Lieberman)
——. *Lieberman's Thief*. New York: Icy Books, 1995. (Lieberman)
Klein, Zachary. *No Saving Grace*. New York: Fawcett Columbine, 1993. (Jacob with Hassidic Jews)
——. *Still Among the Living*. New York: Fawcett Columbine, 1992. (Jacob)
——. *Two-Way Toll*. New York: Fawcett Columbine, 1991. (Jacob)
Lansdale, Joe. *Mucho Mojo*. New York: Warner Books, 1994. (Pine)
——. *The Two-Bear Mambo*. New York: Warner Books, 1995. (Pine)
Lantigua, John. *Heat Lightning*. New York: G. P. Putnam's Sons, 1987. (Cruz)
LaPlante, Richard. *Leopard*. New York: Tom Doherty Associates, 1993. (Tanaka)
——. *Mantis*. New York: Tom Doherty Associates, 1994. (Tanaka)
——. *Steroid Blues*. New York: Tom Doherty Associates, 1995. (Tanaka)
Levitsky, Ronald. *The Love That Kills*. New York: Charles Scribner's Sons, 1994. (Rosen)
——. *Stone Boy*. New York: Charles Scribner's Sons, 1995. (Rosen)
Lochte, Dick. *Blue Bayou*. New York: Simon & Schuster, 1992. (Legendre)
——. *Sleeping Dog*. New York: Simon & Schuster, 1991. (Legendre)
Medawar, Mardi Oakley. *Death at Rainy Mountain*. New York: St. Martin's Press, 1996 (Tay-bodal)
——. *The Witch of Palo Duro*. New York: St. Martin's Press, 1997. (Tay-bodal)
Millar, Margaret. *Ask for Me Tomorrow*. New York: Random House, 1976. (Aragon)
——. *Mermaid*. New York: Random House, 1982. (Aragon)
——. *The Murder of Miranda*. New York: Random House, 1979. (Aragon)
Mitchell, Kirk. *High Desert Malice*. New York: Avon, 1995.
Nava, Michael. *The Death of Friends*. New York: G.P. Putnam's Sons, 1996. (Rios)
——. *Goldenboy*. Boston: Alyson Publications, Inc., 1988. (Rios)
——. *The Hidden Law*. New York: Harper Collins, 1992. (Rios)
——. *How Town*. New York: Harper & Row, 1990. (Rios)
——. *The Little Death*. Boston: Alyson Publications, Inc., 1986. (Rios)
Neely, Barbara. *Blanche Among the Talented Tenth*. New York: St. Martin's Press, 1994.

Page, Jake. *The Deadly Canyon.* New York: Random House, 1994.

——. *The Knotted Strings.* New York: Random House, 1995.

——. *The Stolen Gods.* New York: Random House, 1994.

Parish, Richard. *The Dividing Line.* New York: Dutton, 199 . (Rabb)

——. *Nothing but the Truth.* New York: Dutton, 1995. (Rabb)

——. *Our Choice of Gods.* New York: Dutton, 199. (Rabb)

——. *Versions of the Truth.* New York: Dutton, 1994. (Rabb)

Patterson, James. *Along Came a Spider.* Boston: Little Brown, 1993. (Cross)

——. *Hide and Seek.* Boston: Little Brown, 1994. (Cross)

——. *Jack and Jill.* Boston: Little Brown, 1996. (Cross)

——. *Kiss the Girls.* Boston: Little Brown, 1995. (Cross)

Perry, Thomas. *Dance for the Dead.* New York: Random House, 1996. (Whitefield)

——. *Shadow Woman.* New York: Random House, 1997. (Whitefield)

——. *Vanishing Act.* New York: Random House, 1995. (Whitefield)

Peterson, Geoff. *Medicine Dog.* New York: St. Martin's Press, 1989.

Piesman, Marissa. *Close Quarters.* New York: Delacorte Press, 1994. (Fischman)

——. *Heading Uptown.* New York: Delacorte Press, 1993. (Fischman)

——. *Personal Effects.* New York: Delacorte Press, 1992. (Fischman)

——. *Unorthodox Practices.* New York: Delacorte Press, 1991. (Fischman)

Randisi, Robert. *No Exit from Brooklyn.* New York: St. Martin's, 1987. (Delvecchio)

Resnicow, Herbert. *The Dead Room.* New York: Dodd, Mead, & Co., 1987. (the Baers)

——. *The Hot Place.* New York: St. Martin's Press, 1991. (the Baers)

——. *The Gold Curse.* New York: St. Martin's Press, 1986. (the Golds)

——. *The Gold Deadline.* New York: St. Martin's Press, 1984. (the Golds)

——. *The Gold Frame.* New York: St. Martin's Press, 1985. (the Golds)

——. *The Gold Gamble.* New York: St. Martin's Press, 1988. (the Golds)

——. *The Gold Solution.* New York: St. Martin's Press, 1983. (the Golds)

Rozain, S. J. *China Trade.* New York: St. Martin's Press, 1994. (Chen)

——. *Concourse.* New York: St. Martin's Press, 1995. (Chen)

——. *Lethal Ladies.* New York: Berkeley Press, 1995. (Chen)

Shem, Samuel. *Fine.* New York: Fawsett Columbine, 1995. (Basch)

——. *The House of God.* New York: Fawsett Columbine, 1996. (Basch)

——. *Mount Misery.* New York: Fawsett Columbine, 1997. (Basch)

Simon, Roger. *The Big Fix.* New York: Simon and Schuster, 1973. (Wine)

——. *California Roll.* New York: Villard Books, 1988. (Wine)

——. *The Lost Coast.* New York: Harper Collins, 1997. (Wine)

——. *Peking Duck.* New York: Simon and Schuster, 1973. (Wine)

——. *Raising the Dead.* New York: Villard Books, 1988. (Wine)

——. *The Straight Man.* New York: Villard Books, 1997. (Wine)

——. *Wild Turkey.* San Francisco: A Straight Arrow Thriller, 1974. (Wine)

Stabenow, Dana. *Blood Will Tell.* G. P. Putnam's Sons, 1996. (Shugak)

——. *Breakup.* G. P. Putnam's Sons, 1997. (Shugak)

——. *A Cold-blooded Business.* New York: Berkley Prime Crime, 1994. (Shugak)

——. *A Cold Day for Murder.* New York: Berkley Prime Crime, 1992. (Shugak)

——. *A Fatal Thaw.* New York: Berkley Prime Crime, 1993. (Shugak)

——. *Dead in the Water.* New York: Berkley Prime Crime, 1993. (Shugak)

——. *Play with Fire.* New York: Berkley Prime Crime, 1995. (Shugak)

Stern, Richard Martin. *Death in the Snow.* New York: Scribner, 1973. (Ortiz)

——. *Murder in the Walls.* New York: Scribner, 1971. (Ortiz)

——. *You Don't Need an Enemy.* New York: Scribner, 1971. (Ortiz)

Straley, John. *The Curious Eat Themselves.* New York: Bantam, 1993. (Younger)

——. *Death and the Language of Happiness.* New York: Bantam, 1997. (Younger)

——. *The Music of What Happens.* New York: Bantam, 1996. (Younger)

——. *The Woman Who Married a Bear.* New York: Bantam, 1994. (Younger)

Thurlo, Aimée, and David Thurlo. *Bad Medicine.* New York: Tom Doherty Associates, 1997. (Clah)

——. *Blackening Song.* New York: Tom Doherty Associates, 1995. (Clah)

——. *Death Walker.* New York: Tom Doherty Associates, 1996. (Clah)

Tidyman, Ernest. *Good-by Mr. Shaft.* New York: Dial Press, 1973. (Shaft)

——. *Shaft.* New York: Macmillan, 1970.

——. *Shaft among the Jews.* New York: Dial Press, 1972.

Uhnak, Dorothy. *Victims.* New York: Simon and Schuster, 1985. (Torres)

Wesley, Valerie Wilson. *Devil's Gonna Get Him.* New York: G. P. Putnam's, 1995. (Hayle)

——. *When Death Comes Stealing.* New York: G. P. Putnam's, 1994. (Hayle)

Wiltz, Chris. *The Killing Circle.* New York: Macmillan, 1981. (Rafferty)

Wingate, Anne. *The Buzzards Must Also Be Fed.* New York: Walker and Co., 1991. (Shigata)

——. *Death by Deception.* New York: Walker and Co., 1990. (Shigata)

——. *Exception to Murder.* New York: Walker and Co., 1992. (Shigata)

——. *The Eye of Anna.* New York: Walker and Co., 1989. (Shigata)

——. *Yakuza, Go Home.* New York: Walker and Co., 1993. (Shigata)

Yaffe, James. *Mom among the Liars.* New York: St. Martin's, 1992. (Mom)

——. *Mom Doth Murder Sleep.* New York: St. Martin's, 1991. (Mom)

——. *Mom Meets Her Maker.* New York: St. Martin's, 1990. (Mom)

——. *A Nice Murder for Mom.* New York: St. Martin's, 1988. (Mom)

DANA STABENOW'S ALASKA MYSTERIES

Mary Jean DeMarr

A good brief statement of the need for multicultural emphases in education, at all levels, comes from Otis L. Scott's examination of ways of including multicultural content in various courses. He points out,

We are major participants in a social activity that is intended to shape and frame a reality or sets of realities for our students. We provide our students with both bases of knowledge and skills which will enable them to understand, manipulate, and change their realities. We want our students to be vital participants in their environments, not bumps on a log. To this end, education which includes multicultural learning experiences is vital. We provide students with the ability to better understand the culturally diverse national and international societies they simultaneously inhabit. (58)

These by now obvious conclusions must be, of course, accompanied by consideration of the means by which multicultural learning experiences may be provided for the students. There have been many helpful discussions of methods of pedagogy for students of varied cultural backgrounds. Varied ways of learning, and thus of teaching, which are appropriate to students of differing cultural, as well as linguistic, physical, gender, and other backgrounds have also been examined. Multiculturalism itself has been well defined by David Schoem and others as including "race, ethnicity, culture, gender, sexual orientation, religion, and socioeconomic class" (1). For the purposes of this essay, we will be addressing a question of multicultural content, particularly the ways in which the multicultural subject matter of Dana Stabenow's mystery series set in Alaska may be useful in helping students understand some of the difficulties faced by members of minorities in the United States. In observing the differing assumptions, values, customs, and problems faced by members of several different ethnic groups living in close quarters in Alaska, as depicted by Stabenow, a resident of Anchorage herself, students should find their cultural horizons widened.

Stabenow's series centers around Kate Shugak, a sometime private investigator who lives in an Alaskan cabin located in a national park with only the companionship of her husky-wolf hybrid Mutt and the occasional interlude with her lover Jack Morgan. The novels relate her adventures either when murder invades her world or when she leaves her retreat to investigate crimes, usually at Jack's behest. It is principally the setting and Kate's ethnic background which make this series unique. In many other respects, these novels are similar to other hard-boiled mysteries which use female protagonists. Stabenow explicitly and strongly stresses Kate's Aleut background, and this heritage often also helps to motivate Kate's behavior as well as to give her special knowledge needed to solve particular crimes. Less obvious is the Russian portion of Kate's ancestral history which also colors the setting of these novels. The use of these ethnic materials helps to account for a part of the series' appeal, and readers can learn much about what it is like to be a Native American in Alaska in the late twentieth century from these novels.

Students will find the novels an effective introduction to the world of the Native Alaskan and to the multicultural society of modern Alaska in which Natives and Anglos, Alaskans (both Native and Anglo) and outsiders jostle, sometimes uncomfortably, against each other. The novels depict, from the point of view of a Native Alaskan who knows both cultures intimately, the difficulties of living between two worlds, reveal some of the pressing social problems of the Native Alaskans, and with humor and grace portray strengths and weaknesses of the aboriginal culture. Students may learn from these novels much about how intersecting cultures and peoples can relate to each other.

Additionally, the novels form interesting patterns. The first two books, *A Cold Day for Murder* and *A Fatal Thaw* are set in Kate's home area and illustrate the theme of outsiders and insiders, each group defined in a variety of ways. Outsiders may be those of Native American ancestry or simply long-time residents, while Insiders variously include those of European background or relative newcomers to Alaska. These first two novels also introduce a large cast of characters—Jack Morgan, Kate's occasional lover who, as investigator for the Anchorage District Attorney, is often responsible for embroiling her in her cases; Bobby, the black paraplegic Vietnam veteran whose radio keeps contact with the outside; Billy Mike, tribal chief; Mandy Baker and Chick Noyukpuk, she an outsider who is a dedicated musher and he a Native; Bernie, who runs Bernie's Roadhouse, the unofficial community center for Niniltna, the settlement closest to Kate's homestead; and a variety of relatives of Kate's, most significantly her cousin Xenia (in the first novel, but Axenia in later books), her alcoholic cousin Martin, and most importantly her grandmother, Ekaterina Moonin Shugak. The third and fourth books, however, take Kate afield, first in *Dead in the Water* to a fishing boat off the Alaska coast and then, in *A Cold-Blooded Business,* to the oil fields of the North Slope. In these latter two novels, most of the continuing characters of the earlier books, except for Jack and, mainly in walk-ons, such relatives as Martin, Axenia, and—most significantly—her grandmother—are absent. The following three novels, *Play with Fire, Blood Will Tell,* and *Breakup* are all set on Kate's home turf, with scenes in the park, in Niniltna, and on Kate's homestead. *Play with Fire* is tightly centered around a particular social theme, that of religious fanaticism, while *Blood Will Tell* develops fully the theme of Native corporations and controversies over land use (development versus subsistence hunting and fishing) which are touched on in most of the other books, thus obliquely illustrating some effects of American colonialism. *Breakup* stands apart from other novels because of its more farcical tone but may also be seen as a rewriting of the second novel, *A Fatal Thaw,* treating many of the same materials in a manner that is both more comic and more mature. The first three novels were published as paperback originals, whereas with *A Cold-Blooded Business,* Stabenow entered the world of hardcover publishing.

If there ever was a series for which setting was crucial, it is surely this one. The Alaska scene is central in all seven books, and all are filled with striking—and often loving—descriptions of the locale. Both the beauty and the harshness of the land are well conveyed. Integrally connected with that scene are its people. Most noticeable is the emphasis on the heritage and situation of the Native Alaskans, as depicted through Kate, her extended family, and many of the people she meets. However, aspects of Alaska's colonial past are also dramatically rendered, including both the historical Russian colonial period and the subsequent American colonial exploitation of the region. The Russian connection, relatively superficial, is shown primarily through names and references to the Orthodox church and calendar. The American colonialism, more historically immediate and more central to these novels, is revealed thematically through social and political issues and through direct illustration.

Kate has connections to all these phenomena: to the native Aleut heritage, to both Russian and American colonialism, and to the contemporary world. A college graduate and former employee of the Anchorage District Attorney's office, she moves easily among outsiders; a daughter of Aleuts relocated to the mainland during World War II, she retains ties to her family and people. She speaks only English yet chooses to live in a remote homestead with Mutt, her husky-wolf hybrid, as her only constant companion. Her religious heritage is a mixture of Aleut myth and Russian Orthodoxy, though she practices neither.

Naming is significant in Kate's world. Her own name, in fact, is a mixture: as Kate Shugak she bears an English nickname and a Native family name. However, her full name, as we learn in *Dead in the Water,* is Ekaterina Ivana Shugak (84). Shugak, of course, is Native, but Ekaterina Ivana is interestingly connected to the Russian colonial past. Kate's first name would more accurately today be transliterated "Yekaterina," but it is always spelled in this old-fashioned way (as are all the Russian names, of course, a reminder that Alaska's connections with the old country were cut off well over a hundred years ago) when referring to Kate and to her grandmother and putative namesake. And Kate's grandmother always calls her "Katya," the purely Russian nickname parallel to "Kate." "Ivana" is even more interesting; it appears simply as a middle name, but may be in origin a typically Russian patronymic. "Ivanovna," "daughter of Ivan," which as a Russian patronymic would appear as a middle name, is actually pronounced colloquially by Russians as spelled by Stabenow. Interestingly, Martin, Kate's cousin, bears the middle name Ivanovich, an accurately spelled Russian patronymic, though it seems doubtful that patronymics are in active use in the Shugak family. Nevertheless, the old forms remain, a superficial but consistent reminder of the Russian colonial past.

Other names also serve as reminders of the Russian colonial past. Many who like Kate and her grandmother are of Native or mixed ethnic background bear Russian names. Among Kate's other relatives is her cousin, Xenia (in *A Cold Day for Murder*) or Axenia (in later novels), bearer of a name as distinctively Russian as Kate's own Ekaterina. A few of the many other Russian or Russian-derived names are Demetri Tote-moff (a particularly interesting family name, combining an apparently Alaskan root with a Russian suffix), Samuel Dementieff, Ekatny Kvas-nikof, and Mickey Kompkoff (or Komkoff). Spellings are not consistent but the Russian influence is. These names jostle naturally with such non-Russian appellations as those of Mandy Baker, a purely WASP outsider, her "roomie," Chick Noyukpuk, a Native, Billy Mike, a tribal chief, and Abel Int-hout, the relative who reared Kate.

Other reminders of the Russian colonial past are relatively infrequent and mostly relate to the scene and to customs, particularly religious and calendrical. When Kate is trying halfheartedly to dissuade her rebellious cousin Xenia from leaving her family and going to the city, just as Kate herself had done years earlier, Kate tells her that among other evidences of prejudice, Xenia may expect people to mock her because of her adherence to the Russian Orthodox calendar (celebrating Christmas and New Year's Day later than the Western dates observed by everyone else) (CDM 78). And the conclusion of *Dead in the Water* contains a moving scene which combines Russian Orthodoxy and sea lore. In an Aleutian town, Kate and Jack join a heterogeneous crowd of people, which includes villagers, seafarers, Koreans, Chinese, Americans, and Aleuts, all of them eager to "propitiate whatever the gods might be for a good catch and a safe journey home" (196). A little Orthodox church in Dutch Harbor gives the setting, and an Orthodox priest—"patriarch"—officiates. Jack, the outsider, expresses surprise that so many Aleuts are Russian Orthodox, and Kate, a historical cynic, responds from the knowledge of her family and her people, pointing out that the Aleuts had simply been practical, accepting baptism into the Russian Orthodox faith in exchange for a three-year exemption from taxes (197). Nevertheless, the ceremony of the Blessing of the Sea which follows is moving to both Kate and Jack; the pealing of the bell for those who have died at sea in the last year helps Kate to realize she feels no guilt for the death of the seaman she has killed (198). And this scene is followed by a brief and even more cleansing scene in which an elderly Aleut woman and her handicapped daughter symbolically, by using a traditional Native storytelling method, absolve her—or more accurately depict her as good overcoming evil (199-201). This order is itself significant; while the Russian heritage of Alaska—and of her people, like Kate—is clear and is in their awareness, it is nowhere nearly as powerful as is the Native heritage.

The power of Kate's Aleut—and her more general Alaskan—background is central to these novels. She has chosen to live on a relatively primitive homestead (though she visits Anchorage infrequently to purchase such necessities as toilet paper with cash earned by working on the cases Jack brings to her). Her choice of this relatively primitive life is primarily a reaction to the traumatic fight in which she killed a child molester and was herself grievously wounded. The fight left an ugly scar across her throat, destroying her singing voice (she is an opera lover), and giving her speaking voice a characteristically husky rasp. Her retreat from that ugliness and the violence it has made her participate in is to an area within a national park which is sparsely inhabited by Native Alaskans and by other settlers of the bush. That Kate is to some degree alienated from her Native roots is indicated by her continued involvement in the so-called American culture and by her choice of a home which is not closely connected to her people. Her daily life includes work around the homestead, much reading from her substantial library and listening to her extensive tape collection, and the companionship of Mutt. She can break her isolation when she chooses, by using her snowmobile or her truck, depending on the season, to reach "civilization"—Niniltna, and her American and Native friends there. But she retains control. And the homestead, significantly, had been inherited from her father (CDM 24) and so symbolizes also her connection with her family.

That homestead, however, has no ancestral connections beyond those with her father. She is an Aleut living on the mainland, therefore ironically herself an Outsider. In the third novel in the series, in which Kate works on a fishing boat and travels for the first time in her life to the islands from which her people came, we are reminded that her family had been relocated to the mainland during the second world war. Visiting with Jack the remote island of Anua, whose name means something like "spirit," she explains some Alaskan history to him and reveals some poignant ironies. During World War II, after the Japanese invaded Attu and Kiska, the villagers were removed, by the military authorities who had been given total power over them, to the Alaskan mainland. After the war, few were returned to their original homes, where their villages had been largely destroyed.

"But it was war," Jack pointed out.

"I know."

"If things had gone the other way, they could have wound up prisoners of the Japanese."

"Some of them did. Some Aleuts the Japanese took prisoner off Attu and Kiska. In Japan, they put them to work, and even paid them for it." Kate smiled. "When they were repatriated, their biggest difficulty was in getting their Japanese paychecks cashed." (DW 67)

When Jack asks why Kate knows so much of this obscure history, she reminds him that though she lives in an historically Athaspascan, Eyak, and Tlingit area, she is herself an Aleut, her family having been expatriated with the rest of the Aleuts and settling in the Park because they already had relatives near there (DW 67-68).

A physical description of Kate is generally given early in each novel. That description always includes mention both of her scar and of evidences of her racial background. In the earliest example; Kate is observed by an FBI agent hoping to hire her to work on an investigation:

Twenty-nine or thirty, he judged . . . . Five feet tall, no more, maybe a hundred and ten pounds. She had the burnished bronze skin and high, flat cheekbones of her race, with curiously light brown eyes tilted up at her temples, all of it framed by a shining fall of utterly black, utterly straight hair. . . . She moved like a cat, all controlled muscle and natural grace, wary but assured. . . . .

Then she bent down . . . and he sucked in his breath. For a moment her collar had fallen away and he had seen the scar, twisted and ugly and still angry in color. It crossed her throat almost from ear to ear. That explains the voice, he thought, shaken. (CDM 9-10)

Missing here is one phrase repeatedly used in other descriptions: Kate's eyes have "a hint of epicanthic fold." The importance of physical indications of membership in an ethnic minority is frequently illustrated, both negatively and positively. Kate is sometimes moved to anger when an Anglo unthinkingly assumes a Native must be intoxicated (in *A Fatal Thaw*, for example, when she has been drugged but is assumed to be a typical Native drunk). But there is one telling brief scene in *Play with Fire* when ethnic appearance leads to a moment of recognition.

He took in the color of her skin and the epicanthic folds of her eyes, she the slant of his cheekbones and the thick, straight black hair. He didn't say, "Aleut?" and she didn't say, "Athabaskan?" but they both relaxed a little, the way people of color always do when the door closes after the last white person has left the room. (88)

Though Kate's appearance immediately marks her as an Aleut, she herself is very aware that her racial heritage is far from pure. Arguing with her grandmother, who is a well-known leader and spokesperson for Native causes, she reminds her that their own ancestors and relatives include a Russian Cossack, a Jewish cobbler, and a Norwegian fisherman, and she likens Aleuts to mongrel dogs (CDM 48). Aleuts, then are mutts!—perhaps on some level, Mutt, Kate's wolf-husky hybrid, symbolizes this mongrelization.

Kate's cynical attitude on racial matters mirrors her resistance to being forced into the mould of what her grandmother would call her people. This rebellion, of course, had led her to Anchorage, to university, to employment among so-called Americans, even perhaps to her liaison with Jack Morgan. Others think that her movement from her Aleut culture to the American mainstream has been easy. Her young cousin, called Xenia in this novel, yearning to make the same movement, taunts her with the contrast between their lives, whining that their grandmother insists that she become a good Aleut woman and envying Kate's education and what she sees as Kate's easy choices (CDM 77). And later, Abel Int-hout, Kate's foster father, echoes Xenia's words, telling Kate how easy her own life has been because she has profited from the Native Claims Act (which gave her some land and money, he says), the Bureau of Indian Affairs (which underwrote medical costs for her), and even her father (from whom she inherited her home). Like Xenia, he sees his own life as having been by contrast unfairly difficult (CDM 187). Both assume that life has been easy for Kate and lack any awareness of the struggles she has undergone to get where she is. Kate is distressed by both the adolescent rebellion of the former and the perhaps partly deserved resentment of the latter. To Abel she expresses the built-up anger she feels both at the easy, perhaps envious scorn of her Aleut relatives and at the ignorant prejudice she has met Outside which they both ignore:

"None of you tried to take out a student loan and had the loan officer at the bank tell you you had to have a white cosigner. None of you had to sit in a history class and listen to the white Outside teacher tell you how the Aleuts spread their legs for Alexander Baranov. And none of you has ever had a welder from Tulsa, Oklahoma, call you a nigger." (CDM 197)

Kate is torn. She sees the values inherent in her culture—and she lives by them. She detests waste and the destruction of the land; she is not squeamish about killing animals for food—but she leaves no waste and she abhors those who do. She respects her elders and greets elderly strangers who are also Natives as "Auntie" or "Uncle"; she reprimands Xenia for not showing proper respect. But she also sees the dark side. The alcoholism rampant among Native peoples—responsible for her own parents' untimely deaths—is a constant pain to her. She chooses to be a teetotaler, as a result, and it is surely no coincidence that all of the first four novels turn at least partly on substance abuse, primarily on drug dealing. She understands that the future is limited for young Aleuts. Arguing with her grandmother about Xenia, she foresees for her cousin several possibilities for a grim future. These unpleasantnesses include early pregnancy, welfare dependency, abusive relationships, drunkenness, even a horrible death by exposure while intoxicated. She is nearly shouting at her mother as she finishes this tirade, only to be met by her grandmother's soft words: "Xenia is not your mother" (CDM 52).

The generations flow together here for Kate. Tormented by what had happened in her parents' lives and by seeing her alcoholic cousin Martin throwing his life away, irritated by the self-centered rebellion of her younger cousin, Kate finally does help Xenia escape, and later we learn that this young woman, now referred to as Axenia, is doing well in the city, with a job and a night class at the University (FT 145-46). Her life is not smooth, however, and in *Blood Will Tell,* she becomes involved in some shady dealings with powerful Anglos. Kate also attempts to help others in need—notably an old man she meets in Anchorage and tries to help return to his village, only to learn he has drunk up the money she gave him and has like her mother died of exposure (CBB 114-15, 226-27). And she wishes, equally fruitlessly, to help a deformed girl she discovers living on an isolated island, a girl who turns out to be a victim of fetal alcohol syndrome; strikingly the mother who has caused her handicaps appears in the novel as an admirable—and sober—wise woman (DW 108-09).

From novel to novel, Kate's ambivalences about her worlds are dramatized by her troubled relationship with her grandmother, and the first six novels show her gradually becoming more reconciled to that strong and assertive woman. This progress is motivated in large part by a series of scenes or subplots in the second and third novels, following after the establishment of these motifs in the first book These devices give Stabenow some of her most powerful materials, and some of the author's finest writing occurs in their development.

It is her ties to the values of her culture—respect for elders, a sense of unity with the land, and so on—as well as the tie to her family symbolized by her homestead which was inherited from her father, which underlie her gradual movement toward involvement in tribal matters in later books, particularly after her grandmother's death at the end of *Blood Will Tell.* Her troubled relationship with her grandmother and her rebellion against participation in tribal affairs parallel each other, and her gradual softening toward the grandmother culminates in her taking a leadership role, into which her grandmother has thrust her, in a tribal decision made at the conclusion of that novel. All of this reveals Kate coming to terms with her own sense of identity as someone who belongs in both worlds, not in neither as had sometimes seemed the case in the earliest novels.

In *A Fatal Thaw,* a potlatch occurs shortly before the novel's climax. Typically, the potlatch, quintessentially a cultural expression of Native Alaskans, is here juxtaposed with a high school basketball game, the potlatch being held in the gym before the game which otherwise would have brought the community together. Kate's grandmother is the organizer of the potlatch—merely her announcement that it will occur is enough. Bernie, the keeper of the Roadhouse and basketball coach, tells Kate, "Ekaterina put the word out—the whole Park is supposed to be here. Besides, the first game of the tournament begins right after" (FT 135). As we learn, potlatches are ceremonial gatherings and may be held for many reasons—to celebrate a birth or some other momentous occasion, for example (140). This potlatch is held in memory of the victims of a mass murderer (the killings which opened the novel) and becomes a gloriously multicultural event, joining together members of various tribes, Anglos, and even outsiders. The potlatch at first seems to consist of a potluck supper held in the school gym. But the drums beat and "Ekaterina Moonin Shugak was calling down the tribes" (136). The dance unifies a crowd of ethnically disparate people. All dance the same dance, or at least dance to the beat of the same drums, though their ancestors would have known many different dances. As Ekaterina calls the name of a group, those of its members who are present come to the floor and enter the dance, until everyone there, including Kate, is dancing. The call includes, "Inupiat" (represented by six or so people), "Athabascan!" (and the "oldest chief of any tribe in Alaska," born in 1867, "made his slow and stately way to the floor") (FT 136); "Aleut!" (a large group joins the dancers) (139), "Koniag!"—and then Ekaterina begins calling out some individuals: "Hawaiian!" (and "an enormous man wearing a high, plumed helmet and a floor-length cloak made of brilliant yellow and red feathers took to the floor") (FT 139), and "The black man!" (Bobby, the Vietnam veteran and paraplegic, wheels himself out to the floor and moves rhythmically with the crowd of dancers) (139). Then, she calls out "The white man!" and "There was a whoop and a holler and one lone Rebel yell and a dozen more people took to the floor" (140). Each brings to the dance his or her own cultural memories. And finally, she calls, "Everybody!" and Kate, who has held back when her own people were called, impulsively joins in. The dance which follows, observed through Kate's eyes, unites these disparate people almost mystically until Kate sees not only those who are present and dancing but the spirits of those who were killed. The dance, then, serves as a spiritual and unifying ritual, and Kate stresses to Bernie, the outsider here, that though the ten who were killed were white, that didn't matter—for "They lived here" and some were in fact partly Native; most importantly, they all left people to mourn them (140-41). Contrasting with the "anniversary" of the Tet offensive, celebrated each year by Bobby and some friends in a drunken party,

the potlatch was a paean to life and to those who lived it, a remembrance of the dead, an act of homage. If the dancers mourned the passing of the dead, they also rejoiced in the lives those individuals had lived, and rejoiced as well, unashamed, in their own. (141)

The power of ritual to unite a community is striking here. No less striking is its juxtaposition with that other, more modern—and "American" —unifying ritual which follows, the basketball game. The participants in the potlatch have no difficulty in modulating from the one to the other. This is not the final scene of the novel; it precedes the climax and solution and leads to another mystical scene, this later one, however, a communion with a beautiful and treacherous nature as Kate climbs high into the mountains with only Mutt for companionship and there experiences an earthquake. The social and the natural experiences combine to create a powerful effect.

Similarly strong effects are created in the third novel in the series, *Dead in the Water,* through a secondary plot line and group of characters, an Aleut woman and the girls who cluster around her. Kate makes a brief excursion to the village of Unalaska, a trip rather in the nature of a pilgrimage for her. The narrative sets up this crucial motif by tracing some history: Russian fur traders, New England whalers, gold prospectors, and the United States military during World War II, all suppressed or dispossessed the rich Aleut culture that had preceded them and brought with them the Russian Orthodox faith, commercialism, exploitation, and venereal disease. The history lesson climaxes in the present, with the incursion of modern technological fishing and processing which threaten to destroy the environment with which the Aleuts had lived in harmony (DW 93-94).

The village reminds Kate of her own village of Niniltna on the Mainland (DW 94). Most striking to her is the human element, consisting first of a group of girls she finds on the beach. They are squatting in a circle while one of them, speaking almost unintelligibly because of a cleft palate, is telling a story as she draws in the sand with an ivory knife (DW 95-97). Kate admires the beauty of the knife—but they must explain to her that it is a "storyknife" whose function is precisely what Kate has observed. Her ignorance here underlines her separation from Native tradition. The girls take her to an old woman, Olga Shapsnikoff, mother of the handicapped girl, who explains, in partial justification of Kate's ignorance, that "storyknifing" is "more of an Eskimo custom"— Olga's grandmother was from elsewhere (DW 99).

A long scene follows, in which Kate feels her way into the lives of these women, close to her in heritage and yet distant in almost every other way. Two particular aspects of their culture are emphasized, basket weaving and chanting. Olga has taught the girls to weave baskets, an inherited craft which they employ in order to get spending money (money spent for such things as Michael Jackson albums! [102]). Kate tries her hand and discovers that this skill is very difficult. It will probably die out soon; Olga is the only mature practitioner left, and whether the girls will long continue is doubtful.

During this same scene, while explaining some of her personal history, Olga spontaneously breaks into a chant; she chants twice again, both times on mythological subjects—about the omen of death communicated by the presence of killer whales in a harbor (106) and much later about the creation of the first basket (DW 153-54). All three chants tell stories in a rhythmic cadence and have a particular form: short lines, heavy use of parallelism, and a final line: "That's all." The first two are elegiac in tone, while the third is a creation myth. Because it dramatizes the continuing use of folk traditions in a living culture, I will quote the first of these as an example:

"The Japanese soldiers came.
"Then the army came.
"The army moved all of the people from the islands.
"They put them in towns and in camps in Cook Inlet and Prince William Sound.
"It was too hot up there for the people.
"Many of the people died.
"After the war, the army brought us back.
"The people that were left wished they had died with the others.
"The houses were gone.
"The villages were gone.
"Even the ones where there had been no Japanese.
"The army said they destroyed them because they couldn't leave the villages for the Japanese to use.
"We couldn't go back.
"There weren't enough of us.
"There was nothing to go back to.
"So now we live in a few villages instead of many.
"That's all." (DW 104)

The three chants as well as the use of the storyknife and the weaving of the baskets reveal a still living culture. Nevertheless, the fact that the storyknife is not really central to this particular culture and that the basket weaving is artificially maintained at present, plus the unremarked indication that Olga is alone as a practitioner of the chant, serve as reminders—if any were needed—of the fragility of this culture. However, Kate later, in *Blood Will Tell*, makes use of this storytelling method as she tries to help Jack's troubled son understand the value of learning about history (46-47) and then in her first overtly political act, as she leads the crowd at the Federation of Natives Convention to take the stand toward which her ill and absent grandmother had tried to lead them (168-70). That storytelling is still a living part of her cultural life is underlined by the fact that the first of these stories is one she has made up on the spot while the second is a tale of her own experience killing a moose which had opened the book.

Most of the novels evoke some aspect of Native culture at or near their conclusions, sometimes through use of Kate's grandmother or some surrogate for her. This is most striking in the early novels. In *A Cold Day for Murder*, Kate and her grandmother argue about whether Xenia should be allowed to leave the Park, and Kate's differences from and with the old woman are sharply depicted. But the two women are also alike in their strength and in their love for their people. In fact, it is partly their very likeness that makes the differences so telling. The generational difference is only a part of their disagreement (CDM 194). Almost immediately after their argument, Kate tries to express to Jack how she feels, pointing out her grandmother's use of the Russian nickname Katya to call her back to her Aleut heritage:

"Every time she says it, 'Katya,' . . . . I see fifty generations of Aleuts lined up behind her, glaring at me. . . . she's telling me I betrayed her and my family and the village and my culture and my entire race by running away. . . . I've been preaching, and I quote, 'assimilation into the prevailing culture for the survival of my people.' . . . And I live in a log cabin . . . twenty-five miles from the nearest village. I'm shipping Xenia off to town, but I can't bear to go in myself." (CDM 195)

Her anguish here is not just a result of her general feelings of being caught between two cultures; it is exacerbated by her having revealed that the murderer in this novel has been a Native Alaskan very close to her and that her grandmother has been an accessory after the fact. In her pain, she defends her people to Jack, trying to stress that they are not represented by the common images of them, are not all drunks, adulterers, and murderers but are simply ordinary peoply trying to do the best they can in a world which is hostile to their striving (CDM 195). Here she identifies with her people but her comments on that culture are linked to the negative—she is defending them against the very stereotypes which her solution of the mystery might seem to reinforce.

The immediately succeeding novels, while certainly not underestimating the problems in Native society, show Kate beginning to accept more positive attitudes. Near the end of *A Fatal Thaw* she participates in the unifying dance at the potlatch, directed by her grandmother. And in *Dead in the Water,* she receives a sort of absolution for killing a murderer from Sasha, the handicapped storyknifing Aleut girl, who along with Olga Shapsnikoff has served for this novel some of the functions of representing Native culture usually reserved for her grandmother. *A Cold-Blooded Business* concludes with a brief scene in the grandmother's kitchen. Ekaterina had been horrified by Kate's working for the oil company responsible for a major oil spill, and Kate comes to apologize to her—not for doing her job and trying to put a stop to drug dealing in the oil fields but for hurting her grandmother (CBB 229). Their rapprochement—the fact that Kate now reconciles with her grandmother, in contrast to her rebellion at the end of the first novel—may be credited to experiences in the intervening books: her emotional response at the potlatch and her affection for Olga Shapsnikoff and Sasha along with her failed attempt to help the old drunk return to his home in *A Cold-Blooded Business*. And so the two women drink cocoa together and Kate goes home to her cabin in peace, no longer in anger or alienation.

Of the novels published thus far, *Blood Will Tell* is the one most specifically concerned with Native Alaskan issues—land use, Native rights to subsistence hunting and fishing, the government of the Native corporations. It is structured in part around the annual convention of the Alaska Federation of Natives, which is climaxed by the unexpected death of Ekaterina, the matriarch of the tribes and the most widely known and highly respected of the elders. A chant and dance in her honor spontaneously begins, touching Kate and drawing her once again into its magic. Even the rebellious Axenia in included. Once again, a single dance joins members of many tribes.

> All danced, all together, all as one.
> They danced the dance the missionaries had called heathen and satanic, they danced the dance their parents had been forbidden, they danced the dance their ancestors danced for a hundred and a thousand and ten thousand years, dances to mark a birth, to celebrate a wedding, to heal the sick, to mourn the dead, to thank Agudar for the good hunt, to pray to Manilaq for guidance.
> They danced the dance they would always dance, that their children would dance, that their children's children would dance, in joy and in sorrow, in entreaty and in thanksgiving, and, yes, with beads and with feathers, in button blankets and spirit masks, in kuspuks and mukluks, in jeans and Nikes. . . .
> An elder of the church in Eklutna gave the benediction in a shaken voice, and the convention was over. (BWT 232-33)

The dance, like Kate's use of storytelling which had so recently preceded it, indicates yet again the vitality of some distinguishing characteristics of Native culture. The Christian benediction comes as a surprisingly fitting, if anticlimactic, conclusion.

Breakup, because of its comic tone and relationship with *A Fatal Thaw,* must be seen as separate from the other books, yet at the same time it underscores the progress Kate has undergone. This novel, like its earlier counterpart, is set at the beginning of spring, at the onset of the thaw, and pairs murder and mayhem of various sorts with that new beginning. In *Breakup,* everything that can go wrong does go wrong—bears come out of hibernation and encroach on civilization, parts of a plane fall out of the sky onto Kate's homestead, floods threaten and potholes make road travel uncomfortable, even dangerous. Everything is blamed on the season with the often repeated word, "Breakup!" This is the first novel in which Ekaterina is completely missing, and it is marked also by the almost complete absence of Jack Morgan, Kate's lover, with whom her relationship is almost as stormy as that with her grandmother. One very public telephone call and her happy intent to travel to Anchorage to see him at the end of the book are the totality of his presence. However, the absent grandmother's spiritual presence is strongly felt in the novel's final pages. Kate has just accepted responsibility, has taken a leadership role in an important tribal decision, and she now feels a new understanding of her grandmother. Indeed, it is hinted, she is becoming her grandmother. Out of doors, feeling the breeze and smelling the scents of spring, she has a mystical sense of Ekaterina's being with her.

The bark of the branch smelled strongly of resin. "Emaa," Kate said into the gathering night, "they lean on me. All of them, they lean on me. How do I stand against it? How did you, all those years?" (B 241).

She hears her grandmother's reply in the call of a songbird. And her own response is both acceptance and a love which she had withheld from her living grandmother. She says three things: "All right, Emaa," "I love you, Emaa," and then after a pause, "I need you" (B 243). And the novel's last lines indicate the equilibrium she has finally reached:

Her only answer was the song again, three notes, coming clearly over the wind in the trees, the howl of a distant wolf, the drop of melting snow.

It was enough.

It would have to be. (B 242)

Many thematic and artistic uses of ethnic materials have been ignored here, and the effectiveness of some of the prose developing Kate's Aleut-inculcated closeness to nature has not been conveyed. More to the point are her ambivalence about her background and the gradual change that ambivalence undergoes through the series. Stabenow forcefully depicts a character of deep passions, a woman who has overcome both social and personal traumas (racial discrimination and a near fatal injury) and who is overcoming strong divisions within herself. The novels strikingly portray their Alaskan scene and serve to initiate the outsider into many aspects of a complex social order. They do this through effectively constructed plots and through deftly described scenes and characterizations, all powerfully integrated into moving mysteries. These novels, individually or as a group, are well suited to convey much about being a Native in an Anglo world and about interactions between members of varying cultures. Their greatest usefulness in the multicultural classroom, however, is the sense they give of what it is like to be a Native Alaskan. Because Kate knows Western culture so well—reads, loves, alludes to English poetry, for example—she gives nonNative readers a ready access to the Native world. As she learns about storyknifing, for example, we learn with her. Because she is prepared by her knowledge of her people, she can explain to us. Through her connections with nonNatives, particularly with Jack, we are led into other aspects of Native culture and life. As she explains her people's history, we learn with him. And the view given us is complex and fair. Problems of substance abuse, of rootlessness, of rebellion against old ways by children are depicted along with the values to which Kate clings. Even in her greatest rebellion against the pressures placed upon her by her grandmother, she is unfailingly courteous to her elders—always addressing them courteously as "Auntie" or "Uncle" and taking Axenia to task for being less than polite. And for her, the love of her place, kinship with and careful use of the land and what it provides, is always central and illustrated in a number of beautifully written passages in all of the books. As works of popular literature they are accessible to students at widely varying levels of literary sophistication. Teachers searching for novels which will facilitate discussion of many issues of multiculturalism could do no better than to select one or more of the Kate Shugak mysteries.

Works Cited

Schoem, David, et al. eds. *Multicultural Teaching in the University.* Westport, CT: Praeger, 1993.

Scott, Otis L. "Including Multicultural Content and Perspectives in Your Courses." *Teaching from a Multicultural Perspective.* Ed. Helen Roberts et al. Thousand Oaks: Sage Publications, 1994. 46-59.

Stabenow, Dana. *Blood Will Tell.* New York: G. P. Putnam's Sons, 1996. (BWT)

——. *Breakup.* New York: G. P. Putnam's Sons, 1997. (B)

——. *A Cold Day for Murder.* New York: Berkley Books, 1992. (CDM)

——. *A Cold-Blooded Business.* New York: Berkley Prime Crime, 1994. (CBB)

——. *Dead in the Water.* New York: Berkley Books, 1993. (DW)

——. *A Fatal Thaw.* New York: Berkley Books, 1993. (FT)

——. *Play with Fire.* New York: Berkley Prime Crime, 1995. (PF)

IDENTITY POLITICS:

APRIL SMITH'S *NORTH OF MONTANA*

AND ROCHELLE MAJER KRICH'S *ANGEL OF DEATH*

Priscilla L. Walton

Over the past 30 years, cultural diversity has become a widely discussed and pivotal social concern, and the complications involved in multicultural practices have generated increasingly polarized debates. On the one hand, and in the academic world, cultural acknowledgement of previously ignored theorists, writers, and activists, from disparate backgrounds and of distinct heritages, has led to their inclusion in school syllabi and university curricula. On the other hand, however, these inclusions have engendered resistance, and a growing racial and ethnic backlash. Overall, the cultural climate grows concomitantly more open to and less tolerant of multicultural issues, while, at the same time, the complexities of identity politics have found their way into the mass medium of genre fiction. Although some might argue that such a development points to a trivialization of multicultural concerns, it is also possible to see this same development as a means of presenting the problematics of multiculturalism to a wide and varied body of readers.

Contemporary formula fiction provides a venue for the dramatization of identity politics, since these novels can explore the complexities of cultural diversity in an accessible and readily-available medium. In effect, and as John G. Cawelti argued in 1976, through the process of reading formula fiction, it is possible for readers to address social issues "safely" and in a nonthreatening fashion. For Cawelti, genre novels embody a "controlled space" that allows for the exploration of alternative perceptions and constructions, a space wherein cultural fears and public concerns can be investigated by a wide readership. Accordingly, he contends that formula narratives have the ability to assist in the process of shifting ideological norms on a broad scale. In support of his argument, he draws attention to the transformations apparent in the Western, for it

has undergone almost a reversal in values over the past fifty years with respect to the representation of Indians and pioneers, but much of the basic structure of the formula and its imaginative vision of the meaning of the West has remained

130

substantially unchanged. By their capacity to assimilate new meanings like this, literary formulas ease the transition between old and new ways of expressing things and thus contribute to cultural continuity. (143)

Consequently, the ways in which questions of race and ethnicity, not to mention sexuality, have filtered into the mainstream market indicate that a broad spectrum of readers are engaging with these problems, and point to the commercial market's attempt to incorporate their cultural ramifications (for whatever potential economic reasons).

At least since the 1950s, and the advent of Chester Himes's crime series featuring Coffin Ed Johnson and Grave Digger Jones, detective novelists have embedded racial and ethnic dynamics in their popular fiction. Indeed, a number of popular writers view the genre as an effective political tool. For example, Valerie Wilson Wesley (author of the Tamara Hayle detective series) explains that, for her, writing for the mass market allows her to confront racial issues in a vast public forum:

Because part of a mystery is escaping anyway, I think that there's a sense of travelling in someone else's shoes. These novels take you into a different world for a while. I like the openness of mystery readers. I'm an African American woman, or I should say, I'm a black woman—because the books have been published in England and Germany, and I understand that they're really catching on in Great Britain—[and] I think that a lot of white women who read them say, "Well you know I get into the character and she's just like me." So I think that these books enable readers to get into different worlds. (Jones, "Interview")

Hence, if, as Cawelti has argued, genre fiction provides an important venue through which to explore the complexities of identity politics, or as Valerie Wilson Wesley puts it, enables readers to "get into different worlds," it does so by advancing an opportunity to fantasize alternative subjectivities. That is, readers are invited to identify with the protagonists, and their identification can contribute to political agency. For Theresa de Lauretis, in her recent text, *The Practice of Love,* fantasy identifications potentially function as important means of understanding difference because they point to

the process by which a representation in the external world is subjectively assumed, reworked through fantasy, in the internal world and then returned to the external world resignified, rearticulated discursively and/or performatively in the subject's self-representation. . . . (308)

De Lauretis's position signals how fantasy can disrupt normative self-representations, for it allows subjects to imagine themselves in disparate positions. By placing themselves in the situation of the protagonist, readers may undergo the confusions the protagonists experience, and come to some understanding of the complications involved in identity politics. In this fashion, readers are exposed, in a "nonthreatening" fashion, to "other" practices and self-constructions, and, through the reading process, can explore the pain of racial refiguration.

Two recent mainstream detective novels invite readers to investigate alternative identities by pointedly engaging with the complexities of identity politics from an intriguing bifurcation of insider/outsider perspectives. April Smith's *North of Montana* and Rochelle Majer Krich's *Angel of Death* offer provocative insights into the cultures they examine, at the same that they work to complicate the ways in which such cultures are stereotypically constructed. Through a mainstream medium, therefore, these texts both encourage reflection and put pressure on "normative" perceptions of race and ethnicity. The respective protagonists of *North of Montana* and *Angel of Death* experience identity crises: throughout the course of the novels, Ana Grey, the FBI agent hero of Smith's text, confronts her Hispanic heritage, and Jessie Drake, the P.I. of Majer Krich's, learns of her Jewish background. Moving from a privileged "inside" White Anglo-Saxon Protestant position to an "outside" status, the protagonists must come to terms with ancestries they have not recognized as their own, at the same time that they must reconstruct their pasts and its impact upon their presents. The novels critique stereotypical cultural perceptions, therefore, as they move to interrogate racial and ethnic identity formulations. Examining intersections of race, ethnicity, and subjectivity, Smith's and Majer Krich's novels provide for performative or dramatized critiques of stable identities—and they do so within the venue of mass market fiction.

Demonstrating the fluidity of constructions of "race" and "ethnicity," Smith and Majer Krich manifest accessible exemplars of multicultural theories. In a classroom setting, their texts encourage students to contemplate the more complex scholarly work focussed on race and ethnicity by raising the theoretical issues in a "reader-friendly" fashion. As they explore the permeability of racial constructions, the novels dramatize theses like Joel Kovel's, in *White Racism: A Psychohistory,* and its explanation of the operation of racial categories:

It is hard for us to accept the idea that races are man-made [sic] entities, so indoctrinated have we been by the pseudoscientific distortions of the theories of race. And yet nothing could be plainer than the fact that a race only exists because someone calls it so—or that inflation of the informal idea of race into the massive category, Race, is already a product of white racism. (Wallace 220)

Although "race" as a category tends to denote visible minorities, and "ethnicity" to designate those "nonvisible" groups that are nonetheless distinct from the dominant WASP norm, this separation is, in itself, too simplistic. Racial and ethnic "characteristics," in fact, are fluid, and shift more radically than is generally acknowledged. That is, while racial features are largely understood to be more or less fixed (i.e., black is black), they are in practice quite the opposite. Sander Gilman's work, for example, traces the ways in which the signifier "black" has been used, over the course of two centuries, to denote people of Semitic, East Indian, and African origins (see "The Jew's Nose").

While categorization can be a means of labelling a group of people distinct from the dominant white norm by that white norm, it may also serve as an assertion of agency for those so categorized. Potentially, identity politics offers a venue of resistance, as Trinh T. Minh-ha suggests, a venue that enables a subject to speak his/her own difference. Trinh elaborates by noting:

Difference is not difference to some ears but awkwardness or incompleteness. Aphasia. Unable or unwilling? . . . You who understand the dehumanization of forced removal-relocation-reeducation-redefinition, the humiliation of having to falsify your own reality, your voice—you know. And often cannot *say* it. (12)

Rather than having a cultural designation imposed upon one, then, speaking one's difference can become a powerful tool in self-designation. To say is to assert, and to resist the broad label placed upon one by society at large. Consequently, to define oneself in relation to one's peers offers a means of active self-construction.

Both *Angel of Death* and *North of Montana* underscore the problematics of identification, as Trinh discusses, as they concomitantly point to the oscillation of subject formation and its repercussions. Identification is a complex process, constantly in flux, and Diana Fuss argues, in *Identification Papers,* that identifications shift and contradict each other at different moments and at different times:

at the very same time that identification sets into motion the complicated dynamic of recognition and misrecognition that brings a sense of identity into being, it also immediately calls that identity into question. The astonishing capacity of identifications to reverse and disguise themselves, to multiply and contravene one another, to disappear and reappear years later renders identity profoundly unstable and perpetually open to radical change. (2)

Texts like *North of Montana* and *Angel of Death* portray these complications to their readers by dramatizing the protagonists' confusion and demonstrating how cultural designations have impacted upon the formulation of their respective characters. These protagonists grew up believing themselves to be WASPS, and inadvertently manifested the racist proclivities of their families; each, therefore, finds the discovery of her alternative cultural background difficult to assimilate. The novels portray the complexities of cultural locations by emphasizing the ways in which subjects can shift in their self-definitions; and, by rendering theories of race and ethnicity more accessible, the texts demonstrate what multicultural theorists have long contended—that these issues are far from simple, and that, while racial and ethnic constructions may be fluid, they also manifest very real consequences for those who bear the perceived "non-normative" traits.

As Valerie Wilson Wesley has argued, getting into different worlds can be an important tool in bridging cultural differences, and this is precisely what *North of Montana* and *Angel of Death* offer to their readers. Providing for both "inside" and "outside" looks at social constructions through their presentations of conflicted characters, they lend themselves to classroom discussions of subjectivity. For white students, who begin as normative "insiders" (in tandem with the protagonists), cultural familiarity is disrupted over the course of the novels. For "outsider" minority students, the novels move to affirm alternative heritages as they shift their cultural locus, leaving "outsiders" inside, and "insiders" out; in so doing, they allow space for the operation of alternative identities. Further, the novels serve as springboards from which to examine issues of bigotry, stereotyping, and "authenticity," and, through readerly identification with the main characters, invite students from all backgrounds to familiarize or refamiliarize themselves with such problems.

In both Smith's and Majer Krich's novels, the protagonists begin to deal with identity politics as outsiders. In *Angel of Death*, LAPD detective Jessie Drake is instructed to investigate death threats made to a Jewish lawyer, Barry Lewis, who is defending the rights of Neo-Nazis to parade through a Jewish neighbourhood. *North of Montana*'s protagonist, FBI agent Ana Grey, encounters racial issues coincidentally when a woman approaches her with a tale that her "cousin" from El Salvador, Violeta Alvarado, has been murdered. Unaware that she has such a cousin, Ana denies the familial association. Raised as white, Ana identifies with the dominant norm. She even considers race and ethnic concerns to be appropriate subject matter for jokes—in the following passage, she and her colleagues mock what they have "learned" in a multicultural awareness seminar. Ana begins the exchange by needling:

> "As an Afro-American, I would think you'd be especially aware of offensive stereotyping."
> "Forgive me." Kyle matches her arch tone. "I have misplaced my gender sensitivity manual and I am at a loss as to how to reply."
> "Try this: 'Yo! Honky bitch!'" says Frank, and we all laugh because we have just been through a multicultural awareness workshop that was one big snore. (9)

Discussions like the above underscore both Ana's cynicism toward multicultural politics, as well as her firm belief that she is "one of the boys."

Jessie Drake, less cynical than Ana, nonetheless has problems accepting her new case. A homicide cop, Jessie is infuriated that she has been assigned to a seemingly minor investigation, and she is afraid that her superiors are attempting to trivialize her work. Nonetheless, as a professional, Jessie begins to probe the threats made to Barry Lewis and to assess his position within the Jewish community. Over the course of her inquiries, Jessie meets with a group of rabbis, and is invited to visit the newly built holocaust museum:

> "By the way, Detective, while you're here, why not tour the museum? It'll help you understand our antipathy to groups like the White Alliance and what they stand for. And to people like Lewis, who help them spread their hate." (46)

But Jessie refuses the rabbi's offer, thinking "*Enough is enough*" (46).

While these protagonists succumb to racial stereotyping, then, each, perhaps despite herself, becomes intrigued with the situation that confronts her. Ana vaguely remembers a visit from a young Hispanic woman, whom she brushed off, and begins to feel a certain responsibility for Violeta's fate. She makes inquiries into the murder, and discovers that her "cousin" was the victim of a drug shooting. Dismissing the murder, much as she had dismissed Violeta on that earlier visit, Ana, like the investigating officers, falls prey to the stereotype that most violent Hispanic deaths are drug related. Concomitantly, however, Violeta's situation causes Ana to recall buried memories of her father, an Hispanic migrant worker, who abandoned her and her mother when she was very young:

Suddenly I am very uneasy. Nobody has mentioned my father in years. He was allegedly from Central America but I never even knew which country, since he abandoned us when I was a tiny child and was always a taboo subject in our home. My mother and I lived with her father, a police officer, and I was raised Protestant and white; you couldn't get more white, all the way back to the curl in the horns on the headgear of our Viking ancestors. I happen to have thick wavy black hair but that's as Mediterranean as I get. Hispanics are simply another race to me. (12)

These recollections, along with her own guilt over shirking Violeta, lead Ana to dig deeper into her "cousin's" death, even though the case is officially closed. Feeling ties she does not understand, she decides to visit Violeta's children, who are in the charge of a neighbour. While she urges the neighbor to contact the authorities, the plight of the children bothers Ana, and their presence moves her to remember own past.

In *Angel of Death*, Jessie gets more involved with Barry Lewis's case when the court decides that the Neo-Nazis have the right to parade. Assigned to security duty, Jessie feels that in order to perform effectively, she must familiarize herself with the explosive situation produced by the upcoming parade. She decides to attend a Jewish instruction class, where she learns something of Jewish heritage, and she also meets with a Jewish activist, who warns her that the parade might well turn into a riot. Indeed, as he has predicted, the parade does erupt in violence, leaving several participants wounded and one old woman dead. Now on homicide detail, Jessie, who has become more aware of the Jewish community's position, finds herself questioning her own past. Haunted by the abuse inflicted on her as a child at the hands of her mother, Jessie tries to come to grips with her mother's anti-Semitism and its effects on her:

> *Enough is enough.*
> The phrase popped into her head. It was the phrase her mother uttered every time she saw a reference to a feature film or television movie or magazine or newspaper article that dealt with the Holocaust. "Enough is enough," Frances Claypool would say to her two daughters and husband, even though she herself had some distant Jewish relatives. "How many times do they have to go over this? Can't they forget about it already?"
> Had her attitude rooted itself in Jessie? (46)

Concurrently, the more subtle operations of anti-Semitism are dramatized in the problems confronting Barry Lewis at his law firm. When asked to defend a member of the White supremacist group on a murder charge (for killing the old woman at the parade), Lewis initially refuses: "'See the Jew boy help the Nazis. Round two. . . . Not this time. I won't do it" (145). But he is urged to reconsider by influential members of his law firm—all of whom are WASPS:

> "My parents survived the Holocaust that Kraft says never happened! They almost died in the concentration camps that he and Benning and his organization claim didn't exist!" In a calmer voice he said, "I don't see how I can zealously defend Benning and do his case justice."
>
> "Of course you can, Barry," Haus said softly. . . . "You've impressed me and the other partners with your dedication and loyalty to the firm, Barry. That's why you have a great future with us." He smiled. "I'm sure you wouldn't do anything to disappoint us or to jeopardize the best interests of the firm." (145)

Lewis is in a Catch-22 situation: if he decides to take the case he will be further estranged from his family and community; if he rejects it, he jeopardizes his future at the law firm. Despite his better judgement, yet fearful of his future and that of his partner and children, he accepts the case.

In another vein, the repercussions of race on the work place are foregrounded in *North of Montana,* when Ana begins to learn about the falsity of stereotypes. As she probes deeper into Violeta's murder, Ana discovers that her "cousin" had not been involved in drugs at all—this assumption arose because Violeta was out on the streets in the early hours of the morning. Ana determines that Violeta was returning home from her new job, a job that she was forced to accept because she was fired from her position as a housekeeper. Ana involves herself enough in the case to extract money owing to Violeta from her former employer, and is taken aback at the cavalier ways in which the rich treat their Hispanic servants:

> I feel guilty and deeply conflicted and he is a doctor living in a million-and-a-half-dollar house with a crystal chandelier. "Her children have nobody to take care of them, okay? May I suggest out of common decency, as her last employer, you make a contribution to their welfare?" (67)

Although she is puzzled by Violeta's hold over her, Anna continues to distance herself from her "cousin." At the same time, because she believes herself to be one of the "boys," Ana never hesitates to show off her toughness. At one point, when she is asked if she eats red meat, she responds: "I eat it and I fuck it" (58). But Ana is not one of the boys, as she discovers when a promotion that should have been hers is questioned, and gender issues enter her world:

> ["]You're punishing me because I'm female."
> He squeezes his eyes shut and laughs out loud. "I hope you don't really believe that."
> "Yes, I do, and I'm going to bring an EEOC lawsuit charging sex discrimination against you and the Bureau to prove it." (70)

Ana's exposure to sexism, when she has never questioned her "equal" status in the FBI, opens her eyes to the racism that pervades her world. Bothered by recurring fragments of memory surrounding her father, Ana, who has always idolized her grandfather, tries to question him about the childhood years she cannot clearly remember. But her grandfather avoids her questions and refuses to acknowledge his own obvious prejudice:

> "You didn't like him because he was Hispanic?"
> "I have nothing against Hispanics. I was pissed off because he knocked up my daughter." He says this easily. Authoritatively. As the one in charge of history. "Then the son of a bitch walks away. Abandons her—and you. Why would you care about a guy who left? I'm the one who raised you." (61)

Insisting that Ana is dwelling on a past that is best forgotten, her grandfather is more interested in asserting Ana's whiteness than in helping her to come to grips with her childhood. When she continues to question him about her background, he vigorously maintains her homogeneity:

> ["]I think maybe I am the epitome of multiculturality." . . .
> "Like hell you are. You're an American and if you're not proud of it then one of us has fucked up beyond belief." (61)

Like Ana, Jessie, too, starts to question her past when Barry Lewis is found murdered in his office. Jessie, who must now investigate the lawyer's murder and interrogate a large pool of predominantly Jewish suspects, becomes increasingly disturbed by dim recollections of a picture shown her by her mother and her mother's vague references to "Jewish relatives." As Jessie notes to her Jewish therapist: "[']I've never considered myself Jewish. I still don't. It's just that lately, with the Lewis case, I've been thinking about it more'" (159). Deciding to confront her mother about the mysterious picture, she discovers that her mother is herself Jewish, and that she was a "hidden child"—a Jewish child who looked Gentile and was sent to a Gentile home for safety during the Holocaust. Jessie's mother informs her:

"In Poland during the war, Jessica, six-year-olds were not children. Our bodies were young, but our souls were old. . . . That was in November 1941. The Germans had taken over my father's factory, but my mother had hidden some wool fabric and made me two dresses and a coat. That evening she tied real ribbons on my braids and had me put on one of the new dresses. I cried. I wanted to stay with my parents and my brothers and sisters and grandparents, but my parents promised that they'd come back for me and we'd all be together again." Now Frances's smile was ironic. (220)

Shocked by her mother's revelations, Jessie tries to come to grips with the Jewish heritage that is now her own. At this point, she decides to take up the rabbi's invitation to visit the Holocaust museum, and is overwhelmed by its depictions. Jessie begins to self-identify as Jewish, and to speak her ancestry. Yet her ancestry has repercussions on her personal life, as she discovers when she is confronted by the racism of her lover: "She knew it was going to be fine between them, and she opened her eyes to smile at him and found him staring at her. He shut his eyes quickly and said her name . . . and pretended to moan with pleasure as he moved against her. She closed her eyes and pretended, too" (285). At the office, Jessie's Jewishness renders her suspect, and she is accused of bias in her investigation of Lewis's death:

"Emery Kraft just called. He doesn't like your attitude. . . . He says you've been rude, that you've minimized his concerns about his safety. He claims you ignored information he gave you that could've saved Benning's life. He believes that because you're Jewish, you're unable to conduct this investigation with any degree of objectivity—that you don't give a shit about who killed Benning or, for that matter, Barry Lewis. Any comments?" (315)

In *North of Montana*, Ana, like Jessie, starts to self-identify as Hispanic. Violeta's death, in tandem with her recollections of her father, force her to recognize that she is not white, but half Hispanic:

"She *was* your cousin, right?"
I have not answered John for several moments. Now I cross the marble one square at a time, deliberately walking toward him until we are face-to-face.
"Yes, John. She was my cousin."
In acknowledging this I find I have gained something. Relief. Confidence. (98)

Ana's self-revelation increases her concern for Violeta's children, and, through them, she becomes more familiar with Hispanic culture. Ana commences to speak her own difference, and she begins to align herself with her own minority group as opposed to the white norm of which she has always considered herself a part. When asked about her background, Anna confesses to readers: "For a moment I'm stopped by a surge of anxiety, but I push through it: 'My father was from El Salvador, my mother was American.' It's out on the table and it's not so bad." (149). In Ana's case, this does not alienate her from her co-workers:

> "[I'm] Spanish, actually." I feel myself blush. "Half and half."
> "A Spanish señorita. Or . . . shall I call you señora?"
> "Señorita."
> He nods. For no reason at all, we toast. (102)

Conversely, Jessie experiences the loss of her lover because of her ethnicity, at the same time that she discovers a new bond with her former husband, Gary, who is himself Jewish. Gary provides an outlet for Jessie's confusion: "Anytime you want to talk, call me. Promise?" (312). And, although she is charged with bias by some subjects in the murder investigation, she also finds support in others. One Jewish teacher offers: "'You could learn [about Judaism], if you're interested. You could take classes in Hebrew and Jewish history or whatever appeals to you. I'd be happy to help in any way'" (248). Trying to cope with her conflicted feelings, Jessie discusses them with her psychiatrist, "'You think of yourself one way your entire life, and all of a sudden you're forced to reexamine who you are. It can be confusing and unsettling'" (159). Certainly confused, but able to function within her newly found world, Jessie attempts to understand her mother's abusive behaviour towards her. Indeed, she learns from one rabbi of the problems often faced by hidden children: "'My mother finds it difficult to discuss her life before and during the war.' 'Most hidden children do.' Korbin sighed. 'There's a society of hidden children, you know. They have conventions where they share their experiences and their feelings of abandonment and lack of identity'" (259-60).

Unlike Jessie, Ana cannot fathom her beloved grandfather's behaviour and loses all respect for him. Finally recalling the events of her childhood, she remembers that it was he who killed her father, upsetting all the beliefs with which she had lived throughout her life:

My parents must have just driven in from Las Vegas, where they had gotten married, and Poppy must have been crazy with rage that this ignorant wetback

dared to take his daughter, threatening him with the black policeman's night-
stick, jabbing it into the air. . . . [I]t was my grandfather who raised his night-
stick and smacked my father across the temple and around the shoulders and
neck again and again until blood streaked his temples, he suddenly convulsed
and collapsed and lay still. (245-46)

Realizing that her grandfather's ill health renders the possibility of confronting him futile, Ana recognizes him for the bigot he is. She makes
peace with herself and her shirking of Violeta by constructing a memorial to the dead woman:

I prop up the plastic picture of El Niño de Atocha on the sill of one of the
bricked-in windows and ask him, the guardian of lakes, to bless this unlikely
place where someone has drowned. I set down the candle stubs, memorials to
Violeta and my father, ghosts whom I will never really know. Despite the horns
and the roar of traffic like a jetway and pedestrians on every side, I close my
eyes and stand there and actually pray to El Niño to keep watch over those who
are lost. I pray that Teresa and Cristóbal will walk on a black sand beach where
the warm water will be full of red snapper and shrimp, and that when they reach
the clearing in the bush they will find an older brother who is kind and a loving
grandmother waiting with open arms.

    Violeta's Bible has been bumping around in my glove compartment. I
finally lay it to rest on the window ledge.

    A tight bitter sadness stays in my throat all the way home. (253)

When Violeta's memorial is not only intact the next day, but built upon
by members of the Hispanic community, Ana starts to reconcile her conflicting emotions for her parents:

[T]he picture of El Niño de Atocha is still standing, and furthermore, the win-
dowsill is full of amazing objects. People have left flowers, toy cars, candies,
and coins. The Bible is there, untouched. Nobody has stolen from El Niño.

    In the shelter of the ledge other candles have been added: good luck can-
dles printed with pictures of saints as I saw in the botanica, a fat red and green
one left over from Christmas, a ragtag collection of half-burned tapers standing
in juice cartons or anchored in crumpled bits of aluminum foil. All are lit.
Someone has kept them lit. For the first time I can feel my mother and father
inside me together, then rising together from this tender company of flames;
rising up. (254)

This resurgence of feelings enables Ana to break through her cynicism
and to accept the love offered by a colleague. She even summons him

(illegally) to Violeta's memorial scene: "I lean against the G-ride until Donnato pulls up ten minutes later. . . . He throws the door open and hurries toward me with a worried look. I reach for his hand, in front of that doofball Joe Positano, and everybody" (255).

In *Angel of Death,* Jessie tries to make amends with her mother, although she knows it will be a slow process. Nonetheless, she is encouraged when her mother sends her the picture of Jessie's relatives. As she relates:

"I called and thanked her and told her how much it meant to me. She said something like 'I knew you'd be pestering me about it, Jessica.'" She smiled. "But I swear I heard a catch in her voice." (355)

And, with the reblossoming of her romance with Gary, Jessie begins to find peace within herself and within her community:

"Is this a Jewish home?" His [Gary's] tone was light. His eyes were gazing at her intently.

"I'm interested in learning about Judaism. I'm thinking about taking some classes in Jewish history, maybe a beginner's Hebrew class." She glanced at him to see his reaction.

Gary took the mezuzah case from her hand. He held it a moment, then said, "Want me to help you put it up?"

She smiled. "I'd like that very much." (356).

Both of these novels end on positive notes, with the characters resolving their conflicting identifications. Yet, through their portrayals of racism, bigotry, stereotyping, and self-denial, they work to demonstrate how the problems that confront multicultural practices are far from simple. Although Jessie and Ana come to grips with their unknown backgrounds, characters like Barry Lewis, Jessie's mother, and Ana's grandfather point to the ways in which race and ethnicity permeate and color one's sense of self and social relations. In so doing, the novels provide depictions of reconciliation and self-acceptance in their main characters, while also dramatizing the difficulties "difference" generates, and the pain and bigotry in which it often results.

North of Montana and *Angel of Death* highlight the problematics of multiculturalism, therefore, at the same time that their representations of conflicted and torn individuals make identity politics more immediate to their readers. Through identifications with the protagonists, readers can experience something of the traumas that face Jessie and Ana, since the novels provocatively delineate some of the repercussions of race and ethnicity. Thus, in a classroom setting, these texts can enable white students, who begin in the position of the protagonists, to undergo some of the conflicts that multicultural practices entail, and minority students, who may be "in the know" from the beginning of the works, to be reaffirmed in their own efforts to grapple with the issues involved. By shifting from "inside" the dominant norm to "outside" it, the protagonists and their plights can perform as a bridge for understanding cultural differences, while also potentially aiding minority students in their own quests for self-identification.

Accordingly, these novels not only dramatize the problematics of multiculturalism, they render those politics immediate and accessible. As they do so, texts like *Angel of Death* and *North of Montana* may serve as springboards for students to confront the issues surrounding identity politics, and, by encouraging their readers to identify with the protagonists, the novels provoke discussions of crucial issues in a nonthreatening manner. Through the venue of mass market fiction, these texts, which carefully avoid positing simplistic solutions to the systemic social and cultural problems they detail, invite readers and students alike to explore identity politics "inside" and "outside" diverse racial and ethnic groups. By creating a space wherein difference can be interrogated, deliberated, and debated, then, the novels engage in what is by no means an inconsequential or negligible act.

Works Cited

Cawelti, John G. "The Study of Literary Formulas." *Detective Fiction: A Collection of Critical Essays*. Ed. Robin W. Winks. Englewood Cliffs: Prentice-Hall Inc., 1980. 121-43.

De Lauretis, Teresa. *The Practice of Love: Lesbian Sexuality and Perverse Desire*. Bloomington: Indiana UP, 1994.

Fuss, Diana. *Identification Papers*. New York: Routledge, 1995.

Gilman, Sander. "The Jew's Nose." *The Jew's Body*. New York: Routledge, 1991.

Jones, Manina. "Interview with Valerie Wilson Wesley." Nov. 15, 1995. Unpublished.

Kovel, Joel. *White Racism: A Psychohistory*. New York: Pantheon, 1984.

Majer Krich, Rochelle. *Angel of Death*. New York: Mysterious Press, 1994.

Smith, April. *North of Montana*. New York: Alfred A. Knopf, 1994.

Trinh, T. Minh-ha. "Difference: 'A Special Third World Women Issue.'" *Discourse* 8 (1986-87): 10-18.

THE DETECTIVE AS OTHER:
THE DETECTIVE *VERSUS* THE OTHER

Michael Cohen

I have recently been wondering whether racism is a necessary element in mystery and detective stories. I do not mean racism in the narrowest sense, but fear and hatred of the other, whether it expresses itself in racist and national stereotypes, in misogyny, in the queer-baiting that the hard-boiled detectives cannot seem to avoid, in a specific conviction that Jews, blacks, Chinese, or communists are out to destroy us, or in some more subtle form of exophobia.

Cartooning Racism in Who Framed Roger Rabbit?

It was *Who Framed Roger Rabbit?* that brought the question into my head. My reaction to this movie surprised some of my friends, who thought I had lost my sense of humor completely. But almost from the first moment, the film conjured up for me the features of the worst stereotype of the great American other—the blacks—that could be assembled from the popular arts in America over the past two centuries. If racial stereotyping showed up even in a cartoon mystery, might it not be inherent in the genre? The racial stereotype in *Who Framed Roger Rabbit?* is of creatures distinctly different—not really human by comparison with whites. These "others" bungle work because of shiftlessness and incompetence; they cannot get the simplest thing right, but they work very cheaply. Physically they are strong, practically indestructible, but they are also unpredictable and emotional. They are more affected by liquor than sober whites. They are colorful and interesting, vibrant and alive, but also threatening and dangerous. The danger and the fascination come together in the sexiness that is part of the stereotype as well.

That some of these characteristics contradict each other should come as no surprise. No stereotype ever suffers because pieces of its makeup contradict each other; it does not need internal consistency any more than it needs correspondence with reality.

Now consider the Toons of *Who Framed Roger Rabbit?* The movie presents the Toons as distinctively other. Our first clue to their otherness comes when Roger walks off the set of the opening cartoon—a violent, frenetic animation from which all joy seems to have been deliberately expunged and which inspires, in my experience with the film, only nervous or manic laughter. Roger, hitting himself over the head with a skillet, walks past Bob Hoskins's character of Eddie Valiant, who looks away from him and spits out scornfully, "Toons!" In Valiant's conversation with the studio head, R. K. Maroon, we learn rapidly that Roger is unreliable, physically indestructible, but emotionally a creampuff.

Valiant doesn't like Toontown; his brother was killed there by a Toon's dropping a piano on his head. A little later Maroon throws away the line that Dumbo, along with other Toons that Maroon has borrowed from Disney's studio, works "for peanuts." We also watch Roger's catastrophic reaction to a swig of liquor.

It would be inevitable that some features of the Toons, in their alterity, would coincide with those of any stereotyped underclass. The two things to note here are that *Who Framed Roger Rabbit? chooses* alterity to have the detective play against, and then goes out of its way to make the correspondence with blacks. The "Toon Review" at the Ink and Paint Club, where Jessica Rabbit performs, is an all-Toon show, but the club is, as Maroon says, "strictly humans only." The patrons are humans; the hired help is all-Toon. The parallel with the Cotton Club is unmistakable. When Valiant takes in the show, additional features of the stereotype emerge, specifically the danger the Toons represent to humans and, in Jessica, the sexiness of Toons.

The cannon fired by Daffy at Donald Duck is frightening and genuinely destructive; though its wielders cannot be hurt by it, others can. And Jessica's sex appeal seems like another sort of loose cannon. All of this is uneasily contained in the festival of the club, where humans are served and entertained by those who cannot be admitted as patrons.

The Toons are almost indestructible, and the villain, Judge Doom, turns out to be one of them, though he has been passing as a human. At the scene of the crime for which Roger Rabbit is framed, Eddie Valiant meets Judge Doom. The blatant stereotypical aspects of this scene are many: Judge Doom's flunkies are weasels that caricature pimps; Judge Doom executes summary violence on Toons by substituting "the dip" for lynching, and the judge says solemnly to Valiant, "a human has been murdered by a Toon—don't you understand the magnitude of that?" More subtle are the self-hatred of the judge's actions, along with the racial self-hatred they point to, and the way the reference to *Chinatown* works. "This is the way we handle things down in Toontown," says Judge Doom, recalling the closing lines of *Chinatown* in only one of a number of references to it throughout this movie.

Who Framed Roger Rabbit? is a movie that is supposed to be about tolerance: during its course Eddie Valiant overcomes his distrust and distaste for Toons to the extent that he defends and befriends Roger Rabbit. At the end of the movie the evil genius is defeated, Toontown belongs to its rightful owners the Toons, and the nasty scheme for paving a strip of L.A. all the way to San Bernardino has been foiled. But there are certain problems in these outcomes and the way they have been brought about. The evil genius has been defeated only after he is revealed to be a Toon, though a Toon hater—not an unusual pattern when a villain comes from an underclass. Toontown belongs to its rightful owners only after it has been given them by a human sugar daddy, the gadget man Marvin Acme—the plantation owner—in return for favors received from the sexy Toon Jessica. And the foiling of progress leaves us in a rosy and comfortable nostalgia. This happy ending is problematic because it perpetuates difference by constructing a "Toonship," locally owned or no. There will be no freeway destroying Toontown; the Toons can live happily apart and in the past. This appeal to nostalgia is invidious because it legitimizes the separation; the past cannot be changed.

The ending appears desirable because it defeats Judge Doom and his vision. Doom's "solution" to racial difference is either to conceal it by passing oneself off as the one with the power or to dissolve the differences by simply eliminating the powerless in a corrosive, lethal mutation of the American melting pot. Several reviewers allege that Zemeckis toyed with the idea of calling the dip the "Final Solution" (Johnson 26; Rosenbaum 33).

But finally, what I found most disturbing about the film was that the outcome does not grow out of the exploding of stereotypes, but out of their propagation.

Who Framed Roger Rabbit? is a movie clearly aimed at a wide audience. Its appeal is to adults and to children, though whether it is suitable for children, quite aside from its way of depicting racial difference, is questionable. Its PG rating probably results from the sexual innuendo, the language, and from one kick to the crotch rather than from the rest of its nearly incessant violence. But why would a moviemaker wishing to make a profit on a movie everyone can love risk an accusation of racial stereotyping and the inevitable damage such a charge would cause at the box office?

I think I know parts of the answer. One part is that the moviemakers did not consider the question because they did not *see* the racial stereotyping—did not see it *as* stereotyping. This blind spot is the harder to imagine because Zemeckis has been reported as saying that he was aware of the racial dimensions of what he was doing and because the Cotton Club parallel has been added; it is not in Gary K. Wolf's 1981 source novel called *Who Censored Roger Rabbit?* Wolf's novel is set in a contemporary, not a 1947, Los Angeles, but one with three tiers of segregation: there are facilities for humans, others for humanoid Toons like Jessica, and still others for animal or "barnyard" Toons like Roger. The book begins with a premise the moviemakers attempt to conceal. Wolf's Eddie Valiant dislikes Toons because, as everyone knows, they are worthless. The movie's Eddie Valiant dislikes Toons for a reason. Even Roger admits that if a Toon had killed *his* brother, he would not like Toons either. Eddie's personal prejudice, the extrapolation of his hatred for his brother's killer, is somehow not supposed to read as racial prejudice based on stereotyping. But the racial issue in the story cannot be expunged in that way.

Another part of the answer seems to me to be in American popular culture where *Who Framed Roger Rabbit?* has its roots and in the movies that embody that popular culture—the movies to which this movie alludes so often. It alludes to cartoons as far back as the black-and-white animations of the thirties, to fantasy such as *The Wizard of Oz* (1939), and to the human and cartoon mixture of Disney's *Song of the South,* released in 1946, the year before *Who Framed Roger Rabbit?* is supposed to be taking place. These works have what at best can be called an insensitive attitude to marginal or minority groups. The cartoons of the thirties now look almost incredibly racist in their degrading racial caricatures. My point is that the deeper a work sinks its roots into American popular culture represented by these genres the less likely that it can avoid reflecting their racism.

Encoding racial stereotypes as cartoon characters may be worse than facing the uncoded ugly bias as it is, not because of the automatic appeal to children of a story containing cartoon characters, but because the cartoon characters are by definition not human. "Not human" means by implication "subhuman." This implication combines with characteristics that are transferable or readable as a simple substitution code: the Toons' world is not susceptible to ordinary law; they are unpredictable, dangerous—occasionally deadly—but also sexy. Their part of town is to be avoided at night. Their difference is also seen as festive, but the carnival aspect of the "other" here, instead of stereotypical rhythm and dance, is humor of the cartoon kind, graphically inventive and without logic. It is a sublimation of racial phobia and it would be romantic to suppose that it could effect a catharsis of such fears. It seems to me more likely to be cathectic than cathartic: to concentrate or at least keep alive certain capacities for prejudice rather than to purge them.

But *Who Framed Roger Rabbit?* is not just a cartoon, it is a mystery with human and cartoon characters. Its most frequent allusions are to the 1941 version of *The Maltese Falcon* and to *Chinatown.* How much of its stereotypical construction of otherness has to do with the mystery genre?

Popular Literature and the Mystery

We do not have to go very far to find mystery fiction that is full of stereotypes, ethnic bias, and racial prejudice. The difficulty is in distinguishing between exophobic or alterophobic features that are simply a part of popular literature (in general or in a particular time and place) and those features that are exclusive to mystery fiction. Colin Watson begins his book *Snobbery with Violence* by quoting Lady Mary Wortley Montagu on the way popular writers reflect the "manners of the times" and the "notions that are most acceptable to the present taste" (Watson 15). Watson extends this observation by pointing out how important it has been, since the advent of near-universal literacy, for popular authors in England to be aware of prejudices of various classes—not just those of their own. These authors include but are not limited to writers of detective fiction.

Some detective fiction is pretty thickly xenophobic, homophobic, and convinced that criminality goes along with other sexual preferences, other political views or other—usually nonwhite—races. "Other" here usually means other than the detective's. Colin Watson documents anti-Semitic, racial, and generally xenophobic attitudes in a dozen well-known British writers, including G. K. Chesterton, Edgar Wallace, John Buchan, "Sapper," and Dorothy Sayers (113-36). Otto Penzler points out how many of the arch-villains in crime and detective fiction are foreign in relation to the detectives who oppose them and to the primary readership of the books in which they appear: for examples, English heroes battle Fu Manchu, Moriarty (Irish), Madame Sara (L. T. Meade's antagonist in *The Sorceress of the Strand* is "a mixture of Italian and Indian"), and Flambeau, the Frenchman whom Father Brown catches and turns into a sidekick (Penzler 321-41).

But even a favorable portrait of a character who belongs to another race does not mean that the fiction is not stereotyping or exploiting the other race. At the risk of being obvious I want to emphasize this point. The best illustration can be found in a contrast of those two extraordinary Asians, Dr. Fu Manchu and Charlie Chan. Fu Manchu was created by the English author Sax Rohmer; his first appearance was in a 1913 novel called *The Insidious Fu-Manchu*. (Fu Manchu's name evolved from a hyphenated to an unhyphenated form.) In the 1920s Rohmer brought his character across the Atlantic and discovered that American sinophobia was an even richer vein than the British variety. Fu Manchu is an embodiment of a racial threat, "the yellow peril incarnate in one man" (Rohmer 17). Fu Manchu brings together everything that is frightening in the Chinese stereotype. He is intelligent beyond mere cunning and has mastered English so that the shibboleths of language cannot find him out: he can be mistaken for an Occidental on the telephone, for example. He is utterly ruthless, physically dangerous, and he calls on a network of agents so large it seems to encompass his whole race, playing on the irrational fear that every face with a vaguely nonwestern look must belong to an enemy. As Colin Watson writes, the Fu Manchu books appealed only in proportion to the prejudices they inflamed: "The Fu-Manchu novels went into edition after edition. Their only clear message was one of racial vituperation. Had there not existed in the minds of many thousands of people an innate fear or dislike of foreigners—oriental foreigners, in particular—Sax Rohmer never would have become a bestselling author" (Watson 117).

That everything about Charlie Chan's character is constructed to allay these same fears makes for no less exploitation of them, however. Earl Derr Biggers created his Chinese Hawaiian detective Charlie Chan in six books published between 1925 and 1932, although the character is best known through almost fifty films about him made during the 30s and 40s. Charlie Chan is fat, unemotional, and continually apologizing. As William F. Wu points out in his study called *The Yellow Peril: Chinese Americans in American Fiction 1850-1940,* Biggers's "primary goal . . . is to assure his readers that the character was not threatening to them in any way":

Charlie Chan's calm, apologetic, and passive tolerance of racial insults and harassment is an obvious sop to those who would be threatened by an Asian American detective with normal assertiveness and temper. His rotund figure is also important, symbolizing the opposite of the lean Fu Manchu. Charlie Chan is a middle-aged family man. The existence of his family and his devotion to it further reduce the chance of threat. (181)

But both characters, Charlie Chan as well as Fu Manchu, equally serve "the values and beliefs of white supremacy," according to Wu (182). Chan's actual jurisdiction, even when he is working on the mainland, is Hawaii, and each of his books subordinates him to a young Occidental male character, though Chan is allowed to do the actual crime solving. A sympathetic minority character does not mean the colonizing stops, if the character is also rendered passionless, unthreatening sexually or any other way, or otherwise ghettoized.

Similar stereotyping occurs in the depiction of Arthur W. Upfield's Queensland Detective-Inspector Napoleon Bonaparte, who has an aborigine mother and a white father. What gives him an edge is that his almost supernatural tracking abilities are tempered by imagination (which the aborigines lack in Upfield) and, as we are told on the first page of *The Sands of Windee* (1931), " the white man's calm and comprehensive reasoning." Bony, as everyone calls him, can find evidence of a murder because unlike whites, he can read near the scene of a disappearance a "blackfellows' sign" informing him that a white man was killed there. And while "no aborigine would brave the spirits of the place where, according to the death-sign, violence had been done," the half-caste Bony has no qualms about haunting the site to search for clues (Upfield 14). He has the best of both worlds, and there is no doubt which is the better world—that of "the original, conquering, pioneering British race" (12). Aside from some silly romanticism and nonsense about mind reading, the really repulsive aspect of this book is the objectification of the blacks, whom Bony and others not only use but impassively watch killing one another.

The attitudes in Rohmer, Biggers and Upfield might merely reflect the times in which they write and have nothing to do with the genre of mystery fiction. After all, the fiction of the first decades of the century is more likely to be racist in tone or content, while the end-of-century enlightenment in which we bask now gives us favorable portraits of different races. But this explanation seems to ignore a continuing feature of mystery fiction, an interest in otherness for its own sake. Mystery fiction is very fond of cultural difference, and significantly, that difference is very often viewed from outside. Consider the number of non-black authors who depict blacks (John Ball's Virgil Tibbs, Arthur W. Upfield's Napoleon Bonaparte, James McClure's Michael Zondi), non-Asian authors who depict Asians (Sax Rohmer's Fu Manchu, Earl Derr Biggers's Charlie Chan, Janwillem van de Wetering's Saito Masanobu, John P. Marquand's Mr. Moto, James Melville's Tetsuo Otani), nonIndians, non-native Americans, and non-Chicanos or Chicanas who depict members of these groups (H. R. F. Keating's Ganesh Ghote, Tony Hillerman's Joe Leaphorn and Jim Chee, Dell Shannon's Luis Mendoza, Marcia Muller's Elena Oliverez), as well as a Frenchman created by a Belgian, a Belgian drawn by an Englishwoman, Englishwomen, Irishmen, Italians, even a Tahitian detective, all invented by Americans. Very few authors these days deal in stereotypes, but clearly there is an interest in exotica. Racism or classism can be issues in these books, but as attitudes of characters rather than of the author. The cleverer books exploit race or class friction among their characters. Thus James McClure's Afrikaans police lieutenant Tromp Kramer begins with a stereotypical assessment of his Zulu sidekick, Bantu Detective Sergeant Michael Zondi; their working relationship starts in *The Steam Pig:*

The first time he had seen Zondi was outside the magistrate's court on a Monday when it was thronged so solid with worried wives and families you had to force your way through them. Then the mob suddenly parted of its own volition and through it had come a coon version of Frank Sinatra making with the jaunty walk.

. . . "Cheeky black bastard," Kramer grunted. (McClure 36)

But before long Zondi and Kramer are getting along well, even enjoying each other's company, as long as Zondi remembers who's boss. So it is also with Colin Dexter's Chief Inspector Morse and Sergeant Lewis, where the difference and consequent friction comes from class rather than race. Reginald Hill turns these class and education differences around with his rough-edged Superintendent Dalziel and his sensitive, college-educated sergeant Peter Pascoe. All of these authors are dealing with classes, races or ethnic groups outside their own, and while none of them could be accused of writing from personal prejudice, prejudice in their characters helps to drive their books.

A culture viewed from outside is opaque, with interesting surface features. Viewed from inside, culture is transparent. What I mean can best be illustrated by some of the Japanese mysteries. James Melville begins *The Wages of Zen* by drawing attention to Japanese businessmen's penchant for American social clubs like Rotary and Lions; he notes the Japanese dedication to perfect attendance at meetings. Janwillem van de Wetering, in the first two stories in the collection called *Inspector Saito's Small Satori,* mentions the flowered kimonos that are appropriate for young girls and the "slanting eyes" of Japanese women —both details are noted twice. These are matters that strike an outside observer about things Japanese. Even though these stories are told through the consciousness of Melville's Tetsuo Otani and van de Wetering's Saito Masanobu, the authors have their Japanese characters looking *at* things an actual Japanese would see *through.* Japanese do not think of themselves as having "slanting eyes"—they think their eyes are eye-shaped and that Occidentals have oddly formed eyes. In Shizuko Natsuki's *Innocent Journey,* by contrast, very little is made of the cultural significance of the double suicide Yoko Noda agrees to perform with her lover Takashi Sato—it is merely a starting point for the plot rather than anything distinctively Japanese from their point of view or from Natsuki's. The author looks through the cultural event to how it can be changed and used to drive plot; it has no inherent interest as a piece of exotica for her because it is not exotic.

These days in books using other cultural settings, the atavistic drawing of lines in authors like Sapper has been turned into multiculturalism; difference that once made for simple judgments tends to be valued for local color or even as plot driver. Difference still seems necessary to the genre, but in a different way. Why should it be a necessary feature of mystery fiction at all?

One possibility is an anthropological one—that the social infractions crime literature treats were originally defined in terms of otherness. This cynical view of the relationship between ethics and otherness is that, in the words of Fredric Jameson, "all ethics lives by exclusion and predicates certain types of Otherness or evil" (60). Forms of popular literature that deal with ethical questions, according to such a view, simply turn evil back into otherness. Jameson accepts a Nietzschean model of ethics, in which

the concept of good and evil is a positional one that coincides with categories of Otherness. Evil thus, as Nietzsche taught us, continues to characterize whatever is radically different from me, whatever by virtue of precisely that difference seems to constitute a real and urgent threat to my own existence. So from the earliest times, the stranger from another tribe, the "barbarian" who speaks an incomprehensible language and follows "outlandish" customs, but also the woman, whose biological difference stimulates fantasies of castration and devoration, or in our own time, the avenger of accumulated resentments from some oppressed class or race, or else that alien being, Jew or Communist, behind whose apparently human features a malignant and preternatural intelligence is thought to lurk: these are some of the archetypal figures of the Other, about whom the essential point to be made is not so much that he is feared because he is evil; rather he is evil *because* he is Other, alien, different, strange, unclean, and unfamiliar. (115)

According to this model what occurs in imaginative or narrative practice is a rendering of the ethical otherness of the villain as ethnic or class otherness; the process merely turns back what had already been done in a primordial invention of evil in the first place:

Nietzsche's analysis, which unmasks the concepts of ethics as the sedimented or fossilized trace of the concrete praxis of situations of domination, gives us a significant methodological precedent. He demonstrated, indeed, that what is really meant by "the good" is simply my own position as an unassailable power center, in terms of which the position of the Other, or of the weak, is repudiated and marginalized in practices which are then ultimately themselves formalized in the concept of evil. (Jameson 117)

I find this explanation repugnant and believe it to be wrong and perhaps naive. Some mystery tales and many tragedies show that evil cannot be externalized and demonized, that, in Pogo's turn on Oliver Hazard Perry's phrase, "We has met the enemy and it is us." *Oedipus the King,* for example, seems to point back from its fifth century B. C. version of the myth to a prehistoric recognition of the evil in the self. Moreover, though society begins in tribalism, with a certain amount of usness versus themness, notions of crime and sin are clearly intratribal; what another tribe does to you is not crime or sin but war. I think that the Nietzsche/Jameson formulation must be turned on its head if it is to explain all those others in mystery fiction: what we fiercely desire is that evil should be patent and other when it is so often hidden and just like us. We want, after all, to be able to tell the good guys from the bad guys. What the good guys usually means is guys like us. Mysteries frequently reassure us that the other guys are bad guys and that bad guys are other guys, though once in a while they remind us that neither is necessarily true. The otherness of the orang-utan killer in "The Murders in the Rue Morgue" is countered by the likeness of antagonist and detective in "The Purloined Letter." The reader sees the resemblance between Moriarty and Holmes.

Other Villains, Other Detectives

Mystery fiction isolates both villains and detectives in a conventional otherness. In Edgar Allan Poe's first mystery, "The Murders in the Rue Morgue," a typical reaction to otherness is exploited as one of Dupin's chief clues. The witnesses who arrive as the orangutan finishes his grisly work hear voices, one speaking French in which some words are identifiable, the other shrill and without distinguishable words. The witnesses all assume that the other voice is human, speaking a language they do not understand. The non-Spanish speaking French policeman thinks it is the voice of a Spaniard, the Englishman who does not understand German thinks it the voice of a German, and so on. The point is that it is *other,* unknown to each of them, *foreign.*

Dupin himself is a character of another nationality and language from that of Poe's readers. Dupin is eccentric, different in many ways: he prefers night to day and makes night out of day by shutting up his windows from the light and sequestering himself; he can read others' thoughts—or seems to—by his powers of inference from small bits of evidence, and so on. He is a genius and is full of arcane bits of knowledge. The French rationalist, idiosyncratic character is made as different from the ordinary reader as can be managed.

Both the detective and what he opposes are constructed as foreign to ordinary experience. The differentiation of both is no accidental feature of mystery, but a desideratum. Detective and opponent may converge, as in Dupin/Minister D—or Holmes/Moriarty, but both will still differ from ordinary experience.

The detective is isolated by his mode of being a detective. If he is a crusader such as Chandler's Marlowe or Macdonald's Archer, he has to be alone because he crusades against all those who subvert "ideal" societal values, and most people, if they do not actively promote the subversion, support it because they must in order to get along. If he is a technical genius such as Dupin or Holmes, his intelligence, perception, training, sensitivity, or some combination of these separates him from most people, to whom he seems a wizard. "You would certainly have been burned, had you lived a few centuries ago," says Watson to Holmes in "A Scandal in Bohemia" (Doyle 162). To be a detective is to be separate because of incorruptibility or genius or an extraordinary capacity for thinking like a criminal or any number of other distinguishing mental or spiritual features. Frequently authors add distinguishing physical or behavioral features to their detectives to complement the other differences.

What the detective opposes is also difference. To put it simply, the detective opposes evil. Evil is either us or not-us. When an author forces us to discover that evil resides in the main character with whom we have identified, is ourselves, the realization is shocking and tragic because those depths were unknown to us, parts of the psyche that might as well belong to another person. Mystery more often requires its author to convince us that the nastiness the detective seeks is located in a particular character who is evil and who is identifiably not us. The villain must be unlike us in order to serve the function of scapegoat. W. H. Auden explains the requirement from the point of view of society (of the non-murderers within the story and more importantly of the audience) as "the illusion of being dissociated from the murderer" (409).

Another way to put it is that the detective seeks those who render themselves different or other by breaking the law—law being the codification of the sameness of the rest of society. But this formulation is much too simple. Actually the detective is alienated from those who obey the law—because he or she doesn't—and also from *those who break the law for the wrong reasons*. The qualifier is necessary because the detective breaks the law for the right reasons. Sherlock Holmes reminds Watson that he is "not retained by the police to supply their deficiencies" (Doyle 257), believes that "there are certain crimes which the law cannot touch, and which therefore, to some extent, justify private revenge" (582), and acts on these ideas. He burglarizes the houses of blackmailers more than once, for example. He has no difficulty justifying breaking the law: "Once or twice in my career I feel that I have done more real harm by my discovery of the criminal than ever he had done by his crime. I have learned caution now, and I had rather play tricks with the law of England than with my own conscience" (Doyle 646). Thus he does not turn over to the police the jewel thief in "The Blue Carbuncle" or the killer in "The Boscombe Valley Mystery," two examples from just the first group of Holmes stories. William Ruehlmann has documented in great detail how unlawful the fictional American private eye has always been: Mickey Spillane's Mike Hammer, for instance, simply kills those he feels will be inconvenient to bring to justice. Matters have not changed much with different times or different sexes. While the detectives of Sara Paretsky and Sue Grafton, to name just two examples, are much less violent than their male hard-boiled counterparts, they still break the law. V. I. Warshawski carries a set of picklocks that she uses in almost every case; she and Kinsey Milhone are expert at impersonating officials in order to get information.

Outing Otherness as the Detective's Job

Finally it is not one who acts differently or appears different who is the culprit, but one who thinks differently. The question is not who committed the murder, but who dared to do it. P. D. James takes the modern mystery to its logical extension when she realizes that the important question is not who did it or how it was done, but who *could* do it. And this emphasis on motive is what makes the cozy, closed-circle mysteries as interested in otherness as those in which the antagonists are gangs of roving gypsies, Italian Counts, or polygamous Mormons from the wilds of America. What I have been saying about the necessary otherness of detective and villain would seem to be denied by the Agatha Christie sort of mystery set in a small English hamlet or country house. Everybody in these stories is so dreadfully alike, after all. Even the eccentrics seem to be cut with only two or three different cookie-cutters. While the detective himself in these stories may be eccentric—Hercule Poirot is perhaps the most extreme case, being affected, idiosyncratic, and foreign as well—he or she is more likely to be typical and to fit in very well with the social group. The murderer generally blends in very well with the social group because he or she is definitely of them and not "other." Such stories appear to ignore unpleasant facts about everyday existence, let alone murder; Colin Watson writes that "One cumulative effect of regular reading of this kind of fiction might have been to blunt temporarily the fear of death" (173). But there is a recognition here of what Hannah Arendt called "the banality of evil," the fact that it does not present itself as monstrous but goes on all around us and in us.

Such mysteries conceal the otherness of both detective and villain. Only the victim is demonized in such fiction; he is generally rendered so egregiously heinous and nasty that everyone wants to kill him and there are no tears shed when he dies. What the detective is up against in such fiction does not look like evil at all but rather the murderer's stronger motive and a certain lack of restraint, for of course many of the non-murderers had a motive to kill but did not. Only the lack of restraint separates the murderer from the non-murderers. To look a little deeper we could say that this *is* the monstrous thing about evil, and that the extraordinary genius of the detective is required in order to render visible the dreadful otherness of the murderer, this person who looks just like all the other weekend guests.

The Uses of Otherness

A crude mystery can always assign blame to a Fu Manchu—one who is visibly other. More subtle works, as we have seen, displace the otherness of the villain by emphasizing that of the detective, or displace it entirely onto the victim. Yet more subtle works use visible otherness for yet more complex functions of displacement and distraction. Despite our self-congratulation about enlightened racial attitudes, I suspect that these techniques have not changed much over time; they can be used by James McClure in his contemporary South African setting much as they were used by Wilkie Collins in *The Moonstone* in 1868.

By its very lack of subtlety in racial stereotyping (displaced onto cartoon figures), *Who Framed Roger Rabbit?* points out the uses and power of Otherness in driving mystery fiction. The Toons, segregated, simultaneously dangerous and silly, look like the villains at first when it seems they have dared to commit violence on humans instead of confining it to their own ghetto. Ultimately we discover the villain *is* a Toon, but one who has been successfully passing as human: Judge Doom represents the Other who has internalized the prejudices of the dominant race as self-hatred. Eddie Valiant is the ordinary man who has seen the Others as evil but comes to recognize his kinship with them by working to exonerate Roger Rabbit. The attraction of identifying Otherness with evil, the equivocal or marginal position of the detective, and the vindication of the innocent, all constitute generic desiderata of mystery and detective fiction. Understanding that they do enables authors to take the genre from the crude prejudices of Bulldog Drummond to the sophisticated analyses of cultural friction that we find in James McClure and Tony Hillerman.

Works Cited

Auden, W. H. "The Guilty Vicarage: Notes on the Detective Story, by an Addict." 1948. *Detective Fiction: Crime and Compromise*. Ed. Dick Allen and David Chacko. New York: Harcourt Brace Jovanovich, 1974.

Chinatown. Directed by Roman Polanski. Paramount, 1974.

Collins, Wilkie. *The Moonstone*. 1868. New York: Airmont, 1965.

Doyle, Sir Arthur Conan. *The Complete Sherlock Holmes*. Garden City, NY: Doubleday, 1930.

Jameson, Fredric. *The Political Unconscious: Narrative as a Socially Symbolic Act*. Ithaca: Cornell UP, 1981.

Johnson, Brian D. "Review of *Who Framed Roger Rabbit?*" *Maclean's* 4 July 1988: 26-27.

The Maltese Falcon. Directed by John Huston. Warner Brothers, 1941.

McClure, James. *The Steam Pig*. 1971. New York: Pantheon, 1972.

Melville, James. *The Wages of Zen*. 1979. New York: Ballantine, 1985.

Natsuki, Shizuko. *Innocent Journey*. 1976. Trans. Robert B. Rohmer. New York: Ballantine, 1989.

Penzler, Otto. "The Great Crooks." *The Mystery Story*. Ed. John Ball. Harmondsworth: Penguin, 1978.

Poe, Edgar Allan. *The Short Fiction of Edgar Allan Poe*. Ed. Stuart and Susan Levine. Indianapolis: Bobbs-Merrill, 1976.

Rohmer, Sax. *The Insidious Doctor Fu-Manchu*. 1913. New York: Pyramid, 1961.

Rosenbaum, Jonathan. "*Who Framed Roger Rabbit?*" *The Chicago Reader* 1988: 33-37.

Ruehlmann, William. *Saint with a Gun: The Unlawful American Private Eye*. New York: New York UP, 1984.

Song of the South. Directed by Walt Disney. RKO, 1946.

Upfield, Arthur W. *The Sands of Windee*. 1931. New York: Macmillan, 1985.

van de Wetering, Janwillem. *Inspector Saito's Small Satori*. 1985. New York: Ballantine, 1987.

Watson, Colin. *Snobbery with Violence: English Crime Stories and Their Audience*. 1971. London: Eyre Methuen, 1979.

Who Framed Roger Rabbit? Directed by Robert Zemeckis. Touchstone Pictures and Steven Spielberg, 1987.

Wolf, Gary K. *Who Censored Roger Rabbit?* New York: Ballantine, 1981.

Wu, William F. *The Yellow Peril: Chinese Americans in American Fiction 1850-1940*. Hamden, CT: Archon, 1982.

IN SEARCH OF OUR SISTERS' MEAN STREETS:
THE POLITICS OF SEX, RACE, AND CLASS
IN BLACK WOMEN'S CRIME FICTION

Nicole Décuré

The politics of sex as well as the politics of race and class are crucially interlocking factors in the works of Black women writers.
—Barbara Smith

But I who am bound by my mirror
as well as my bed
see causes in colour
as well as sex

and sit here wondering
which one will survive
all these liberations.
Audre Lorde (a: 49-50)

At the beginning of the 1990s, it could have been said of black[1] women's crime fiction what Toni Morrison said when she began writing: "[T]his person, this female, this black did not exist center-self" (Russell 45). It was a "virgin territory" (Paquet 11). The first black women detectives, in the 1980s, were written by white women, Susan Moody and Dolores Komo. And then, at the beginning of the '90s, nine years after Sara Paretsky and Sue Grafton, and even longer since Marcia Muller and *Edwin of the Iron Shoes,* Nikki Baker made a pioneering entrance for black women with a black protagonist. She was followed the next year by Barbara Neely[2] who created quite a sensation with the unusual character of Blanche White. And then, in short order, appeared a handful of other black women writers. Still, when Sally Munt wrote her chapter on "Race politics in crime fiction by women" in 1994, she deplored having found but five black women writers.[3]

At the end of the twentieth century, there are still only about a dozen black women crime writers with black heroines.[4] In a field as thriving as women's crime fiction this represents but a token minority. Yet, publishers do not seem reticent. Reading their opinions on current trends, it seems that today, in this market-oriented genre, they have come to see black fiction as able to offer "alternatives to the standard proto-types," "extra pizzazz," a "sense of place and insight into a special world or special group of people and the way they love" (Anthony 43). In other words anything new, exotic, might sell and is worth a try but I hope it represents more than that.

Black women's detective fiction is not a case of re-reading or re-constructing, as in mainstream fiction. These novels have not been ignored, they have not yet been written, or at least not published until recently. Why this lateness? Lack of models? Lack of equal opportunity? Is the fact that there have been cat and dog fictional detectives before black women any indication of their status in society? Is crime fiction a genre alien to black consciousness because it "is not a logical choice for those positioned outside the hegemonic institution of law enforcement" (Munt 85)? All these reasons probably have to be taken into account.

But black women are now beginning to create their own fictitious heroines. Considering, with Maya Angelou, that image-making is of paramount importance, who better can do it? Therefore, we will examine here those black women writers who have chosen black women as sub-jects of their narratives, who put them center-stage.

Detective Fiction as a Forum for Politics

In today's novel of detection, crime occurs and social and political problems are revealed. Women's novels deal more particularly with issues related to women's oppression: abuse, rape, pornography, prosti-tution, abortion, etc. Claudia Tate describes thus the contribution of black women writers to literature:

Being both black and female, these writers write from a unique vantage point. They project their vision of the world, society, community, family, their lovers, even themselves, most often through the eyes of black female characters and poetic personae. Their angle of vision allows them to see what white people, especially males, seldom see. With one penetrating glance, they cut through layers of institutionalized racism and sexism and uncover a core of social con-tradictions and intimate dilemmas which plague all of us, regardless of our race or gender. Through their art, they share their vision of possible resolution with those who cannot see. (Tate xvi)

The words "black" and "woman" call up social and political issues, and we have come to expect writers who fit in these categories to address those issues. The way these issues are addressed or ignored is a personal statement about whether the author chooses to identify with the broad category(ies) in which she is placed, category(ies) based on oppression. If she chooses to deny oppression, it may mean that she has never felt it (which requires strong powers of denial) or that she has chosen, for reasons of survival or expediency, to ignore it. Being black does not imply that one automatically will place the issue of race at the core of one's fiction. Sally Munt asserts that "White writers do not inevitably construct racist narratives, nor black authors emancipatory ones" (Munt 105). In the same way, not all women, far from it, write feminist books.

Nikki Baker puts in the mouth of one of her characters the following analysis:

Mystery novels can never be truly feminist . . . because they must either assume that the state of the world is good and our system of justice is benign or that things are so screwed up there is nothing the individual can do about it. (*The Lavender House Murder* 155)

Beyond the fact that no two persons would agree on a single definition of what is "truly feminist," Nikki Baker's dichotomy appears too restrictive when one considers the diversity of the recent narratives by women: individuals, especially in the P.I. novel, act according to their own lights and outside the system of justice. Resolution, at the end, often leaves a bitter taste. They might not be "truly" feminist statements, whatever that is, but might we not settle for "plain" feminist in these years of backlash? Feminism is expressed in more diversified ways than considerations about the justice system.

Class is a less obvious characteristic than race or gender because it is not immediately visible. Working-class literature seems to be a contradiction in terms. Crime fiction, with its conventions, finds it hard to accommodate class considerations. As detectives, police(wo)men cannot be said to be working class, nor can P.I.s. Amateurs could but who has the time to detect when one has to work for a daily wage? Only Barbara Neely's protagonist Blanche White, when on the job, can do it. But not for long. In the second book, she is on vacation at a bourgeois black resort. Clients need money to hire a P.I., which excludes working-class clients (the police deal with these). So, that leaves us with working-class or lower-class victims and incursions, or rather excursions into poorer neighborhoods. Not surprisingly, black women's fiction, with the notable exception of Barbara Neely's, will focus primarily, when it does focus on political issues, on race and gender.

If black women are in the position of being able to write from at least two perspectives, as women and as people of color, each category being a "prism through which to perceive human experience" (Friedman 8), black lesbian women can write from three perspectives. Barbara Christian defines the contributions of black lesbians to Afro-American women's literature as "the breaking of stereotypes so that black lesbians are clearly seen as *women,* the exposure of homophobia in the black community, and an exploration of how that homophobia is related to the struggle of all women to be all that they can be—in other words to feminism" (Christian 199-200).

From their position, through these prisms, black women can and must be innovative. When they claim the mystery for their own, they cannot occupy it in the same way as white women (or black and white men for that matter) because their perspectives, their background, their concerns are different. There is no tradition of black crime fiction because for so long blacks have been excluded from the law making as well as law enforcement agencies. They have been deprived of power and have been on the side of outlaws rather than sheriffs. Coffin Ed Johnson and Grave Digger Jones were part hoodlums, part cops. A social group which needed a Civil Rights Bill as late as the 1960s cannot be expected to feel at ease on the side of law and order; in the same way, women who got the right to vote late in history, less than a century ago, are still far from achieving parity in politics and other centers of power.

There is no question here of putting black women writers in a ghetto, setting them apart (separate and unequal). But, all fiction having a "power of representation" (Rabinow), we can try to assess what this particular social group which has not had access to publication until recently, is bringing to the genre. The emergence of black women writers in mainstream fiction has brought on original voices, as varied as Maya Angelou's, Toni Morrison's or Alice Walker's, to name but a few. Can the same be said of crime fiction?

A crime novel is neither a psychological treatise nor a political manifesto. We should not expect the authors to solve millennial problems in a nice, tidy way as they are, by essence, a murky, messy, irrational domain. But it enables the authors, if they so wish, to tackle serious issues while retaining the fundamentals of the crime novel: escapism and entertainment.

Therefore, it is interesting to see "where" black women writers "speak from." Do they speak as women? As blacks? As black women? As colourless people? As lower/middle-class people? As lesbians? And how do they deal with various forms of oppression? But, whatever point of view they choose to favour, these are new voices, who are speaking for themselves, defining themselves and that alone is, unfortunately, still subversive.

Black Women and the Genre

There is no idle amateur among the black detectives. In fact, they have all but disappeared from today's crime fiction. The detectives are working women, professional women who detect on the side: Virginia (Ginny) Kelly in Nikki Baker's fiction is a financial consultant; Simone is an attorney's clerk in Nora DeLoach's books and her mother is a social worker; Theresa Galloway, in Terris McMahan Grimes's series, is the personnel officer for the department of Environmental Equity; Penny Mickelbury has two heroines, an investigative reporter, Montgomery (Mimi) Patterson and Gianna Maglione, a policewoman; Eleanor Taylor Bland's series also features a policewoman, Marti MacAlister; the only professional P.I., Tamara Hayle, appears in Valerie Wilson Wesley's fiction.

The plots run along conventional lines: a woman encounters a crime or a mystery in the course of her job or private life. She investigates. Successfully. Often, near the end, there is a confrontation with the murderer which puts her life at risk.

It is difficult to make generalizations about such a small sample as if these authors, in their diversity, were representative of a whole social group but two features emerge as important and original in black women's crime fiction: the heroines' personal relations with family, friends and lovers/husbands and their relations with white America. The former differ quite markedly from white women's fiction in that the family plays a greater role; the latter breaks the pall of silence that surrounds the subject of inter-racial relations.

Personal Relationships

If the black women of crime fiction mostly work in racially mixed environments, they all, except the lesbians, live their private lives in a black one. "Essential identity (takes) place within the family and community," wrote Gayl Jones (Tate 93).

With the exception of Virginia Kelly, there is no lonely heroine in black women's crime fiction, no "friendless orphan" (Grafton 113). Her quest is more than a quest for truth and justice. It is a quest for self-fulfillment, happiness, a better life, meaningful relationships. Some of Claudia Tate's definition of the black heroine apply to detective fiction:

[T]he black heroine seldom elects to play the role of the alienated outsider or the lone adventurer in her quest for self-affirmation. . . . [S]he is ensconced in her community, dependent on friends and relatives for strength during times of hardship and for amusement during times of relaxation. (xx)

Whereas white women write about orphans and single childless women in the hard-boiled and procedural categories, black women may live on their own, but hardly alone.

Mothers

One distinctive characteristic of black women's fiction is the role played by the detectives' mothers, positively or negatively. Some are omnipresent to the point of being stifling, others hurt through lack of love and understanding. Terris McMahan Grimes, who dedicated her first novel to her mother and mother-in-law, begins and ends *Somebody Else's Child* with Theresa's mother and that sets the tone:

Mother has always been rather excitable. What can I say, she's my mother and I love her (9).
[T]he phone rang. I picked it up. It was Mother (262).

Mrs. Barkley lays down the moral law, summons her daughter in the middle of the night, generally bosses her about and Theresa runs to do whatever she is required to do, abandoning husband, children and work. Her mother is the reason she detects, a strong figure who is also her anchor, the one she turns to in times of stress. This character serves a triple purpose at different levels, narrative, emotional and social: Theresa's strong connection to her mother justifies her amateur detecting as Mrs. Barkley gives her missions she cannot refuse. The relationship adds a rich human dimension to the stories through the conflicts and the tensions brought on by this relationship which competes with all the other demands on Theresa's time and attention. Finally, clashes between mother and daughter on fundamental issues such as abortion, inter-racial marriage or homosexuality enable the author to present the points of view of two different generations, the mother's, conservative and big-oted and Theresa's, liberal and open-minded.

Another strong matron is Mama in Nora DeLoach's *Mama Solves a Murder* and *Mama Stalks the Past*.[5] Simone, the narrating daughter, also starts with her mother, whom she obviously loves and admires:

My mama's name is Grace. Everybody calls her "Candi," like candied sweet potatoes, because of her skin, a golden brown color with yellow undertones that looks as smooth as silk. (*Mama Solves a Murder* 7)

Simone's all-powerful mother is a clichéed matriarch who rules masterfully over husband and children. Simone obeys her meekly.

Whenever Mama finds something that she thinks is worth sleuthing she calls on me, and I'm obliged to join her in the hunt. To be perfectly honest, Mama is my Sherlock Holmes and I'm her Dr. Watson. (*Mama Solves a Murder* 9)

In *Mama Solves a Murder,* Mama takes over the investigation of the crime Sheryl, Simone's former college roommate, is supposed to have committed and drags her daughter into another investigation concerning family matters. As a result, the narrator, who has been "playing detective since [she] was a little girl" (8) with her mother, is maintained in a child-like status. The fact that neither mother nor daughter are ever identified by their surnames in this book adds to the infantilism of the relation and the lack of substance of the characters. Simone is like putty in Mama's hands, running back and forth between Atlanta and South Carolina at her mother's bidding, not really allowed a private life in which she could make her own decisions.

Simone yields all the time. Theresa Galloway rebels briefly from time to time but always gives in in the end. She feels guilty if she neglects her mother, even though her mother's demands and lack of understanding make her literally sick. In spite of this, the relationship between mother and daughter is basically good. They love each other, do not clash on fundamental issues or, on Theresa's part, agree to dis-agree. Nikki Baker's fiction offers a different story. Ginny's parents appear in the third book of the series. The relationship between parents and daughter is a tense one, due to their refusal to accept her as a les-bian, an adult in her own right. They persist in their attempt to get her to marry a proper black man. In part, this explains Ginny's existential dif-ficulties, her inability to be happy, to have loving and equalitarian rela-tionships. Her parents' lack of acceptance also leads her to reject her roots, at a more general, political level. An iconoclast, she sees Mother Goose tales in the stories of the Civil Rights Movement told by her par-ents. She considers Martin Luther King, not as the hero of black people but as a womanizer. The difficulty, for Ginny, is to find herself without the support of family or community and she has not managed it so far: she is the only truly isolated character in black women's crime fiction.

To add to the diversity of views, in Valerie Wilson Wesley's[6] *Devil's Gonna Get Him,* Tamara Hayle lives with the painful memory of a mother who treated her with "rage and brutality," "cruelty and bitter-ness," "*knocking the black off,* as if she were determined to go to the center of who I was and erase it" (56). Her response is that of all battered children, a mixture of love and hate. That this lesson in self-hatred should come from a mother shows clearly how racism can be constructed from within and explains the narrator's anger when her own son becomes a victim of racism. Ultimately though, Tamara understands that in order to find peace for herself she has to forgive her mother, understand her past, her roots, connect in some way with this other black woman. That is the really important resolution of the book.

Children

Three of the central characters have children, good children, loved and loving, intelligent and resourceful, grown enough to look after themselves if need be. They do not cramp the style of the detectives who can rely on other people for help (a husband, friends) when they have to pursue murderers. Children do not come first. Tamara Hayle, for instance, in *When Death Comes Stealing,* considers her independence as important as her son, whom she cherishes.

Concern with children, and not only one's own, is strong in these books. In three novels out of four, Marti MacAlister deals with children's abuse and neglect, which contrast all the more with her own safe, warm nest. Theresa too drives around very poor neighborhoods, trying to save and protect the three children next door to her mother's and keep two others in check. It is in these two authors that the notions of class, or rather of poverty, as class is not tackled in Marxist terms at all, are most present. Poverty is described in emotional, moral terms rather than in social, economic and political ones. The roots of the problem are not named nor are possible solutions apart from personal ones like love and care. This is one of the limitations of fiction and not only crime fiction. It can describe and denounce social conditions which are often the causes of violence but it cannot offer solutions except at the personal level.

Theresa Galloway's teenage children enable Terris McMahan Grimes to tackle the problems of growing up black in America, the question of identity and the question of race and gender relations. They add the viewpoints of another generation. Both Terris McMahan Grimes and Valerie Wilson Wesley, at some point, deal with the question of racism through the children: Tamara's son is wrongly arrested with a group of black youths and Theresa's is called a "nigger" at school. Because their children are concerned, neither mother can do what she often does when she alone is concerned, that is to say ignore the insult, ignore the pain: motherhood forces them to react. The children, in an ambivalent way, represent both a future as bleak as the present with its racism and a brighter one where one feels less powerless, and is in possession of some tools and the courage to fight back.

Female Friends

When the detective's mother is absent, friends feature as all important. In this, black and white women's fiction is alike. Marti MacAlister shares a house and parenting with another woman, Sharon, who looks after the children when Marti has to be on the job. As they are good friends, this is an ideal world. Blanche White enjoys the strong support of her friend Ardell, with whom she discusses her problems over the phone. In Penny Mickelbury's books, friends are good, no matter what the sex or the color. Tamara Hayle can rely on both male and female friends but she counts on women's solidarity as the one firm anchor in life:

Black women and food, sisterly comfort when you need it—brothers may fail you, money may fly, but there's always good food and the grace to offer it. (*When Death Comes Stealing* 241)

Again, the only exception to this rather rosy picture of friendship is Nikki Baker. In the first novel, *In the Game,* Ginny's best (and only black) friend almost kills her which leaves her lonely and lost as Naomi, a white woman who always remains aloof cannot fill this place.

Men

In women's crime fiction generally and black women' fiction in particular, men do not play a large role. The books usually feature a strong matriarchy and women as heads of one-parent families. Men come in several categories. They can be dead, like Marti's husband, which enables the heroine, at the same time to affirm that she is a true woman (she once was married), not a castrator (the dead man is idolized) and gives her some much needed freedom to exercise her detecting skills. A dead brother in Wesley's fiction serves a similar purpose by giving the heroine a deep sorrow, therefore, an intense inner life. The men can be meek, totally dominated by matron-like women: Simone's father in DeLoach and Ben, an idealized male, innocuous, bland, gentle in Bland's fiction. They can be sulky like Theresa's Galloway's husband who resents the power of strong women, particularly his wife and mother-in-law. They can be no-good ex-husbands, the notorious black man, philandering and irresponsible like DeWayne in Wesley's fiction. They can be nonexistent, marginalized in Neely's books: Blanche wants a man but there are none good enough. In lesbian fiction the men are work mates only, or else gay and therefore acceptable as friends.

The only active husband is Theresa's who wants his wife where she belongs: doing *her* job at home, looking after him, the kids and the house, letting him do *his* work, blaming *her* when things go wrong. His name is Temp which seems to be short both for temper (he *is* short-tempered) and temporary and although Theresa seems to agree with him, his outbursts, his attempts at curtailing her freedom, may well lead to a subsequent estrangement if he and the series carry on. Theresa finds it really hard to keep her autonomy of action and a colored man happy at the same time. "Husband maintenance activities" (*Blood Will Tell* 25) take time and, although sex with Temp is good (it even seems to be the only good point about him) she feels that "men can sometimes be more trouble than they're worth" (59). Since, at the end of the second novel, Theresa's husband and mother enter into an improbable alliance via a business partnership, it is to be feared that she will be even more tied down by her various obligations.

In Valerie Wilson Wesley's fiction, relations with men are, to say the least, difficult. There are two categories of men in *When Death Comes Stealing:* the bad ones who are nothing but "trouble" and the nice ones who are unattainable for various reasons. Tamara's ex-husband is bad through and through. A chronic liar, involved in shady business, his only apparent redeeming quality, taking care of his sons, turns out to be ironically false: married seven times, he has had six children, one with each of his wives except the last one. The first one dies by accident and the blame is put on an innocent child to enable DeWayne to escape harsh treatment. Thus the politics of sex and race are inextricably intermingled. Once grown up, the child kills the other sons, one by one, in retaliation. This story paints a picture of black manhood which is not only grim but extremely critical. Jake, a male friend, warns Tamara: "DeWayne is one of these dudes that evil seeks out like pins to a magnet, so don't get too close or it will stick to you too. The gods don't like ugly" (78). The other baddie is Basil Dupree to whom Tamara is attracted. But then, as her friend Annie says: "Have you ever known a brother as fine as Basil who wasn't trouble?" (129). These are not tender remarks for black men.

In her second novel, *Devil's Gonna Get Him,* another bad man is introduced, a former boyfriend who used her and left her hurt and bitter. In contrast to these men, stereotypes of bad black men, are two "goodies." First, Tamara's brother Johnny who committed suicide and whom she mourns. As so often in crime fiction as in life, the dead are perfect people whose loss is felt as irreparable. The other man, Jake, to whom she is also attracted, is out of bounds because he is married to a woman who is seriously depressed and dependent on him. So, the two good men are unapproachable. That seems to tell us that the reality consists of real men who are no good and good men who are ideals, who do not exist yet. To make up for this rather negative attitude, Tamara acknowledges, on the political level, how hard society is on black men and watches warily as her son Jamal grows into manhood.

Sex hardly exists as an option for the heroines. Marti MacAlister, a widow, works her way slowly toward it. She enjoys frank sexual talk with her friend Sharon but a sexual relationship would mean commitment to Ben and then where would her independence go? And what about the wonderful memory of her husband? Blanche has rejected a boyfriend and refrains from sex with a killer. Simone has a boyfriend but sex is not mentioned. Theresa Galloway is the only one to have sex with her husband when she is not too busy running around and Tamara Hayle is rescued from supposedly torrid sex by a convenient deus ex machina device: she has to leave. Tamara, aware of being attracted to the wrong sort of man, tries to fight it, but she is not always successful. Still, in the process, she emerges as a strong woman. The overall picture is that of women who may feel the lack (or the shortcomings) of a man in their lives but who are self-reliant, with a good support group of friends and families, who cherish their independence and are reluctant to compromise it.

Black/White Relationships
Anne Petry said in an interview:

We write about relationships between whites and blacks because it's in the very air we breathe. We can't escape it. But we write about it in a thousand different ways and from a thousand different points of view. (O'Brien 157)

Our six writers exhibit various attitudes towards race relations from ignoring them to denouncing racism. Denial is one common way of dealing with oppression. Acknowledging oppression means having to confront the situation, the oppressor(s), and do something about it if one wants to retain some self-esteem. On the personal level, it often means getting out of oppressive relationships; on the societal level, nothing short of a cultural revolution will do, a group effort. Women more readily acknowledge the existence of sexism in society as a whole than in their personal lives. It is less painful (except when it becomes personal as in rape). But, however hurtful, the option exists: one can start fighting one's nears and dears while society changes. For blacks, the oppression is mostly at the global level of society, hence more difficult to deal with because the oppressor has so many faces and little can be achieved on a personal level. The whole of society has to be tackled and the task is formidable. For black women, things are even more difficult. Who is attacked, the black, the woman or both? This is a recurrent question in black women's fiction. Their anger will range from repression to sporadic outbursts.

Many black detectives meet white people, at work, in the street, in offices and have to deal with racism in their own way. But, except the lesbians, they stick to lovers and families of the same colour. The irruption of a white person in a family is seen as transgression. So, racism will be examined at the global, more impersonal level of society, rather than at the personal level. The issue of racism within the black community, based on shades of black, is not ignored either. All writers broach it at one point or another and Barbara Neely, in particular, puts this question at the very core of her second novel.

When Claudia Tate wrote the introduction to her book about black women writers in 1983, the definition of the black heroine heralded the arrival of fictitious black detectives.

Another characteristic of the black heroine is that she, like her counterparts in real life, not only carries the double burden of racism and sexism, but must also stand erect under their weight, must also walk, run, and even fight. She is a guerilla warrior, "fighting," as DeVeaux insists, "the central oppression of all people of color as well as the oppression of women by men." She wages this struggle with self-confidence, with courage and conviction, and her principal strategy is her self-conscious affirmation of black womanhood. Her battle cry gives pitch and timber to the countless unheard voices of armies of black women. (Tate xxiii)

In matters of crime, white women writers refrain from having black criminals (and having blacks at all, until recently, even as secondary characters): it might be construed as racist. Black women have more combinations at their disposal: black kills black, white kills white, white kills black. But black never kills white: this would reinforce the commonly held prejudice about black violence and could be interpreted as racial hatred and retaliation. Race relations are a minefield.

Nikki Baker

The only exception to this is Ginny's friend, Bev, in Nikki Baker's first novel, *In the Game,* who kills her white lover out of jealousy, then her black lover to cover up the first murder and almost kills Ginny. It may look like a crime of passion but racism is at the root of it: Kelsey, Bev's white lover, has "a thing for black women" (140), whom she sees as sexual objects, not persons in their own right. Bev dies, as retribution for her crime, but there remains a bitter taste: Ginny has lost her best friend to racism and sexism. It also reveals the deep *mal de vivre* that black lesbians endure: strangers in their own communities who reject them for their sexual preference, strangers in the white world, they have no place to call their own.

Her attitude to whites is ambivalent. Ginny lives in a white world because her black world would not accept her white woman lover. In this "alien" environment, exiled somewhat against her will, she feels happy when she sees a brown face after some time. With black women, connections of race, class and experience are immediate and do not require words. Yet, a white gay man feels as close to her as a blood relation and, sexually, she is mostly attracted to white women. "A series of blondes" has "marched though (her) love life" (*Long Goodbyes* 22). Her lovers are white, even if she feels contempt for their politics, the "white feminist patter" (*The Lavender House Murder* 35), or even their legs that look like "fascist art" (*The Lavender House Murder* 76). In her love relationships, race never comes up as an issue. In the first book, she lives with a white woman. Em's working-class background enables her to understand "the difference between right and privilege" (*In the Game* 21) and Ginny feels this is a strong connection to her own experience as a black person. At one point, the narrating voice explains this attraction to white women in terms of "good old-fashioned American racism" that leads to self-hatred: "It is staggering how deeply we must know and love ourselves as black women to kiss the mirror with open eyes" (*In the Game* 16-17). Ginny has a rather desperate vision of the "running joke" of her life as a black woman (*In the Game* 136).

In spite of this attraction to white women and lack of racial tension in her private life, the picture that emerges from inter-racial relationships is one of control of whites over blacks: Em manages Ginny's finances, Susan is a "control freak" (*In the Game* 116) who orders Ginny's food for her, Rosey Paschen in *Long Goodbyes* leads her along on false promises, white Kesley wants a black wife. After her breakup with Em (over her unfaithfulness) Ginny goes from one woman to the next, drawn to them but not committing herself. The writer puts in other characters' mouths a distrust of white women. A young woman in *The Lavender House Murder* expresses the impossibility of a relation with a white woman:

"white women can no more banish their racism from their dealings with me than men can banish their sexism from dealings with women. In some cases it's just less damaging . . . I could never commit myself to a white woman. It says too many conflicting things sociologically, you know." (160-61)

On this occasion, Ginny refrains from commenting. But, in the following book, when her friend Sandra speaks on similar lines: "White women are the only people in this life who have it easy and they will fuck you over to keep having it easy," Ginny reacts strongly. She has no patience with what she calls "talking shit," the "African American nationalist soap box" which she compares to a downhill freight train (*Long Goodbyes* 130-31). Strong generalizing statements, racist statements with a clear hate content do not suit her, wherever and whoever they come from.

She is not at ease in the white world (the firm for which she works is ironically called Whytebread and Greese); she is not at ease with blacks like her parents who do not accept her homosexuality, nor her friends Sandra and Andre who have both a "straight" and a classist attitude, nor blacks who have racist attitudes towards one another. Ginny and her black women friends are on survival trips, trying to make it in the middle class, but conscious that they are barely tolerated. This leaves her in limbo, a drifter lost in a maze of contradictions, with no direction, no purpose, no politics. She drifts more and more with each book, always wanting the impossible, bent on destroying what she has as soon as she gets it, a woman without strong ties to anyone, without a community where she would feel accepted.

Nikki Baker is the writer who best and most abundantly expresses the complexity, the contradictions, the ultimate despair of being a black woman in America.

Eleanor Taylor Bland

Very different is Eleanor Taylor Bland's quietly optimistic fiction.

Marti MacAlister respects everyone and everybody respects her, blacks and whites. People tend to move out of her way, and not only because of her impressive physical presence. She gets positive responses, as a policewoman, from older women in the black community who feel she represents progress.

Her working environment is mixed, blacks and whites get on fairly well together, with no racism mentioned within the police. She lives in an integrated town where all sorts of ethnic groups mix. Only in her private life are people all black. On the force, she is paired with a white sexist (but not racist) male partner who thinks women's job in the police should be restricted to typing reports and making coffee and she wins his grudging respect through sheer persistence and constant good humor. The other two cops, Slim and Cowboy in Vice, are also of different races and form a good working team.

Hers is a rosy view of the situation: a black woman is making it on her own with her children and her friends, leading a good, useful life. There is emphasis on her humanity rather than her color. Recognizing her own racial prejudices makes her an even more real human being.

Bland explores racism, not through the main character, but through secondary ones. For instance, in *Done Wrong,* she exposes the crude secret thoughts of a former chief of police, not embellished by illocutionary precautions. In the case of this character, racial prejudice goes hand in hand with sexism and antigay feelings. Or it can go with child abuse: the racist passes easily from verbal abuse to physical abuse. Daily, ordinary racism is also described in little touches here and there: the blue eyes of a woman staring at Marti from the other side of a burglar chain, the lack of understanding and even hostility of a police officer about black mourning rites. Marti's reaction in the latter case is one of understanding (there is a lack of social contact between the communities) and a pedagogical attitude: she is ready to explain differences. At other times a racist situation is denounced in a cold statement of facts. There is no apparent anger in Marti. The third person narrative helps keep this distance. She emphasizes the positive: the immediate bonding, understanding within the black community, especially women, the positive changes that are taking place: dolls with brown faces, black attorneys, black policewomen. Nor does she ignore the problems within this community: women's passivity when faced with men's abuse, the hierarchy of colors. She tries to present a balanced view, dispassionate and optimistic. She (and her partner) get commended for their good work in *Gone Quiet:*

I am recommending you because that's what policing is all about. Going into the community, treating its members with respect, exercising discretion and common sense. (317)

The essence of her character is exemplified in her attitude towards language. She has a sense of the black community in that she is very sensitive to and appreciates black language, the way people address each other, idioms of certain parts of the country. At the same time, she is open to other languages: she speaks Spanish fluently and understands Polish. Her presence is one of quiet affirmation that with good will, peace can reign on earth.

Nora DeLoach

Nora DeLoach plays down the black/white issue as if it didn't exist. Why not, after all? It is one way of dealing with it, projecting oneself into a better reality. But it deprives the author of a means of showing concern with wider issues, confining her to a rather narrow world. Since Agatha Christie (whom Mama admires, probably overlooking some unsavory racist remarks), we have come to expect more of the crime novel.

Simone's private world is black and secure. Everybody, blacks and whites alike, talk readily to Mama, so engaging is her personality. Her white boss, Mr. Jacoby, is a nice man who worships Mama and trusts her blindly; the sheriff (probably white) relies on her to help him solve his most difficult cases; Cheryl, Simone's accused friend is white and meek and a victim. There is equal opportunity among both victims and murderers: first, a white man and then two black women are murdered. Does the author create a black child molester and a white one to show that the same evil exists in men, no matter what race? The white one has a little more substance though and is given more attention. The black one is literally left in the backwoods.

The main criticism of Nora DeLoach is that of blandness. The narrator lives in such a rosy world that it is hardly disturbed by murder, let alone societal ills such as racism and sexism. Secure in her job, secure in the love of her parents, her boyfriend, her friend Donna, nothing in the world at large comes to ruffle this tranquillity. There is nothing wrong with being happy but it has never made for great literature. It especially clashes with the causes of murder which are mostly negative: hate, greed, power, madness, etc. So the reader feels removed from the pain, which isn't shown, and removed from the happiness, because happiness excludes others.

Crime novels ought to leave you feeling a little bit angry.

Terris McMahan Grimes

Terris McMahan Grimes's first novel, *Somebody Else's Child,* which also features a prominent mother and looks resolutely on the bright side of things, is firmly grounded in "the community" (10) and its harsh realities, in spite of Theresa Galloway herself living comfortably and safely with husband and children in a part of Sacramento called "Greenhaven." Her frequent ventures into her mother's (and her old) neighborhood sound like expeditions into foreign territory: those streets, she feels, have become too mean for her. She is afraid of potential muggers and rapists, of the rampant violence behind closed doors as well as outside. At the same time, she feels compassion, understanding and concern for the children and the old people trapped in this poverty. She feels responsible, she wants to help. She belongs to the Christian, church-going, "we shall overcome" generation (34), peace-loving, courteous, faithful, "loyal, trustworthy, and friendly" (77); she does not feel better than anybody else, just better-mannered than the "get out of my face, mother" generation (34), marking their territory loudly but not necessarily justifiably. Her stance is a race variant on the "I am not a feminist but" defense formula that wishes not to antagonize. She restricts her comments on race relations to "safe" topics like the environment, "white male Homo sapien bureaucratus" (33), the paternalism of white employers. She deals mostly with racism in an oblique way, by describing the conditions of life in the black community, the brutalization of poverty, drug abuse, ignorance, the lack of schooling, of contraception. This environment is quite different from her own sheltered life as a member of the "black stable class if not middle class" (27), with Jordan shoes, fiberglass nails, silk blouses and a $90 haircut, a husband that plays golf and children who attend a mostly white private school. Which is not to say that she does not encounter racism. But she prefers to ignore it. She hides the hurt either by joking about it, pretending, for instance, that her car was insulted and not herself or shutting up and choosing contempt, or plain saying she is tired, not allowing herself even to feel anger. In the second book though, as already mentioned, racism hits home and she has to discuss strategy when her son, Shawn, receives a racial slur from a schoolmate. She suppresses the "hot, white flash" (138) of anger quickly. She does not approve of his violent physical reaction (although her husband does) and tries to argue in favour of explanations. She wants to believe in the power of words.

Theresa only lets her violence erupt in the black community. When she goes to her old neighborhood, she feels physically threatened and needs to respond in kind. There comes a point when she, a black woman, has to separate herself from "those other folks out there" (77), other blacks. When she considers killing, she surprises herself and feels ashamed and guilty. She certainly does not identify with whites and neither does she feel a traitor to the black community, even though she gets accused of thinking herself white (which rankles) because of her accession to the middle class.

This is where the contradictions of race and class come into play and Terris McMahan Grimes expresses the complexity of the problem with sensitivity, especially in Theresa's private life. When she was young, black girls just did not date white boys. Races and classes remained apart. But times have changed and now it seems that black middle-class boys will date any girls (white, Asian, Hispanic) except black girls, a fact the latter resent. Theresa's brother has married a white woman, which is seen as a "defection" by her own mother and forces Theresa to make up for it by being more available to her. Theresa's daughter feels that her brother ought to be taken out of his white academy because he is starting to date white girls (and the supreme horror would be to bring them home) and, above all, is losing touch with the black community, "real people, Black people" (144) which may cause him problems later. The barrier of race stays up at the front door for the older as well as for the younger generation. Theresa herself does not comment on the desirability of races mixing and the question is left in suspension, probably to be raised again in subsequent books. The overall impression here is that the black community is a battlefield but that there can be safety out of it, in the middle class, provided one's private life remains black.

The criminal, in the first novel, turns out to be a white woman who kills an old black woman to protect her family's reputation and to get her son elected as mayor. Although she makes no overt racist statement, her whole attitude is one of condescension for "you people" (247, 249), servants who are called by their first names only. Making the criminal insane may serve two purposes: alleviating the charge that whites kill blacks easily and implying that racism is a form of madness.

Blood Will Tell, apart from the crisis with Shawn, is full of little snapshots such as an old black man calling a white man "boy" (20) or Theresa declaring to a white man that "white is beautiful, too" (134). The latter comes just before the scene with Shawn, making it all the stronger as we can see that, in spite of appearances, one should not be dulled into a false sense of security and achievement: racism is still alive and well. The author uses perceptive little touches to show the complexity of relations between races and sexes and among blacks and women themselves.

Penny Mickelbury

Penny Mickelbury's heroines also lead middle-class lives but their public and private lives are wholly interracial. As the love relationship between Mimi, the black journalist and Gianna, the white policewoman (with Italian roots) develops, the question of race never comes up between them, only the question of bodies: perfect bodies. It is the muscles that matter, deep down, and the heart, not the skin. They are more separated by their jobs, their conflicting interests in discovering the truth, their professional rivalry than by their color, which is a non-issue.

In *Night Songs,* the author tackles the question of race hatred. At the beginning, she shows caution in making sociopolitical commentaries and tries to avoid sweeping generalizations. "In D.C., as in other big cities, poor people, and especially poor people of color, believed they got short shrift from an over-burdened justice system, and they quite often were correct" (*Night Songs* 15-16).

When it comes down to specific people, the black voice, Mimi is ready to generalize and exhibit her disgust at the behavior of rich white men. There is little doubt that violence is on the white side. White boys kill black prostitutes as an initiation rite, an expression of power. White neo-nazis harass a Jewish woman to the point that she commits suicide. Even Black Men on Guard, an antidrug gang of black anti-Semites, are not enough to help her. There is a double message here: some violence (retaliatory) is admissible, and that is black violence, but violence based on hatred is not; and prospects for the future are grim. Along the same lines as Terris McMahan Grimes, Penny Mickelbury sends us a double message: the world around us is bad, violent, racist, homophobic; but individuals can be good and tolerant.

Valerie Wilson Wesley

Tamara Hayle's world is almost wholly black. Contrary to Marti MacAlister, she left her job in the police because of the racist aggression of fellow cops toward her son. There are few white characters: her ex-boss, DeLorca, who supported her as a black and a woman when she was in his command, is seen in a favorable light; on the other hand, a white woman, one of her ex-husband's ex-wives, is portrayed as messed-up, unpleasant and racist, despite her having a colored son.

I couldn't believe what she'd just said. *Who you calling a nigger, white girl?* I hadn't heard a white person say that word since I'd left the Department and heard it every day. My reaction was pure reflex: I pushed the anger down to that place inside me where I'd always put it when I'd been on the force. Nigger bitch. Nigger whore. Nigger bastard. Nigger son of a bitch. I'd heard it so much it had lost its meaning. Just another word. (*When Death Comes Stealing* 87)

Of all the black heroines, Tamara is the most often, most openly angry. She gets very angry at the way blacks are dealt with, by whites, by the police, but she does not act on it. She has been trained to keep the anger in check, to anesthetize herself to the hurt. Her silence, the repression of anger express the hurt powerfully.

In *Devil's Gonna Get Him,* Valerie Wilson Wesley's approach to race is more diversified. While still condemning institutional racism, Tamara also blames blacks for espousing white racism and discriminating against each other on the basis of shades of black. She also acknowledges, somewhat surprised, that it is possible to like a white person and wonders if what women have in common can "overcome the chasm and discomfort that race always seems to create between people who might otherwise easily become friends" (78).

Sisterhood as an antidote to racism sounds like a good idea. Although wariness justifiably remains, there is a desire and hope for good interracial relationships in these women's fiction.

On the subject of racism, black women evidence great restraint in crime fiction. I do not think it is a question of trying to attract as wide a readership as possible. I believe it reflects a very common way that women have had for centuries of dealing with oppression. Anger is still considered unbecoming in women and so they keep their feelings bottled up, trying to ignore the aggression, not acting on the anger.

The Question of Definition

We have seen that the six authors discussed here have a great variety of viewpoints on what it means to be a black woman in America today.

Being discriminated against as a black person or as a woman is inescapable because tangible: people see what they hate and hate what they see. With antigay feeling, there is a way out: as long as one keeps in the closet there is nothing to fear. The hatred against gays is analyzed in terms of insanity, morality, sin, evil. It is indeed different from racist or sexist oppression which are based on the rationalization that the other is inferior (with pseudo-scientific justifications) because different, the rationalization itself being based on the fear of difference, on insecurity, the need to feel powerful by rendering others powerless. Antigay sentiment is based on the feeling of threat to one's values and certainties and it is more difficult to develop a theory of "separate but equal" since it is homosexuality itself which has to be eradicated. People must be changed.

In black women's crime fiction, all these oppressions come into play, illustrating Audre Lorde's statement:

I am not one piece of myself. I cannot be simply a black person and not be a woman too, nor can I be a woman without being a lesbian . . . What happens when you narrow your definition to what is convenient or what is fashionable, or what is expected, is dishonesty by silence. (Lorde, "My Words" 262-63)

The authors combine the various elements differently. For some racism comes first, for others it is sexism and for others still, homophobia. The way each author combines these various elements gives their books their special flavor.

Marti MacAlister mostly feels hostility toward herself as a woman, probably because blacks were admitted in the police before women were. She cannot afford to act in some ways, showing emotion for example, for fear of being called a "female cop" (*Done Wrong* 67). It is as a woman that Marti has to prove herself. She has to work twice as hard as a man to be accepted. Even Isaac the tramp acknowledges that women are better at the job than men because they are never satisfied, they are perfectionists. It is as a woman that she claims power and respect for herself, taking pride in the position she has achieved. She sees herself as a strong woman, well able to combat sexism on the job. "Sometimes you confront [men], sometimes you ignore them. Most of the time I just do my job . . . You change the things you can. The rest will just get you frustrated" (*Done Wrong* 152).

For instance, she describes nude calendars "adorning" the walls of the precinct rather dispassionately but lashes out at her colleagues, Slim and Cowboy, at a sexist superior, at a suspect (she "deballs" him) and leaves another awed and subservient: "Lordy, Lordy. A colored woman cop an' I done got her mad" (*Dead Time* 31). At the level of race, she is not submitted to harassment, either personally nor through her children.

Her relationship with Jessenovik, her white male partner, evolves gradually through the books from mistrust, on his part, toward the woman to understanding, respect, consideration, affection even. Marti keeps him constantly on his toes, does not give an inch. They complement each other. Vik even defends her against the sexist remarks of their colleagues, helps her with her investigation into her husband's death on his free time, loves her food. A family man and a churchgoer, ready to help people, he has a lot in common with Marti. And she has excuses for him: he was brought up in a male environment so that explains his attitude to women.

Marti makes up her mind, as a woman, about abortion. She does not buy into the black genocide theory and claims the right to abortion, as a principle if not for herself (she is personally against it as a Christian). Slavery denied blacks the right to their bodies, a right Marti cherishes and she sees abortion as a question of control and power, something she well understands.

Strong statements about racism and sexism are not made through Marti but through other characters. At one point, her colleague Leotha bursts out about the difficulties she has encountered as a black police officer.

Marti, I'm pushing fifty—hard. I'm black—no, African-American—and I'm female. That puts me in three protected categories according to the labor department and doesn't mean shit anywhere else . . . I've always played it safe, done whatever was politically correct, said purple when I knew damn good and well that the sky was blue, held my liquor, covered my ass. I laughed at their stupid jokes, put up with their sexist behavior and ignored their racist remarks . . . I work twice as hard, take three times as much shit and they still don't want me to have rank. (*Done Wrong* 79)

Marti refuses to be drawn into what she calls a "vendetta," prefers to see it as a specific rather than a generic problem. She is no militant. Her priorities are "family values": "family, home, church, a few friends" (*Done Wrong* 99), a relief from the horrors she encounters on the job. Hers is a compassionate, helping, tolerant attitude. The author refrains from making her a mouthpiece either for blacks or for women, to make her more widely likeable, no doubt. What she has to say is more easily put in the mouths of secondary characters who just pass through the stories.

Terris McMahan Grimes also gives importance to Christianity, with Theresa Galloway coming from a church-going family in which the Bible is passed from mother to daughter through the generations. The Christian attitude is one, not necessarily of turning the other cheek, but of forgiveness and this explains in part the lack of anger in Bland's or Grimes's characters. There are no considerations on being a woman in the latter's first book but most of the characters are women: black and white women in Theresa's mother's neighborhood who struggle through poverty to bring up their children properly, who look after each other's children when the mothers are in prison or on crack, concerned with their safety, their schooling, their manners; strong women who may even use a gun (or shears) to defend themselves. The men are all but absent from the black community. When they are there, they are portrayed as idle, violent, delinquent. Yet the issue of women's oppression is never mentioned. But the subject of abortion is brought up several times as it is at the root of the reason for the murder of old Mrs. Turner. Theresa almost apologizes for uttering her conviction about a woman's right to control her own body in front of her mother who is opposed to it on religious grounds. But she is more vocal in front of a white politician, trying to make him take a stand.

In her relations with her husband, who constantly lectures her on her role as mother, she wavers between feeling guilty and ignoring him, carrying on with whatever she feels she has to do. There is a strong contrast between Temp's archaic attitude and the advice Theresa gives to her daughter Aisha about choosing a supportive boyfriend who will be her equal. Theresa preserves peace at all costs, with her mother, with her husband, with her children. This makes her run around in circles and leaves her exhausted. In matters of racism and sexism, she is too conciliatory for her own good and, as a character, lacks some fighting spirit.

At first sight, Nikki Baker's priority, as seen through Virginia Kelly, seems to be her identity as a lesbian. A lot of space is devoted to gay issues and gay politics, particularly coming out and outting in *The Lavender House Murder*. This is what Ginny is most openly vocal about. At the beach, the world is not separated by a color line but into three sexual categories: lesbians, gay men, heterosexuals of both sexes. But her identity as a black woman, mixed with considerations of class, is ever-present as well. Nikki Baker finds it hard to say which oppression is strongest and changes her mind from time to time, but that should not be surprising: it is just a shift of emphasis according to the situation. Being gay is a question of politics: staying in the closet or not. It can be hidden. But blackness and racism are inescapable. The strongest oppression is as a lesbian (it is as a lesbian that she fears harassment from the police) but the deepest hurt is as a black. The bitterest comments are about race, about the history of black people in America.

To her, the root of all evil is white patriarchy which accounts for all forms of oppression:

It's all about power. White men want to have all the power for themselves . . . It all comes down to power. Patriarchy, imperialism, racism, sexism. They're all the same . . . If we want an education that tells the truth about women and gays and people of color in this country, we have to rewrite the book . . . We have to re-educate ourselves or we're going nowhere. (*The Lavender House Murder* 61)

At one point Ginny gives some sort of order to the oppressions: gays are most discriminated against in the business world, then blacks, then women. "Women are valued for (their) bodies" and "blackness is valued not at all" (*In the Game* 135). She opposes "newer, whiter, more feminist causes" to "Negro rights" with a clear priority to the latter (*The Lavender House Murder* 85). And yet, little in her behavior bears this out. At another point, she contends that money is all powerful and supersedes considerations of color or class. In some situations, as a black woman, she finds it impossible to say who is discriminated against, the woman or the black.

Ginny, as a character fails to engage us because of her lack of commitment to causes. If the narrating voice speaks, the character is silent. Most of the time, when issues are raised, Ginny does not take a position. She lets her "politics drop," unable to comment or elaborate on political issues. "Avoidance is one of my special gifts," she says in *Long Goodbyes* (72). She avoids issues, discussions, confrontations. She weeps in her corner.

Ginny's bumbling, stumbling ways (reminiscent of Rebecca O'Rourke's *Jumping the Cracks*) with her alternately trying to make sense of her life and avoiding it, reflect the confusion encountered in real life situations and would perhaps suit better a mainstream novel than a mystery which requires heroines to have more grip on their lives. More and more, with each book, the crime element is relegated to the background, all but forgotten. We are left with the overall impression of a woman stifled by overwhelming odds and no sense of direction.

Penny Mickelbury also writes as a lesbian. Wrongly called on the front cover "A Gianna Maglione Mystery," her books give about equal space to Gianna Maglione and Mimi Patterson. Both are extremely beautiful, competent, financially well off. Life would be perfect for Gianna and Mimi if they did not, at times, feel oppressed because of their homosexuality. Straight off, Mimi says:

Being queer in America . . . was one of the few things worse than being black. It was possible to be forgiven the color of one's skin, the assumption being that one had no choice in the matter. But to love one's same sex—that was something else. (*Keeping Secrets* 47)

Gianna heads a Hate Crimes Unit, with a rainbow team. She is concerned with crime based on group hatred, race, or sexual preference. Hate is "big business" in America (*Night Songs* 14). Women, as a group, are not considered as a target of generic hatred and Gianna fights for them to be included, as she sees violence against women as a "fundamental issue" (26). This is an interesting perspective as it is the most widespread and least recognized oppression on earth, affecting half the human race, and Gianna's stand makes (common) sense. In the first book, *Keeping Secrets,* Penny Mickelbury deals with homosexuality, in the second, *Night Songs,* with prostitutes (who are also black).

Gianna may not care about "why" people hate certain groups and may just want to stop the violence, but she is still aware of the workings of hatred: hatred in itself is not a crime in the eyes of the law, which makes it impossible to "impose morality" (*Night Songs* 34). And she understands that it is a question of "power and control" (*Night Songs* 26). She also offers us shrewd insight into the contradictions involved in hate against women as embodied, literally, by prostitutes: "[W]omen hated because they used their bodies to bring pleasure to those who hated them" (*Night Songs* 18).

As a black woman, Mimi faces a double oppression: white men associate those two characteristics with the epithet "prostitute" and she feels hatred when a white man in a bar assumes that, because she is black, she is a prostitute.

She knew there was no logical reason or way to mistake her for a prostitute; but there was also no mistaking her Blackness. And the white man saw a Black woman and reached what for him was a logical conclusion. She hated him and people like him and all the forces of evil and ugly that had conspired over time to allow him to think he had the right to make such an assumption about her. (*Night Songs* 21)

Penny Mickelbury echoes Nikki Baker in that she thinks that women are perceived as being of "no value" (*Night Songs* 214) and so are blacks.

Penny Mickelbury describes race and sex relations on two levels: that of reality with the societal violence of whites against blacks, of men against women and that of an idealized version of society, on the personal level, where the races get on well together, like and respect each other. The two main characters, Mimi and Gianna, do not take refuge in this private world. They have chosen to fight against the ills of society at the institutional level. Mimi, being personally involved where race is concerned, is the emotional voice, Gianna the more rational, theoretical one but both are equally committed to fighting discrimination of any kind. This makes Penny Mickelbury the most militant of the group of writers we have discussed here.

At this point, I will discuss briefly a recent addition to this group, Judith Smith-Levin with her first novel, *Do Not Go Gently*,[7] because, although she writes mostly on the same lines, she takes questions of sex and race a little bit further. She uses standard stereotypes of crime fiction: the good-looking detective is a woman alone, without a family but with a good (black) friend; the father died on the job and the daughter follows in his footsteps. Starletta Duvall, a police lieutenant, is in a position of authority; her partner, a handsome white man is nice and supportive; the rich handsome white doctor (the medical examiner) falls in love with her and interracial romance enters the scene. But these are mere appearances and cracks soon appear under the smooth surface: her father died because of the racist assumptions of a fellow policeman; the handsome white salesman turns out to be a vicious rapist, cruel, twisted. What Judith Smith-Levin exposes far more nakedly than any of the writers above is the hatred that forms the basis of racism, in this case hatred against black women, "black" and "woman" being inseparable. The black is punished as a woman, through rape (and murder). The fact that the murderer finishes off what the rapist does is not successful in the narrative, stretching our powers of credibility too far, but it works at the symbolic level of the conspiracy of white (men) against black (women): it makes the hatred personal.

This serial killing of black women echoes the serial killing of gays and black prostitutes in Penny Mickelbury's fiction. Here, we see not only the results of this hatred but we get into the thoughts of the rapist who expresses his hatred time and again. We see hatred at work and it is frightening. "Anger" and "rage" are used repeatedly to characterize Starletta's reaction to the crimes. But even though the crimes are horrible, the author resorts to the old "attraction-repulsion" trick between the detective and the criminal to finally justify her ultimate overpowering of the criminals as if women needed extreme provocation to be finally able to take action. It is probably as a form of atonement that the author, in parallel, presents two good white males (too good to be true) in counterpoint to the violence of the two other men.

Conclusion

To Toni Morrison there is something "very special and identifiable about [black literature]" (Awkward 9). Not all of black mystery fiction seems to bear out this statement. There is no innovation in form, but the genre does not really permit it. There is simply a shifting of the place of the characters: no longer in menial occupations (with the exception of Blanche White but she is the main character, not an adjunct) they are now middle class and they reflect the accession of a number of blacks to that status. Furthermore they are the main characters if not the only characters.

Black women writers' attempts at dealing with the subject of race has probably encouraged white women, in turn, to approach the issue of inter-racial relationships. Barbara Wilson faced the issue of racism in 1984 but the subject remained more or less taboo in other white writers' fiction. More recently, several writers (Sara Paretsky, Linda Barnes, Julie Smith) have made interracial relations an important feature, both in narrative and commentary, in their latest books.

In black women's fiction we find two of the scripts defined by Susan Friedman to classify white women's writing about race: scripts of denial and scripts of accusation. The majority are scripts of affirmation though. Whereas white women writers try to escape into fantasy, imagining women living on their own, encountering all sorts of dangers, black women's tales are more realistic, more concerned with the social conditions in the black community, paralleling life and statistics. All but one of the authors discussed here deal with today's perceptions and analyses, the latest developments in the debates on race, gender, class, and culture. Their books are a good medium to apprehend contemporary society. They are finding ways to be themselves, to tell new stories, create characters, open new paths. Within the constraints of the mystery genre, this is no mean feat.

Notes

1. Black, in this paper, will refer to people of African descent only. White will refer to people of European descent, excluding Latinas or any other "ethnic" characters and authors.

2. I will not examine Barbara Neely's work here in any depth as Frankie Bailey is doing it in another chapter and I wish to concentrate on lesser known writers.

3. She mistakenly included Dolores Komo among the five.

4. Grace F. Edwards and Charlotte Carter will not be discussed here as their novels have not been available to me in time. Judith Smith-Levin's first novel will be briefly examined at the end, as an illustration of one of the directions black women's crime novel may be taking.

5. Nora DeLoach has also published *Mama Traps a Killer* (Holloway House) and *Silas* (Holloway House), a noncrime fiction novel.

6. Valerie Wilson Wesley's third book in this series, *Where Evil Sleeps* (Putnam), is not included in this study.

7. I received her book just before the deadline for this article, making it impossible to weave her contribution into the body of the article. This is the problem with (and the interest of) contemporary crime fiction: it changes fast.

Works Cited

Anthony, Carolyn. "Many Ways to Mayhem." *Publishers' Weekly* 17 Oct. 1994: 43-54.

Awkward, Michael. *Inspiriting Influences: Tradition, Revision and Afro-American Women's Novels.* New York: Columbia University Press, 1989.

Baker, Nikki. *In the Game.* Tallahassee, FL: The Naiad Press, 1991.

——. *The Lavender House Murder.* Tallahassee, FL: The Naiad Press, 1992.

——. *Long Goodbyes.* Tallahassee, FL: The Naiad Press, 1993.

Bland, Eleanor Taylor. *Dead Time.* New York: Signet Books, 1993.

——. *Done Wrong.* New York: St Martin's Dead Letter Paperback Mysteries, 1995.

——. *Gone Quiet.* New York: Signet Books, 1994.

——. *Slow Burn.* New York: Signet Books, 1993.

Carter, Charlotte. *Rhode Island Red.* London & New York: Serpent's Tail, 1997.

Christian, Barbara. *Black Feminist Criticism: Perspectives on Black Women Writers.* New York: Pergamon Press, 1986.

DeLoach, Nora. *Mama Solves a Murder.* Los Angeles: Holloway House, 1994.

——. *Mama Stalks the Past.* New York: Bantam Books, 1997.

Edwards, Grace F. *If I Should Die*. New York: Doubleday, 1997.

Friedman, Susan Stanford. "Beyond White and Other: Relationality and Narratives of Race in Feminist Discourse." *Signs* 21.1 (1995): 1-49.

Grafton, Sue. *B Is for Burglar*. New York: Bantam Books, 1985.

Grimes, Terris McMahan. *Blood Will Tell*. New York: Signet, 1997.

——. *Somebody Else's Child*. New York: Onyx/Penguin Books, 1996.

Lorde, Audre. *Chosen Poems: Old and New*. New York: Norton, 1982.

——. "My Words Will Be There." *Black Women Writers (1950-1980)*. Ed. Mari Evans. New York: Anchor Books, 1984. 261-68.

Mickelbury, Penny. *Keeping Secrets*. Tallahassee, FL: The Naiad Press, 1994.

——. *Night Songs*. Tallahassee, FL: The Naiad Press, 1995.

Munt, Sally. *Murder by the Book? Feminism and the Crime Novel*. London: Routledge, 1994.

Neely, Barbara. *Blanche on the Lam*. New York: St Martin's Press, 1992.

——. *Blanche and the Talented Tenth*. New York: St Martin's Press, 1994.

O'Brien, John. *Interviews with Black Writers*. New York: Liveright, 1973.

O'Rourke, Rebecca. *Jumping the Cracks*. London: Virago Press, 1987.

Paquet, Anne-Marie. "Breaking Ground. An Interview with Toni Morrison." *AFRAM Newsletter* 31 (1990). Paris: Université de la Sorbonne Nouvelle.

Rabinow, Paul. "Representations Are Social Facts: Modernity and Postmodernity in Anthropology." *Writing Culture: The Poetics and Politics of Ethnography*. Ed. James Clifford and George E. Marcus. Berkeley: University of California Press, 1986. 234-61.

Russell, Sandi. "It's OK to Say OK." *Critical Essays on Toni Morrison*. Ed. Nellie Y. McKay. Boston: G. K. Hall & Co., 1988.

Smith, Barbara. "Toward a Black Feminist Criticism." *The New Feminist Criticism: Essays on Women, Literature and Theory*. Ed. Elaine Showalter. New York: Pantheon, 1985. 170.

Smith-Levin, Judith. *Do Not Go Gently*. New York: HarperCollins, 1996.

Tate, Claudia, ed. *Black Women Writers at Work*. Harpenden, GB: Oldcastle Books, 1983. (First publication: Crossroad Publishing Co.).

Wesley, Valerie Wilson. *Devil's Gonna Get Him*. New York: Avon Books, 1995.

——. *When Death Comes Stealing*. New York: Avon Books, 1994.

BLANCHE ON THE LAM,
OR THE INVISIBLE WOMAN SPEAKS

Frankie Y. Bailey

As editor Paula L. Woods notes in her introduction to *Spooks, Spies, and Private Eyes,* a recent anthology of mystery, crime, and suspense fiction by African American writers, Barbara Neely[1] in her Blanche White series "debunks the stereotype of the stupid black maid while simultaneously addressing issues of race, color, and class consciousness" (xviii). Barbara Neely says of her novels: "I wanted to write about social issues in a way that was accessible and entertaining. I also wanted to pay homage to working women because they are the bridge that got us over. [My work] is about the people who are assumed not to have a world-view" (qtd. in Woods 288).

This essay examines Barbara Neely's first novel in the Blanche White series, *Blanche on the Lam.* The novel is examined as a vehicle for addressing social issues through use of the mystery genre. Barbara Neely's character, Blanche, is considered within the historical context of the evolution of black characters in mystery and detective fiction. Barbara Neely's work is considered as a contribution to the body of literature by African American writers of both genre and non-genre crime fiction. The role of Barbara Neely as an African American female writer attempting to make other African American women "visible" as women is also discussed.

Black Characters in Mystery Fiction

"Oh, Lord!" Blanche lifted her apron to her face as she'd seen Butterfly McQueen do in *Gone with the Wind.* If the subject had been anything other than Nate's death, she'd have had a hard time keeping a straight face. It was the kind of put-on that gave her particular pleasure. But now she only wanted to appear convincingly simple. (Neely, *Blanche on the Lam* 153-54)

As this parody of a maid enacted for the benefit of her employer implies, Blanche (and Barbara Neely) believe whites in the South—and elsewhere—still base their assumptions about blacks on stereotypes that date back to the era of slavery in the United States. In short, some whites assume black inferiority and are unable to recognize a put-on when they see one. Blanche uses this white "blind spot" to her benefit. So does Nate, the old family retainer, whose "Uncle Tom" act is so good even Blanche has her doubts at first. But when Nate is murdered—for knowing too much—Blanche uses her employer's gullibility as a mechanism for finding out what she needs to know to avenge Nate's death.

Such role playing, requiring both intelligence and insight, is something of which black characters in early mystery fiction were assumed not to be capable. Created by white writers, early black characters reflected the prevailing stereotypes of African Americans used to rationalize and defend the system of black slavery which had existed in the United States since the colonial period. In "The Gold Bug" by Edgar Allan Poe ("the father of the mystery short story"), there is a black character who is "Sambo" personified. The servant of an aristocratic Southern recluse, Jupiter is so ignorant he does not know his right hand from his left. Poe uses him to provide the story's "red herrings" in the form of Jupiter's malapropisms and misunderstandings. That Poe could and did create such a character is not surprising. Poe was a nineteenth-century Southerner. He was writing in the prevailing tradition of the pro-slavery writers of the antebellum period (Bailey, *Out of the Woodpile* 3-6).

Such depictions of African American characters in the mystery and detective fiction of writers in the United States and in England reflected the class and racial/ethnic biases rooted in centuries of colonialism and empire building. White Europeans superiority was taken for granted. The darker skinned "natives" of India, Africa, Australia, and the Caribbean and the conquered "Indians" and "Mexicans" of the land that was claimed as the United States were seen as inferior and less "civilized" beings. As Colin Watson states: "Thrillers were packed with despicable and evil-intentioned foreigners, while even writers of the more sedate detective stories devoted some of their talents to remarkably splenetic portraiture of characters with dark complexions or guttural accents" (129).

These attitudes toward people with dark skins and/or foreign accents can be found in the works of British writers from Charles Dickens and Wilkie Collins to Arthur Conan Doyle and Gilbert K. Chesterton. The routine acceptance of racial slurs and stereotypes is exemplified by Agatha Christie, the grand dame of mystery novels, who titled one of her mysteries, *Ten Little Niggers* after the popular nursery rhyme (see Bailey, *Out of the Woodpile,* Chapter Two).

In the United States, which shared a common heritage with Great Britain and which had its own long history of racial/ethnic domination and oppression, the mystery fiction of the late nineteenth and early twentieth century reflected those stereotypes and attitudes common in American society. In popular culture—movies, radio, the theater, magazine ads—the members of minority groups were presented as occupying menial positions in society. They were presented often as caricatures—as walking, talking personifications of racial stereotypes.

In the case of African Americans, these caricatures were based on beliefs about the intelligence, sexuality, religiosity, loyalty, and work habits of blacks. These caricatures had been popularized in the minstrel shows of the nineteenth century which featured singing, bragging, shuffling, dancing, lazy blacks—the "Sambos" and "Zip Coons." They encapsulated the history of black-white relationships in the United States. There was "Nat," the rebellious black male who was to be feared. There was "Uncle Tom." He was a distortion of Harriet Beecher Stowe's character, a loyal, humble, God-fearing old man. There was "Mammy," big, fat, sassy. Mammy had nursed many a white babe, was more devoted to her white family then her own, offered a sturdy black shoulder for her white mistress or master to cry on. And, of course, there was the oversexed black female—alluring, dangerous to both white men and black. She was often a light-skinned mulatta (of mixed white and black ancestry). These caricatures and others—including the happy go-lucky and hapless black child ("pickaninny")—appeared in mainstream literature and in genre fiction.

In mystery fiction, servants—whether black, Irish, or Chinese—were generally "walk-on" characters. In the case of African American servants, when they did appear, they often provided comic relief. In moments of crisis or danger, they engaged in racially stereotyped performances—eyeball rolling, shrieking, being struck dumb, fleeing the scene to hide. Even relatively "liberal" writers of "classic detective" fiction such as Ellery Queen and Rex Stout sometimes portrayed black characters who behaved in this manner (Bailey, *Out of the Woodpile* 35-36).

In the more proletarian "tough guy" fiction of the 1920s and 1930s, the roles of black characters were still restricted. However, writers such as Raymond Chandler and Dashiell Hammett took their private eyes into the urban neighborhoods inhabited by blacks. These neighborhoods were alien places for white investigators such as Philip Marlowe and the Continental Op. In these settings, as the writers acknowledged, whites were viewed with distrust and suspicion. At the same time, the white heroes often viewed black characters with disdain.

In the 1940s, in the aftermath of the atrocities of World War II and in the midst of protest and agitation by homefront organizations, the level of racial sensitivity in the United States showed some—albeit minor—improvement. Lynching and other acts of violence against racial and religious minorities continued. But there was a climate in which writers could offer new twists on old racial themes. In this post-war period of the 1940s and 1950s, an occasional writer in the mystery genre reconsidered racial stereotypes and introduced black characters that were more fully developed and who played more than walk-on roles. As early as 1938, Rex Stout in *Too Many Cooks* had presented a group of black cooks and waiters, including among them a Howard University anthropology student.[2] In *Murder by the Day,* Veronica Parker Johns went further, offering a black manservant named Webster Flagg as the amateur sleuth and hero of her novel. Webster, a retired actor, turns his hand to detecting when his employer is murdered. As a servant—and therefore "invisible" to those he serves—Webster is able to probe into the lives of the suspects in the case. He can sleuth as he serves dinner. In the same vein is Sammy, the black housekeeper of aristocratic New York homicide detective Gridley Nelson. Sammy appears in the series by Ruth Feninsong. Six feet tall and moving "like dark honey poured from a high-held jug" (Feninsong 69), Sammy goes undercover as a maid to help her boss investigate. She is equally as useful in Nelson's kitchen, where she is said to be a culinary artist.

With the 1960s, a new cast of black characters appeared in mystery fiction. During a period in which the racial status quo was being challenged both in the courts and on the streets, mystery writers began to incorporate these changing social mores into their work. As more blacks were recruited into police departments in American cities, they also began to appear more often in mystery fiction. First in John Ball's novel *In the Heat of the Night* and then in the film based on the novel, Virgil Tibbs, African American homicide detective, joined the ranks of fictional police officers. He was not the first black cop to appear in mystery fiction. He was, however, the first to get such prime time play. Tibbs had his civilian counterpart in the form of Harlem P.I. John Shaft. A "tough guy" detective, *Shaft* was created by Ernest Tidyman. As in the case of Tibbs, Shaft made it to the movies, bringing the character to those who might never read a mystery novel. The same was true of two films, *Cotton Comes to Harlem,* and *Come Back Charleston Blue,* which brought the raucous exploits of Chester Himes's police detective duo, Grave Digger Jones and Coffin Ed Johnson to the screen.

What the success of these movies featuring black heroes did was usher in what came to be known as the era of "black exploitation" films. These films of the 1960s and 1970s featured strong, assertive black heroes, villainous whites, violence, romance, action, and plots crafted to please a young black urban audience.[3]

In the post-Civil Rights era of the 1980s, white mystery writers continued to create black characters—sometimes with sensitivity and thoughtfulness, sometimes falling back on old stereotypes of pimps, prostitutes, and servants. But by the 1990s there was also a flowering— or a minor explosion—of black mystery writers creating black characters. Barbara Neely is one of these African American writers. Like her peers, she comes out of a tradition not only of mystery writing but of blacks writing fiction that was considered non-genre but that focused on crime, violence, and injustice.

Black Writers and Crime Fiction

In *Native Son* Richard Wright presented a story of crime and punishment that was aimed with deliberate forethought at what he perceived as one of the deepest fears of white Americans—that of the violent and lustful "bad nigger" who would boldly rape and kill. In this novel Wright considered what might happen if a "Bigger Thomas," one of the many oppressed, angry young black males he had encountered, found himself in a setting that was inherently threatening and to which he was conditioned to respond with fear and anger. In *Native Son,* Wright depicted an urban setting in which the boundaries of the ghetto separated blacks from whites. In earlier works, Wright had explored race relations and racial violence in the South. Although Wright's work caught the attention of white readers and earned the praise of critics, he was not the first African American writer to consider such themes.

In their oral tradition, African Americans during slavery and in its aftermath, had used their folklore and their songs to share tales about crime (comic and serious) and violence (defensive and horrific). In the literature of the late nineteenth and early twentieth century, a first generation of educated black writers brought to their writing the tradition of storytelling of their ancestors. They wrote about the violence—lynchings, riots, beatings, and rapes—that plagued the lives of blacks in the rural South and in the urban North and Midwest. They placed these events within the everyday context of a system of racial segregation which proscribed and restricted the lives of African Americans. At the same time, they wrote with an awareness of the vibrant black culture that made such tribulations bearable.

Looking at the mystery genre, Paula L. Woods finds that African Americans whose stories and novellas appeared in black magazines and periodicals were engaged in experiments with mystery fiction that paralleled those of their white contemporaries. However, "[t]he extent of the black presence in mystery fiction has yet to be 'discovered' by many mystery enthusiasts, regardless of race, or by many mystery scholars"

(Woods xiv). Among those black writers whose contributions to the mystery genre have been recognized are Rudolph Fisher and Chester Himes. Fisher, a physician and writer during the Harlem Renaissance, set his 1932 novel *The Conjure-Man Dies: A Mystery Tale of Dark Harlem,* in that black community. In this classic detective novel, Fisher presents both a cast of characters that is a cross-section of Harlem and a pair of sleuths, Dart and Archer, who are black. Years later, Chester Himes also wrote about Harlem, presenting blacks cops and black professionals, black crooks and black laborers. But Himes's tales of "domestic Harlem," written in the 1950s and 1960s, presented a much more violent Harlem. It was a Harlem that his two protagonists, police detectives Coffin Ed Johnson and Grave Digger Jones, were hard-pressed to control.

Other writers, lesser known, also explored this terrain. But it was in the 1990s with Walter Moseley's detective series featuring Easy Rawlins and set in 1940s' Los Angeles, that black mystery writers began to receive attention. This period marked the debut of writers such as Eleanor Taylor Bland and Gar Anthony Haywood—and of Barbara Neely with *Blanche on the Lam.* Barbara Neely's mystery series is significant for two reasons: first, because of her purposeful use of the mystery genre to address social issues; second, because her character, Blanche White, comes out of a tradition of literary writings and scholarly discussions about black females as women and as workers. The remainder of this article will focus on Blanche White as a domestic and on her importance as a character in the mystery genre who speaks out about social issues.

Blanche White and the World of Black Domestics

Barbara Neely's protagonist, Blanche White has chosen to be a domestic—a maid or housekeeper, a servant. This choice is both surprising and thought-provoking because of the low status assigned domestics in contemporary society. Why would Blanche, resisting the urging of her mother to become a teacher or a nurse, deliberately choose to be a domestic? Why would she work at a job that as the novel opens has been paying so poorly that she has for the second time written a bad check and this time been sentenced to 30 days in jail? Why choose work in which she is constantly demeaned by her employers whose assumptions about who and what Blanche is are very different from her own? From Blanche's perspective, her present predicament has more to do with her decision to move with her two children from New York City back to Farleigh, North Carolina. In the small town of Farleigh, the "so-called genteel Southern white women" have no concept of how to treat a "full-service domestic" (4). However, Blanche's sustaining view of her work is that she is a professional. She is excellent at what she does and she takes pride in what she does (65).

As a domestic Blanche is descended from that long line of black women who have labored outside their homes to support their families. The importance of their work to their families and to their communities has long been realized by African American fiction writers—particularly female writers. More recently, domestic workers have been the subject of research by social historians and discussion by black feminists. Collins writes: "Black feminist research on Black domestic workers allows a closer view both of how African-American women perceived their work and of the actions they undertook to resist its exploitative and dehumanizing aspects" (55). As Andolsen observes: "Black writers stress that their social experience is not that of white women . . . Black feminist perspectives on rape, work (especially domestic work), female/male solidarity, and female beauty demonstrate these differences" (xiii).

As Collins and other scholars (Katzman, Gray, Omolade) assert, historically the prevailing social structure—one of racial oppression—determined the types of work available to black women and the conditions of their employment. Even when they left the South, many black women found that the only jobs available to them were as servants. Collins writes: "In 1910, 39.5 percent of all employed Black women were domestic workers. By 1940 that number had risen to 59.9 percent" (55). This concentration of black women as paid domestic laborers continued (with brief respite for some in World War II industries) until the 1960s and 1970s when significantly more black women—often the daughters and granddaughters of domestics who had struggled to provide for their education—began to enter other occupations.

Yet, historically, the work of the domestic has represented not only a reality of black women's lives but the prevailing stereotype about their status as women. Collins writes:

The first controlling image applied to African American women is that of the mammy—the faithful, obedient domestic servant. Created to justify the economic exploitation of house slaves and sustained to explain Black women's long-standing restriction to domestic service, the mammy image presents the normative yardstick used to evaluate all Black women's behavior. . . . the mammy symbolizes the ideal Black female relationship to elite white male power. (71)

African American novelist and folklorist Zora Neale Hurston put it more succinctly in her novel *Their Eyes Were Watching God* when she has Nanny, an old black woman, tell her granddaughter that the black woman is "de mule uh de world" (16). In this role black women labored in their own homes and in those of white folks. They bore both the psychological and the physical burdens of being at the bottom of the white patriarchal structure, below not only the white male but the white woman and the black male.

With regard to their work, African American women as domestics could depend on neither unions nor the courts for support and protection.[4] They were forced to negotiate their own working conditions. This was complicated by the special nature of the employer-employee relationship. Omolade writes: "Black female household workers had to fit into the 'family' in order to make a living in the highly emotionally charged private sphere of the white home" (44). There were regional differences in how black domestics were expected to fit in. In the South "servants" were assumed to be black. The employer-employee relationship was governed by the racial caste system and traditional racial etiquette. In the North employer-employee relationships were shaped by the fact white immigrants also worked as servants and by the spatial distance separating white neighborhoods from black ghettos (Katzman, Gray).

But as Clark-Lewis notes: "African American women in domestic service usually developed ways to achieve a measure of control over their lives despite the social restrictions. The first step was to master the work environment" (104). Attempts to achieve mastery of their work environment were constrained by efforts of employers to control the black domestic. Andolsen writes: "Employers who demanded live-in arrangements were sometimes particularly exploitative. Their domestics often worked . . . longer hours, got little disposable income, and were separated from their families" (91). Therefore, one mechanism black domestics used to gain control over their work environment was to work as day workers rather than live-in servants. But day work generally did not pay as well and the income was less reliable (91). In the North, during the Depression, black domestics found themselves standing on street corners waiting for employers to choose them for a few hours or a day's labor.[5]

Katzman states: "In the South, many mistresses preferred the live-out system because they thought live-in service would bring into their homes the worst types of Negroes and that would corrupt their households" (160). On one hand, white Southerners swore by the loyalty of their old black retainers. On the other, they suspected all blacks were thieves and reprobates and not to be trusted. They were also concerned about the "worthless" black males who might be supported by their black female servants (see Bailey, *Boundary* 145-46).

In fact, it was the black female domestic who had more reason for concern and more to fear from her relationship with her employer. Sexual harassment was commonplace for black domestics working in white homes. This was one of the reasons black parents and community leaders were reluctant to see young black girls go to work in domestic service. It was one of the reasons black women preferred to be day laborers rather than live-in servants. For the black domestic faced with sexual harassment, her options were few—attempted avoidance, submission, or quit the job.

Alexander writes:

In general, black women understood that neither verbal rejection, attempted escape, nor physical resistance served any deterrent purpose, and that they sometimes had to compromise their own sexual integrity to protect their lives and the lives of their loved ones. (8)

Alexander is describing the experience of black women during slavery. Black feminist scholars and other historians describe this situation as continuing to exist in the post-Civil War Reconstruction era in the South. Decades later, economic survival continued to dictate the responses of black women to sexual harassment by their white male employers.

However, black domestics were not passive in the face of economic and physical victimization. They engaged—continue to engage—in daily acts of resistance.[6] They fought back on the job by working at their own pace, misunderstanding instructions they did not wish to obey, taking home the food from the kitchen they needed to feed their own families—and occasionally by spitting in Madame's soup. And sometimes they simply made their displeasure known by quitting a job with an intolerable employer.

In her mystery series Barbara Neely presents Blanche White, domestic, as a resistance fighter who speaks for the often invisible working class.

The Invisible Woman Speaks

Katzman, in his study of domestic servants, writes: "One peculiar and most degrading aspect of domestic service was the requisite of invisibility. The ideal servant . . . would be invisible and silent, responsive to demands but deaf to gossip" (188). In literature, black domestics suffered from a similar invisibility. Mullen in his anthology of short stories by African American women asserts: "Black female domestics had been literally and figuratively silent in American fiction until Alice Childress found the voice for the character who inhabits the vignettes in *Like One of the Family: Conversations from a Domestic Life*" (251). Childress's black domestic engages her friend Marge in a one-sided conversation about topics ranging from the ways of the white folks she works for to the lurking dangers for black people in a trip to a public beach. She also comments on the depiction of black people in movies. She makes this incisive observation about the movie domestic:

As soon as I see a colored maid that's workin' for somebody, I know that she will have a conniption-fit cause the lady she works for won't eat her dinner. . . . I know that maids don't be carryin' on like that over the people they work for, at least none of em that I've ever met! (Childress, in Mullen 260)

Harris traces the evolution of domestics in African American literature "from mammies to militants." By the 1970s, black domestics were being portrayed as not only no longer being mammies but as sometimes being lethal. For example, in Ted Shine's play "Contribution," a militant young black man learns his seemingly submissive old Granny has been aiding the civil rights movement by poisoning the bigots for whom she cooks. Just before the sheriff goes out to confront the young demonstrators, including her grandson, she sends him a basket of food. The sheriff dies of a "fit" in the street.

In mystery fiction, the transition from a black domestic such as Melville Davisson Post's loyal and white-identified Mammy Liza[7] to Barbara Neely's Blanche White is radical. Blanche, a domestic for the 1990s, is determined in her resistance to what she (like black feminist scholars) terms "mammyism." She thinks:

Loving the people for whom you worked might make it easier to wipe old Mr. Stanley's shitty behind and take young Edna's smart-ass, rich-kid remarks. And, of course, it was hard not to love children, or to overlook the failings of the old and infirm . . . What she didn't understand was how you convinced yourself that you were actually loved by people who paid you the lowest possible wages; who never offered you the use of one of their cars. . . . (Neely, *Blanche on the Lam* 48)

Blanche's other term for this delusion on the part of some black domestics is "Darkies' Disease." Although she is able to resist any fleeting urge to offer her employer a shoulder to cry on about her husband, Blanche finds herself tested by Mumsfield, the cousin of the family. Mumsfield is "special," slightly retarded from Down's syndrome. Mumsfield is also intuitive and gifted with his own brand of intelligence. He and Blanche share an empathy that makes it difficult for Blanche to maintain her distance from him. But as she reminds herself, in spite of the connection between them, Mumsfield is a white man. His ancestors might have owned her ancestors—have bought them and sold them (Neely, *Blanche on the Lam* 182).

When Blanche meets Nate, the old black man who works in the garden, she is afraid he is suffering from Darkies' Disease. Nate tells Blanche the story of how years ago he was saved from the Ku Klux Klan by Blanche's employer, Miss Grace. Blanche realizes the truth of the story is that Grace saved him only because Grace's dog was about to have puppies and she wanted Nate to help with their whelping. Blanche sees no reason at all Nate should still be grateful. But gradually Blanche comes to realize Nate is not as stupid or as bowed as he pretends. He is also, as she puts it, "a storytelling man," in the oral tradition of other black people she knows. She is delighted when she realizes this. She hopes to have her questions about the household answered. But Nate is not as informative as she would like. And then Nate is murdered: "A thick, hot rage began to roil in her stomach at the thought of the deaths of all the poor black Nates and, yes, Blanches at the hands of the privileged white Everetts of the world" (Neely, *Blanche on the Lam* 148-49). In her rage, Blanche rejects the "declining significance of race" thesis proposed by some social scientists (e.g., Wilson). She rejects the idea that "class [doesn't] exist and color [doesn't] matter anymore" (Neely, *Blanche on the Lam* 149). It does for working-class black people like her and like Nate.

Even before Nate's death, Blanche has commented on her sense of class stratification and racial injustice. Just before she "takes it on the lam" from the courthouse, escaping from the 30-day jail sentence, she compares her plight with that of the county commissioner charged with accepting bribes. She is sure the worst he will suffer is a "little bad publicity, and a lot of sympathy from people who might easily be in his position" (Neely, *Blanche on the Lam* 5). And later when the sheriff shows up at the country house where she is hiding out as the housekeeper, Blanche wonders if he will spend tax dollars trying to recapture her because he considers her escape "a personal affront to all decent, God-fearing white people. She remembered the wanted posters for Joanne Little, Angela Davis, and Assata Shakur" (43). And Blanche remembers the murders and beatings by cops of young black and Puerto Rican males in Harlem. In her mind, she links white Southern cops to the "paddyrollers" and overseers of slavery time (89-90).

Clearly, Blanche views the criminal justice system as less than just—often criminal in its treatment of the poor and of racial minorities. In this respect, Blanche speaks from what social scientists refer to as a "conflict" or "radical" perspective on the criminal justice system (see e.g., Reiman). Blanche rejects the idea of consensus. She does not believe there is general agreement in society about what the laws should be and how the law should be enforced. Blanche believes the criminal justice system favors the rich and powerful.

As a poor black woman who works as a domestic, Blanche has experienced personal victimization. She was raped by the brother of her first Farleigh employer. But Blanche did not bother going to the police. She doubted they would believe her and she knew if the circumstances of the rape had come out she would have had trouble getting another job. She was naked in her employer's bathtub at the time. She had been invading her employer's private space, using her personal things—not something that would be acceptable behavior by a black servant in the eyes of the people who might hire her (Neely, *Blanche on the Lam* 63).

But this invasion of bathtubs and other space is something that Blanche feels she needs to do. She uses her employers' stereos and telephones and sits in their chairs because these are her "ways of getting some of her sold self back" (Neely, *Blanche on the Lam* 63). As Blanche confides, even though she prefers domestic work to a factory assembly line, she wouldn't be doing it if she didn't need the money. She would like to retire to the Caribbean and open a guest house for other working women (63-64).

In Farleigh, the other women with whom Blanche shares bonds are her mother, her friend Ardell, and Miz Minnie, an old woman who knows everything that is going on in the town. Blanche thinks of Miz Minnie as being like the "wise women elders who chose chiefs and counseled them" among some African peoples (Neely, *Blanche on the Lam* 115). People in the black community come to Miz Minnie to tell her their troubles and their business. Because of her connections among the black people—who work for whites as their domestics—Miz Minnie also has sources of information about the white community. When Blanche finds herself trying to solve the mystery of what is going on with the white people she is working for and later of Nate's murder, she turns to Miz Minnie. Or, rather, she turns to her mother and Ardell and has them consult Miz Minnie. Blanche's relationship with her friend Ardell is as close as sisters. They are on the same wave length. Her relationship with her mother, Miz Cora, is more problematic. Miz Cora disapproves not only of Blanche's choice of profession but of her decision to go off to California. She disapproves of the fact that when Blanche's sister died and left her two children in Blanche's care, Blanche took the children and moved to New York. And she disapproves of the fact that Blanche is single—and had intended never to have children. Still, when

Blanche finds herself in trouble, Miz Cora comes through, helping her to plan her escape to her cousin who lives in Boston.

But Blanche can't leave town until her income tax check comes. And in the meantime, there is Nate's murder to solve. At the novel's climax, Blanche discovers she herself has been making certain assumptions about who was capable of what. When she discovers who the real killer is and why, Blanche is disconcerted. She feels "like someone who'd been tricked by a red spade." Her error in reading the killer's character is disturbing to Blanche because she depends on her wits. Being a shrewd judge of character is essential to her livelihood (Neely, *Blanche on the Lam* 184).

But Blanche does survive. As the novel ends she is on her way to Boston to stay with her Cousin Charlotte. She feels very little compunction about having taken the "hush" money she was offered and then going to a reporter with what she knew. She considers the money "aggravation pay, not hush money" (Neely, *Blanche on the Lam* 213). Actually, Blanche has what she considers a good and sufficient reason for taking the money. She intends to use it toward the education of her children Taifa and Malik.

The Continued Adventures of Blanche White

In *Blanche among the Talented Tenth,* Blanche is living in Boston and sending her children to a private school. It is through them that she meets a wealthy couple who invites them to Amber Cove, an exclusive, all-black resort in Maine. It is here that Blanche (and Barbara Neely) speak out about the "color complex" that exists among African Americans.

In *Blanche on the Lam* the reader learns that Blanche White finds it annoying when people like her employer's husband are amused by the contrast between her name and her skin color. But she is accustomed to "some people getting the chuckles" when they hear that she—a black woman—has "a name that mean[s] 'white' twice" (30). Blanche believes her parents' had a right to name her anything they pleased. Moreover, she is proud of her deep black skin color. Therefore, Blanche is not delighted with the people she encounters at Amber Cove who are obsessed with skin color. They are members of a light-skinned elite who consider themselves better than poor, black people like her.

But, as Blanche discovers, the summer people at Amber Cove have their problems too. They are enmeshed in complicated relationships, protecting secrets that someone appears willing to kill to protect. Blanche finds herself drawn into unraveling the mysteries behind an apparent accidental death and a suicide. Among the residents of Amber

Cove to whom she is drawn is Mattie Harris, a regal black matriarch, widow of a wealthy white sociologist, now renowned in her own right as a feminist writer. There is also a young black woman being courted by the son of one of the founding families of Amber Cove. His mother objects to the young woman because of her dark skin color. And there is the local pharmacist, elegant, handsome, and connected to Amber Cove since childhood. He threatens to sweep Blanche off her feet.

But Blanche has come to Amber Cove with a mission. Aside from staying with her own children and her friends' two children, while the couple go off on a week-long boat trip, Blanche intends to perform her own private ritual. She has been advised by her spiritual adviser, Madame Rosa, that she needs to go to the water and carry out a ceremony at sunrise. Blanche hopes this will help her to recover the equilibrium in her life that has been upset by her move to Boston and by her long-time suitor/lover Leo's marriage to another woman.

In this novel, Barbara Neely has Blanche consider the matter of African American spirituality. Blanche has rejected organized religion and created a religion of her own based on her own rituals. She worships her ancestors at an altar she made for them and she "routinely call[s] on all the forces in the universe for power" (Neely, *Blanche among* 61). Blanche's mother originally objected to Blanche "playing around with them roots and such" (59), but Miz Cora has come around enough to send Blanche a rock for her altar. To Blanche, it makes more sense to believe in her own religion than in Christianity because as a child she came to realize Christianity was "the religion of the people who had enslaved her ancestors" (60). Neither is Blanche satisfied with Islam or the other male-dominated religions she has considered. So she has created her own personal form of worship. And in Maine, she goes to the ocean to perform her rituals and comes away feeling cleansed and centered.

Soon after, Blanche found herself dealing with the secrets of the "Insiders" (the members of the elite old money families) and the anger and displeasure of the "Outsiders" (who are allowed to stay at the resort but treated with contempt). It is in her discussions with the Insiders and the Outsiders that Blanche comments on intraracial class and color discrimination. Earlier, before her departure for Maine, during a telephone conservation with her friend Ardell, Blanche observes:

Everybody in the country got color on the brain—whitefolks trying to brown themselves up and hate everything that ain't white at the same time; black folks puttin' each other down for being too black; brown folks trying to make sure nobody mistakes them for black; yellow folks trying to convince themselves they're white. (Neely, *Blanche among* 9)

Blanche is not particularly concerned about what the snobbish Insiders at Amber Cove think of her own "eggplant" black skin or her unstraightened hair. As she tells the reader in *Blanche on the Lam,* when she was a child bemoaning her blackness because she was taunted and teased, a female relative told her the other children were jealous because Blanche had the night in her. And Blanche became "Night Girl" with "a sense of herself as special, as wondrous, and as powerful" (59). But Blanche is concerned that her children, particularly her preteen daughter Taifa, exposed to the lifestyle of their classmates, will come to look down on her. She is disturbed by Taifa's suggestion on the telephone that Blanche get her hair straightened before coming to Amber Cove. And she is wounded when Taifa makes a comment about Blanche's blackness.

But Blanche is aware that the uneasiness between her and Taifa has less to do with Blanche herself and more to do with Taifa's budding sense of herself as a young woman. Blanche—who never planned on being a mother but who loves her children dearly—fears Taifa is growing away from her. She feels the pain and anxiety of this imminent psychological separation. She wonders if she will lose Taifa to a world of which she is not and cannot be a part.

In this mystery novel, Barbara Neely focuses perhaps more on relationships than on murder. There is the mother-child relationship between Blanche and her children and Mattie Harris and her godson. There are the couple relationships between the godson and his wife, between the young woman Blanche befriends and her wealthy fiancé, and between Blanche's friends who are moving toward divorce. And there is Blanche's own budding romance with the handsome pharmacist. Blanche fears her attraction to him has more to do with her hormones and pure lust than with her good sense. She tells her friend Ardell this. She talks often to Ardell. To Ardell, Blanche talks from the heart. At Amber Cove, Blanche tries to connect with Mattie Harris, who she admires as "a diva" by engaging her in "heart talk."

Heart talk. . . . Her term for the way women gave each other bits of lives and history as a way of declaring their good intention toward each other. Why would you mess with someone who knows your business? (Neely, *Blanche among* 93)

But as Blanche discovers to her disappointment, the barriers are not so easily overcome. She finds neither lasting friendship nor lasting romance at Amber Cove.

Using Barbara Neely's Works in a Diversity Course

As should be obvious from the above discussion Barbara Neely brings to her mystery writing a sense of social mission. She uses the mystery and her amateur sleuth Blanche White as vehicles for social commentary. At the same time, she does this in a highly entertaining fashion. Some mystery purists who are more concerned with plot than character may be bothered by the slow development of the plot. The murder does not occur on the first page in either of the two novels in the series. In fact, in *Blanche among the Talented Tenth,* the crime—if there is one—is secondary to the social commentary. But one may argue that in the Blanche White series, Blanche is concerned not so much with criminal justice as with social justice. Given that the crimes must be placed in context of setting and social relationships. ʌ

As works for use in a diversity course, both novels—which should be read in order—are superb. Barbara Neely writes out of a black feminist perspective. In the two novels, she presents Blanche White as a single mother, working class, struggling to provide for herself and her children. Blanche is neither at ease in the city—where she fears for her children—nor in her Southern hometown—where she cannot find enough work. Blanche faces the relationship dilemmas of the modern woman. She has declared her independence. She had chosen not to marry Leo, who loves her but wants too much from her. But at the same time she has the need for male companionship and a sex life. She must deal with all of the concerns inherent in modern male/female relationships. At the same time, she is negotiating her family relationships with her mother and her children—and even her dead sister. She has connections, people she loves. But Blanche is also searching for spiritual meaning in her life. All of the complexity and richness of Blanche White's life occurs within a social structure that oppresses and disdains her because she is poor, black, and works as a domestic.

Using Barbara Neely's mystery novels, the instructor can explore issues of race, class, and gender. *Blanche on the Lam* used in conjunction with assigned readings on domestic workers can be used to engage students in discussions about the working lives of black women. The novel is also useful for a discussion about the relationship between the criminal justice system and African Americans. *Blanche among the Talented Tenth* can provide a springboard for discussion of the "color complex" among blacks. Russell et al. write: "Intraracial color discrimination is an embarrassing and controversial subject for African Americans" (1). Blanche White's no nonsense comments about the color complex may help to ease students into a discussion of the subject. The novel should also dispel notions that students might have that until recently there was no black elite. As Barbara Neely points out, since the antebellum era there has been a black elite, often with white ancestry, who enjoyed a more privileged lifestyle than the black lower class. However, even the elite faced the barriers created by racial discrimination— hence the need to establish exclusive black resorts such as Amber Cove. This novel may be used in conjunction with a discussion of the works of African American sociologist W. E. B. Du Bois who coined the phrase "the talented tenth" to refer to the educated African Americans elite who would serve as the leaders of their race.

In addition to the mysteries in this series, Barbara Neely is also an author of short stories. Paula L. Woods includes "Spilled Salt" in her anthology. This story is told from the perspective of a mother, who is probably black but who is not identified by race. The issue here is that the woman's son—a convicted rapist—has been released from prison and returned home. The mother struggles to cope with her own revulsion for the son she loved so much as a boy but who has committed a crime that she can neither comprehend nor forgive. How could a young man reared by women and loved by them destroy another woman's life?

Young writes: "African-American writing began with a woman" (47). Barbara Neely is a descendant of those African American women who wrote of their own experiences and those of their people. Like her predecessors, Barbara Neely helps us to understand—to enter into the minds and hearts—of those who others have tried to render both voiceless and invisible.

Notes

1. This author's name appears on her books and in her copyright as one word "BarbaraNeely."

2. African American college students took jobs at spas and resorts to earn their college tuition.

3. Although not directly related to this trend in which African American characters were featured as heroes, the film *The Pawnbroker* should be mentioned here. This 1965 film, starring Rod Steiger as a Jewish survivor of a Nazi concentration camp who runs a pawnshop in Harlem, New York, was important—groundbreaking—in its use of location shooting and its focus on the African American and Hispanic residents of this ghetto whose lives intersect (in the end, violently) with that of the mentally tormented pawnbroker.

4. See Katzman and Gray on the less than successful efforts of black domestic workers to organize and to strike for better working conditions.

5. A female investigator for the African American owned newspaper *The Amsterdam News* did a series of articles in 1935 about the streetcorner hiring of domestics. She and colleague characterized this hiring situation as "slave markets" (Gray 57-58).

6. Historians have also noted the significant role played by black domestics in the Civil Rights movement as activists and workers.

7. An early twentieth-century mystery writer, Post set his stories in Jeffersonian Virginia. Mama Liza appears in "The Devil's Tools."

Works Cited

Alexander, Adele Logan. " She's No Lady, She's a Nigger': Abuses, Stereotypes, and Realities from the Middle Passage to Capitol (and Anita) Hill." *Race, Gender, and Power in America: The Legacy of the Hill-Thomas Hearings.* Ed. Anita Faye Hill and Emma Coleman Jordan. New York: Oxford UP, 1995. 3-25.

Andolsen, Barbara Hilkert. *"Daughters of Jefferson, Daughters of Bootblacks": Racism and American Feminism.* Macon, GA: Mercer UP, 1986.

Bailey, Frankie Y. "Boundary Maintenance, Interest-Group Conflict, and Black Justice in Danville, Virginia, 1900-1930." Ph.D. dissertation, State University of New York at Albany, 1986.

——. *Out of the Woodpile: Black Characters in Crime and Detective Fiction.* Westport, CT: Greenwood, 1991.

Childress, Alice. *Like One of the Family: Conversations from a Domestic's Life.* Selected vignettes (1956). *Revolutionary Tales: African American Women's Short Stories from the First Story to the Present.* Ed. Bill Mullen. New York: Dell, 1995. 251-62.

Clark-Lewis, Elizabeth. "For a Real Better Life: Voices of African American Women Migrants, 1900-1930." *Urban Odyssey: A Multicultural History of Washington, D.C.* Ed. Francine Curro Carry. Washington and London: Smithsonian Institute Press, 1996. 97-112.

Collins, Patricia Hill. *Black Feminist Thought: Knowledge, Consciousness, and the Politics of Empowerment.* New York: Routledge, 1990.

Feninsong, Ruth. *The Butler Died in Brooklyn.* Garden City, NY: Crime Club-Doubleday, 1943.

Gray, Brenda Clegg. *Black Female Domestics During the Depression in New York City, 1930-1940.* New York and London: Garland, 1993.

Harris, Trudier. *From Mammies to Militants: Domestics in Black American Literature.* Philadelphia: Temple UP, 1982.

Hurston, Zora Neale. *Their Eyes Were Watching God.* 1937. Greenwich, CT: Fawcett, 1969.

Katzman, David M. *Seven Days a Week: Women and Domestic Service in Industrializing America.* New York: Oxford UP, 1978.

Mullen, Bill, ed. *Revolutionary Tales: African American Women's Short Stories from the First Story to the Present.* New York: Dell, 1995.

Neely, Barbara. *Blanche on the Lam.* New York: Penquin, 1992.

——. *Blanche among the Talented Tenth.* New York: Penquin, 1994.

Omolade, Barbara. *The Rising Song of African American Women.* New York and London: Routledge, 1994.

Reiman, Jeffrey. *The Rich Get Richer and the Poor Get Prison.* 1992. Boston: Allyn and Bacon, 1995.

Russell, Kathy, Midge Wilson, and Ronald Hall. *The Color Complex: The Politics of Skin Color Among African Americans.* New York: Anchor Books, 1992.

Watson, Colin. *Snobbery with Violence.* London: Eyre, 1971.

Wilson, William J. *The Declining Significance of Race.* Chicago: University of Chicago Press, 1982.

Woods, Paula L., ed. *Spooks, Spies, and Private Eyes: Black Mystery, Crime, and Suspense Fiction of the 20th Century.* New York: Doubleday, 1995.

Young, Mary E. *Mules and Dragons: Popular Culture Images in the Selected Writings of African-American and Chinese American Women Writers.* Westport, CT: Greenwood, 1993.

WRITING BLACK:
CRIME FICTION'S OTHER

Claire Wells

The 1990s have seen important and radical additions to British crime fiction as the genre as a whole has mutated from a traditional form marked particularly by the collapse of the safe and distinct boundaries of writer, criminal, detective, and reader. That is to say that the boundaries which have previously divided these elements are eroded as the collapse between the literary and real life (and indeed between genre and mainstream fiction) becomes ever more blurred. These previously understood categories in crime fiction were little traversed, for the perception is that crime fiction has traditionally been a formulaic type of fiction. Black crime writers are, however, increasingly challenging this literary tradition. In contemporary cultural production generally, there is a more sophisticated discourse of race than ever before with a wider range of accessible racialized identities to read. Detective fiction accordingly now operates from many different cultural and social perspectives, of which race is one important strand, but which has also seen the coming to prominence of several gay and feminist writers. Clearly in terms of the racial strand, this is a genre whose time has come in the United States with the rise of the popular black American authors like Walter Moseley, Barbara Neely, and Eleanor Taylor Bland. Yet in Britain it is a genre which is yet to become established—the black British writer Mike Phillips is one of the most important writers in the field. Mike Phillips was born in Guyana and came to Britain in 1956. He went to school in Islington, London, and then studied for a degree and postgraduate degrees in English, politics, and teacher training. After a variety of jobs in factories, garages, and the Post Office, he started and lived in a hostel for homeless black youths in Notting Hill, leaving to become a community activist in Manchester and Birmingham. He entered journalism in the 1970s and subsequently taught at the University of Westminster. As well as a number of books and screenplays, he has published two Sam Dean novels. The first *Blood Rights* was serialized for BBC-TV and the

Reprinted from *Diegesis: Journal of the Association for Research in Popular Fiction* 1 (Winter 1997) with permission.

second, *The Late Candidate,* won the Crime Writers' Association's Silver Dagger Award. By looking at his work and tracing some of the contradictions and obstacles that he as a black crime writer faces, it is possible to outline the sort of boundaries which have traditionally dictated the English crime novel, particularly in terms of race, and to examine how Phillips's work offers a critique of the system of white power which threatens time and again to subsume his and others' black specificity and writing.

Crime fiction is a notoriously conservative genre and an examination of how the boundaries are breaking down in terms of racial positionings in this genre is perhaps representative of the wider postmodern slippage which is generally occurring in the field of literary production. This article seeks to draw attention to the extent to which this hitherto conservative genre is being adapted and subverted by those who have traditionally been marginalized and made crime fiction's other.

In my recent interview with Phillips, he states that when he began writing crime fiction he assumed that all he needed to do was to reproduce the conventions of the genre, substituting his own black persona for that of a white person. An initial uneasiness however soon developed into a certainty that, "this was a genre whose conventions were part of a racist polemic about society."[1] It is important to highlight the nature of what the black crime writer is confronted with in the genre of crime fiction and moreover how such *racist polemic* is being challenged by writers such as Phillips. He states,

I had the sense as a black writer that there were certain categories reserved for me, I could work as a children's writer, I could write about the Caribbean, about Africa—I could even write about Afro-America, but I couldn't write about being a black person in England. Nobody was stopping me but it was in the sense that I wouldn't be published and even if I was nobody would pay much attention. I thought if I write a crime story then I could say a number of things about what I wanted to say about my life and about society in a format in which people would let it pass, even that they wouldn't notice or would accept it as part of the story. That's why I really started writing in the crime genre. (Interview)

English crime fiction has traditionally been concerned with the formation of ideas about the social and moral order and its role in policing the boundaries of class and race. Julian Symons comments,

[T]hese were very special fairy tales. Social and even political attitudes were implied in them. It is safe to say that almost all the British writers in the twenties and thirties, and most of the Americans, were unquestionably right wing.

This is not to say that they were openly anti-semitic or anti-radical, but that they were overwhelmingly conservative in feeling. It would have been unthinkable for them to create a Jewish detective, or a working-class one aggressively conscious of his origins, for such figures would have seemed to them quite incongruous. It would have been equally impossible for them to have created a policeman who beat up suspects . . . Acknowledging that such things happened, they would have thought it undesirable to write about them, because the police were the representatives of established society, and so ought not to be shown behaving badly. And although an unemployed man might be seen sympathetically if he was trying to be helpful to his social betters, he was usually regarded as somebody who just refused to work. (118)

Moreover crime writing has to some extent endorsed the social and legal systems by which criminals are punished. The elements in crime writing which define and reinforce a particular version of the social and moral order are almost self-evident so that you find that sense in the classic English mystery of a stratified society with a distinct social and moral hierarchy. As Julian Symons helpfully comments, "The social order in these stories was as fixed and mechanical as that of the Incas" (119). For example, in much of Agatha Christie's writing the classic model is the closed middle-class society. In *The Murder of Roger Ackroyd,* the villain is particularly threatening because, astonishingly he is *one of them*—he is revealed in the final chapter as good Doctor Shepherd; the bastion of polite village society and supposed upholder of the middle-class system of values—a figure of absolute trust. The book caused a literary sensation when it was published and its resolution is still shocking today because it violated the code of detective fiction of the time so espoused by critics and writers like Monsignor Ronald Knox in his "Ten Commandments of Detection" in 1928. The Detection Club in Britain, shortly after its foundation in 1930, asked its members to swear an oath promising that their detectives would "well and truly detect the crimes presented to them" without reliance on "Divine Revelation, Feminine Intuition, Mumbo-jumbo, Jiggery-Pokery, Coincidence or the Act of God."[3] The trick of making the local "good doctor" into the story's narrator, Poirot's Watson, *and* the murderer outraged such literary rules.

These social and moral hierarchies are often indicated by a character's gender or class but race has traditionally been the other classic signifier of criminality. Phillips's insistence upon the importance of the racialized context of his work is supported by reference to the work of Stuart Hall, the noted black British critic and theorist. He contends in his important essay, "Minimal Selves," that black identity is not a fixed position; it has always been mediated through the white eye, so that black identity has in some ways been a response to the racializing white perspective. His work on issues of race and the diaspora is of use to us in approaching the question of how black crime writing, and the work of Mike Phillips in Britain specifically, is breaking down traditional barriers in crime fiction. "Blackness" has impacted dramatically upon the British literary scene in terms of the critical and commercial success of diasporic writings, but also inasmuch as any contemporary British writing cannot fail to take into account the black presence in Britain today. The notion of diaspora, particularly in British cultural studies, is a relatively emergent area and it is only latterly that there has been sustained critical engagement with it. I have taken the word diaspora broadly to mean those peoples whose ancestral (or more recent) roots are not within Britain. Traditional understandings of Englishness. it seems to me, signal the sort of cultural and sociohistoric parameters that diasporic writers such as Phillips are resisting. The writing of the diaspora affords new possibilities, new understandings, and new awarenesses of what literature is and can attain. It is in some sense contemporary British literature's lifeblood. Hall emphasizes (in common with many other black writers and theorists, Paul Gilroy and Kobena Mercer notably) that black history as a narrative has traditionally been written *elsewhere.* That is to say that there has always been a black cultural and intellectual agenda but one which has not been able to flourish and develop in the same manner which has been enjoyed by white cultural society for example. (An appropriate measure of this is the manner in which black in crime fiction has traditionally been reduced to the criminal by the white perspective.) It is only through acknowledging difference that an honest and positive dimension for black identity and subsequent cultural production is negotiable and indeed desirable, "Constituting oneself as black is another important recognition of self through difference: certain clear polarities and extremities against which one tries to define oneself" (Hall, *Real* 136). Mike Phillips's black characters do not have to be criminal to feature; he is foregrounding the racial issue through his positive characterization of black people in his texts. His insistence upon the racialized context of his work is, as he himself has pointed out, a way of insisting and drawing attention to this important difference. This foregrounding of racial identity allows him to explore racial tensions in a number of ways. The character which Phillips has constructed in Sam Dean, his successful black journalist and private eye, is doubly disconcerting to the established crime fiction order, for here is a black character, the principal character, who is educated, sophisticated, attractive, street wise, and very much aware and proud of his racial identity. Stuart Hall says,

The fact is "black" has never been just there either. It has always been an unstable identity, psychically, culturally and politically. It, too, is a narrative, a story, a history. Something constructed, told, spoken, not simply found . . . so the notion that identity is a simple—if I can use the metaphor—black or white question, has never been the experience of black people, at least in the diaspora. (*Real* 136)

Hall, along with the theorists outlined above, are optimistic about this new found attention to difference. He claims that in creating texts and other forms of cultural production which challenge the status quo, these artists are claiming a space of power for the black voice. In a highly popular genre such as crime fiction, it is evident that the mixture of black voice and social commentary that is so much a part of Phillips's work has important potential in terms of the numbers of readers it can reach. Stuart Hall says,

Paradoxically in our world, marginality has become a powerful space. It is a space of weak power but it is a space of power nonetheless. The emergence of new subjects, new genders, new ethnicities, new regions, new communities, hitherto excluded from the major forms of cultural representation, unable to locate themselves except as decentered or subaltern, have acquired through struggle, sometimes in very marginalised ways, the means to speak for themselves for the first time. And the discourses of power in our society, the discourses of the dominant regimes, have been certainly threatened by this decentered cultural empowerment of the marginal and the local. (*Culture* 34)

Mike Phillips's work is an answer to these old discourses of white power. He is by his own admission attempting to turn the usual binaries of crime fiction upside down so that the idea of black carries new meanings and new spaces for identity.

In contemporary British cultural production there is an historical re-evaluation going on in terms of race (and other previously marginalized groups such as gay, feminist, working-class, etc.). This important challenge to the critical and social orthodoxies of the past has brought about the reshaping of previously held notions of Englishness and this obviously has an important impact on cultural and, specifically here, literary production.

In white crime fiction, being on the other side of the racial divide is typically a symptom of criminality and deviance. To be black in such a world of crime fiction is to be an irretrievable outsider. So, for black crime writers squaring the circle presents intense problems, which may be one reason why there are sadly so few of them in Britain. Crime fiction speaks to social identity and beyond that to national identity and political identity. What crime fiction has traditionally dealt in is racial stereotypes shaped by white structures of power and these stereotypes have become versions of definitions of what it means to be criminal that even now have social and cultural reverberations. Stuart Hall comments upon this phenomenon and talks about the manner in which black cultural and literary agendas are now addressing this inequality in order to transcend these orthodoxies of the past:

> . . . black experience placed, positioned at the margins, as the consequence of a set of quite specific political and cultural practices which regulate, governed and "normalised" the representational and discursive spaces of English society. These formed the conditions of existence of a cultural politics designed to challenge, resist and, where possible to transform the dominant regimes of representation . . . There was a concern not simply with the absence or marginality of the black experience but with its simplification and its stereotypical character. (*Stuart Hall* 442)

Phillips's texts share some of the classic preoccupations of American private eye fiction like Dashiel Hammett's and Raymond Chandler's inasmuch as his work is concerned with corruption in local government, with organized crime, and a preoccupation with the alienation and anomie of individuals in a large urban situation. But, again, their version of reality, their version of the social and moral order excluded people like him completely. He says,

> I would not exist in their fiction or I would be a crook or a con man, to be a person like me in their world view would be to be a confidence trickster or madman or whatever. So for me it could not simply be a case of changing the colour of the protagonist I had to challenge the order of the convention in order for me to exist in the genre. (Interview)

Phillips's project is twofold in his writing. Not only is he interested in contributing a positive black authorial voice to the crime fiction genre, he is also very keen to retrieve the black character within that crime fiction as a construct more than simply the criminal. The concept of dominant white hegemony which he takes issue with also has important implications when considering the way of defining law and order as keeping a check on certain elements of society, that is keeping certain elements of society out or excluding them. Phillips's project is also interested beyond the idea of the crossword puzzle of crime solving in his fictions, he is additionally very interested in the redemptive quality that crime writing can offer the black critical agenda. He says,

What I write is normally described as crime fiction, but that is not necessarily my description. I like to think of myself as a novelist, I like to think of what I do as more to do with the social landscape, more to do with describing people than with describing crime. There is a strange sense if you like in which I find the obsession with crime as a crossword puzzle slightly disgraceful because you are very aware sometimes that life is serious, that notions like physical assault very often happen. People ought not to think about it as if it were some sort of a game. (Interview)

In this sense then Phillips is actually engaged in critiquing a genre which has traditionally been notoriously conservative at best and exclusionary at worst.

It is clear looking at the history of the genre that black writers can not easily enter into such narratives because, according to the tenets of crime fiction their own identity places them firmly on the side of evil. For example, the earlier North American black crime fiction writer Chester Himes, writing in the late 1950s, invented two black detectives, Coffin Ed and Gravedigger Jones, brutal characters driven by a deep rage to beat and kill other blacks—a sort of psychotic reaction to systematized racial self-hatred. White readers were introduced to the moral underworld in which they operated which Himes made into an analogy for black life. In the time in which he was writing and being published, his work was popularly perceived as an accurate representation of black life, which only fuelled racist expectations and thought prevalent at the time. In his work Himes created characters who seemingly without much sense of authorial irony conformed to and confirmed such racial expectation. In a sense, Himes seemed engaged in publicly taking revenge on his blackness, reworking an internal conflict about himself into an urban fantasy and the nature of this psychological outline was credible within the racist confines of a particular moral view of the world then. His novels document the everyday struggles of the black underclass in a part of New York City that had become indelibly associated with blackness in the American popular imagination. Himes records the prostitution, numbers games, small time cons, and drug dealing that existed as strategies of survival in this hellish environment. Phillips says that when he began writing he "took Chester Himes as a dreadful object lesson" (Interview). Chester Himes's vision of the black community was a world typically peopled by violent brutal black males, freakish black hermaphrodites, and garish black prostitutes amongst other black caricatures. With this sort of writing as the only tradition of black crime fiction that Phillips had access to, the project of addressing the imbalance between the black self as a manifestation of evil and of the white person as hero becomes of utmost urgency as he attempts to be admitted to the crime writing genre and to introduce black characters who in turn are the "heroes," returning the world at the narrative's end to its status quo but allowing acceptable and honest treatment of its black characters.

It is perhaps indicative of a certain consensus about what has traditionally been commercially viable in black crime writing that more recently several writers have followed Himes's descent into the moral underground, from U.S. narratives about gangster life on the street by Iceberg Slim to the drug dealing chic of the so-called Yardie novels by Victor Headley.

By contrast, Phillips has said that he wanted to locate his stories and moral choices in a multiracial world but also in the type of narrative framework in which the nature of crime is ambiguous which depends rather more on an understanding of social and moral worlds and social and moral hierarchies. The problems, obviously, are that social and moral hierarchies have traditionally been dictated by white power so that any statement about morality is contrived through the perspective of white power and a white definition of what it means to be criminal.

Certainly, the colonized Other was constituted within the regimes of representation of such a metropolitan centre. They were placed in their otherness, in their marginality, by the nature of the "English eye," the all-encompassing "English eye." The "English eye" sees everything else but is not so good at recognising that it is itself actually looking at something. It becomes coterminous with sight itself. It is of course, a structured representation nevertheless and it is a cultural representation which is always binary. That is to say, it is strongly centred; knowing where it is, what it is, it places everything else. And the thing which is wonderful about English identity is that it didn't only place the colonised Other it placed everybody else. (Hall, *Culture* 20)

What Stuart Hall outlines here as the self-confidence of the position of Englishness was arrived at over a long period of time and depends upon having a fairly fixed understanding of Englishness which sets itself at the center and around which the satellites of the marginalized identities revolve. Thus the establishment of this concept of an English identity is deep-rooted and more than a little difficult to shift or write against. The problem with this "all-encompassing English eye" is that, as Hall points out, it is so strongly centered that it deals in binaries or either/or positions. Phillips's work represents a challenge to this established order because his work refutes such binary, "either/or" positionings and looks rather at the politics at play in structures of power at work in contemporary society.

Traditional crime writing (and there are still some writers that think like this today, P. D. James notably) has stated that moral choices are most interesting amongst middle-class people because people in the inner city and people who are socially confined by poverty have fewer choices. Mike Phillips strongly rejects this idea. His rejection is the real social value of his work in terms of teaching and learning because it sets a multicultured agenda and it allows a theoretical discussion of the sort of shared assumptions that crime fiction has traditionally relied upon. The study of a particular writer in a racially defined context means that theoretical discussions of issues focussing on the wider cultural and social impact of the genre arise. Readers are forced to question their own assumptions.

The result is that readers who identify with our heroes have their universe turned upside down. In our worlds we are the goodies, and the real threat of the mean streets is the paranoia of the white world about our presence. Around us are conditions which, for our families and friends, have often squeezed shut the avenues to economic survival, except for petty crime. The real crimes are to do with cruelty, with physical and social confinement, with racial oppression and hatred. (Interview)

Crime writing is an extremely popular genre and speaks to a wide and varied audience. As such, it is an important vehicle for discussions of the nature outlined above. By challenging his white readers with reversal of stereotype, Phillips's work opens up debates around race and ethnicity which are then made available to a cross section of the crime fiction reading populace. Phillips's writing highlights the ambiguous nature of morality. His writings show that white morality which has traditionally been used as a yardstick with which to judge black morality is redundant and moreover a suspect position in itself. Part of Phillips's agenda is to expose the ambiguous nature of the morality with which he is faced. He is interested in confronting stock images and representations. In this sense he is engaged in rewriting black experience through the vehicle of crime fiction. He is reclaiming it as part of a wider black critical agenda; he is keen to create stories which deal with blackness honestly and within a less narrowly (white) constructed moral framework and perspective.

Crime as a disruption of social and moral sensibilities has traditionally made claims about the nature of moral authority and has also recreated the protagonist and the characters as moral enforcers—people who reinforce that consensus and demonstrate how it works. Much contemporary crime fiction, then, is interested in recreating the protagonist and the characters as a sort of stronghold of the moral majority; for example, Morse and Dalgliesh are moral guides. It is very difficult to conceive, however, of an equivalent black guide. It seems the guides have to be patriarchal, white, and advanced in years!

The crime fiction tradition also provides a model for certain ways of talking about the nation—the way that John Major would have England described, for example—"warm beer and cricket on the green and solid middle-class community types." Crime fiction traditionally encapsulates the outline of an imaginary paradise of unchallenged white nationalism where "everyone knew their place." There is an unspoken reference in such understandings which evoke a time when crime was isolated in slum areas, boundaries (racial, gendered, and sexual, for example) were not traversed and people who crossed such social barriers were dealt with accordingly, and social order was therefore secure. This points up the nastier side of the nostalgic elements of crime fiction— England is evoked as an island of traditional order threatened by alien criminality which might be gender, class, or racially based.

Reading the work of black crime writers like Phillips, it becomes clear how the gap between black and white perceptions of crime and punishment has been established and reinforced. For them, this gap is a manifestation of the ambiguity of the racialized context in which they live. The idea of the detective as double sided or living two lives as a result of this ambiguous racialized context is usefully thought of in terms of the Du Boisian model of double consciousness.

It is a peculiar sensation, this double-consciousness, this sense of always looking at one's self through the eyes of others, of measuring one's soul by the tape of a world that looks on in amused contempt and pity. One ever feels his twoness—an American, a Negro; two souls, two thoughts, two unreconciled strivings; two warring ideals in one dark body. (DuBois 2)

This term refers to the black experience of being a member of a racist society which excludes or marginalizes black people. The overwhelming psychic perception is that of being an outsider in that society but nevertheless living in it. There is something in the nature of this idea of the outsider looking in which makes the black detective peculiarly suited to questioning the world, particularly the white world; the detective is critical of the world and the sphere of everyday life.

Although a crime writer, Phillips is additionally keen to investigate this ambiguity—he is interested in the social landscape and how people are driven to crime. His writing often demonstrates a sympathy with how people live or more often struggle to live and he builds into his work his own experience of institutional harassment, authoritarian cruelty, repression by the class system, and the distortion of law and order as the socio-economic backdrop to his fiction. In *An Image to Die For,* Phillips locates part of the action on a working-class London housing estate where the underclass are the inheritors in economic terms of the Thatcher and Major years. A murder occurs and Sam Dean is pulled into the mystery. The other part of the narrative is set in the world of media/TV executives who want to exploit the tragedy of the initial murder to make an interesting documentary about a possible miscarriage of justice. The Sam Dean novels, however, resist the famous Thatcher declaration of "There is no such thing as society." They insist rather on a nurturing and supportive community of black people. This positive black network or society adds to Phillips's agenda of transgressing the acknowledged framework of racial identity and allows him to deal with the mystery of self, of being black in a dominant white world which demands the critical engagement or involvement of both white and black readers who will read either questioningly, challengingly, or affirmatively according to their own identity positioning.

In order to represent black experience faithfully, Phillips has to deal with the sorts of prejudice which daily touch the lives of black people and of which the average (white) crime readers are mostly unaware. Phillips is keen to highlight the racialized context of his work and in a subtle manner he manages the lesson very well; there are criticisms in the text of the way white people have an unconscious perspective about black people which they would not perhaps consider racist but which nevertheless holds the black subject within the all powerful white gaze. For example, in *An Image to Die For,* Phillips writes,

The statements about Helen's visitors had come from whites, and white people were notoriously unobservant about physical differences between black people. Hypnotised by skin colour, the average English person often failed to pick out the most dramatic differences of height, weight and shape. Not surprising in the normal run of things. (42)

In *Point of Darkness* he mentions the sort of racial stereotyping which black people have been subjected to and which is still so prevalent and pernicious today:

[T]he irony was I thought, that white people's notions about African America were bounded by images of jazz, blues, and rap music; tap dancing; riots and heavyweight boxing; street violence, guns and poverty. (6)

This sort of white expectation holds the black subject in a limiting racial stereotype and reduces the black individual to other. These extracts are typical of Phillips's agenda. Within the framework of the crime narrative Phillips is offering the black voice and the black perspective which requires that the reader reflect on the status of racial identity. He also writes about the more overt, recognizable forms of racism which people again encounter on a daily basis. For example, when Mary, the young mixed race woman he has been searching for in *Point of Darkness,* tells Sam Dean about an encounter with white cousins:

I grew up outside of everything. We didn't belong anywhere. Nobody wanted me. What do they call us? Half breed. Half-caste. I had some cousins I went to stay with once. They took me to the beach and then left me there while they went off to play with some other kids. All day I was sitting there. They never even spoke to me. I couldn't tell my Dad even. He thought they were being nice to me. When I came back he asked if I had a nice time. (190)

In this example, Phillips demonstrates the loneliness of a little girl who is effectively rejected by members of her own family by dint of her mixed racial origin. The episode highlights an example of racial prejudice which is experienced on a frequent basis by black people everywhere.

If traditional crime writing constructs for itself a time where everyone knew their place, and not least a black character, then Phillips is keen to re-map or re-envision that sense of place. In *Point of Darkness,* he does it in New York where his main character Sam Dean looks for a good friend's lost daughter amongst a diasporic community made up principally of Hispanic and Caribbean peoples. Such a character is a threat to the old order of things precisely because he is able to negotiate both white and black territory successfully because of his twoness. To a certain extent, this ambiguous racial position mirrors some of the tensions Phillips himself encountered, as he says of himself,

When ever I read any crime fiction I would put myself in it and I would be the criminal and I would be a very bad kind of criminal because here I am brought up a black kid in Islington, gone to university got a yard long arm full of degrees, done a lot of jobs. There was no place in the imaginative scheme of things for me. (7)

The character of Sam Dean is unusual in that he, as a black man, confronts and challenges corruption in white authority which he encounters while unravelling the mystery of the disappearance of the young woman.

Crucially his blackness is always foregrounded in Phillips's writing; it is by dint of his black identity that he is able to negotiate the tough diasporic nature of New York and the impoverished black and white underclass of the London housing estate in *An Image to Die For.* Dean's capability of traversing black and white terrain and language as an indication of this comparatively easy social mobility is an important signifier in this text—the different layers of language highlight and reflect his ability to negotiate place and a wide range of social space. His black characters speak in dialect to each other which is faithfully recorded for the reader for it is also part of his agenda to demonstrate how English has been/is being reshaped by the immigrant experience. Kobena Mercer writes,

Across a whole range of cultural forms there is a "syncretic" dynamic which critically appropriates elements from the master—codes of the dominant cultures and "creolises" them, disarticulating given signs and re-articulating their symbolic meaning. The subversive force of this hybridising tendency is most apparent at the level of language itself where creole, patois and black English decentre, destabilise and carnivalise the linguistic domination of "English"—the nation-language of master-discourse—through strategic inflections, re-accentuations and other performative moves in semantic, syntactic and lexical codes. (57)

This extract serves to reinforce what Phillips's work is interested in doing. In particular, the attention to preserving the authentic dialect by reinscribing it phonetically is a specific instance of the reclaiming and moreover rewriting of traditional English.

Dean talks about the expeditiousness of adopting a voice which makes him sound like "someone who'd known Robert Morley" which generally shocked white Americans "when they realised that the black person in front of them was speaking with a real English accent" (*Point* 69). In the opening of *Point of Darkness,* he is speaking French to a Haitian taxi driver in New York, a city constituted of many different diasporic identities as he explains,

Past White Plains Road Caribbean English suddenly gave way to Caribbean Spanish, then after the Montefiore Hospital and down past the Bronx Museum I was in a street so Irish it could have been Kilburn, every detail precisely similar. (24)

There is a touch of irony in the reference to Kilburn, for it is one of the areas in London (not Ireland) which has a very large Irish population.

This reflects playfully on the status of white diasporic peoples in a larger dominant culture.

New York is a useful location for it is racially varied enough to cater for the wide range of racial mix which Phillips takes as his story's background. Throughout this particular text he negotiates with all manner of peoples in his search for his friend's daughter—rich white people, aspiring young black middle class, and so on. As such, this text constitutes a challenge to the established social order normally reproduced in classic crime fiction.

Phillips uses this racial landscape to comment upon the existence of a network of black people who enable Sam Dean to trace the errant Mary—the young mixed-race woman he is searching for. Phillips is very keen to locate his narrative in a black environment where the usually white characters are exchanged for black characters—there is a whole network and community of people who, were they to appear in classic detective fiction, would, as Phillips has said, be the villains. Here they figure as lawyers, UN ambassadors, journalists, photographers, and researchers, to outline but a few of the characters he constructs; he is foregrounding the black professional or achievers.

Phillips is keen to preserve a sense of cultural heritage and pride for these characters—he often has them discuss notions of home meaning the Caribbean island where the family originally hails from (in Phillips's own case Guyana) in an extremely nostalgic and affectionate manner. As has been, stated his characters fall into dialect when talking amongst themselves, their friends, and their family and there is accordingly an insistence all the way through the text on articulating what home means.

According to Paul Gilroy (a black British cultural theorist) implicit within the identity of the diasporic individual is the suspension between "where you're from" (for example, Jamaica or more metaphorically, an imaginary Black Africa) and "where you're at [Britain]" (383).

In other words what the diasporic position opens up is the possibility of developing a post-imperial British identity-one based explicitly on an acknowledgement and "vindication" of the "coming home" of the Colonised Other . . . The diasporic project problematizes "Britishness" from within, from the experience of the marginalised. (Stretton and Ang 283-85)

In *Point of Darkness,* there is an important scene where Dean articulates what his racialized, diasporic identity means to him. He says,

[W]hen we were kids back home none of us ever imagined what would happen to us, where we would be now and how it would turn out. When I left home I was ten, eleven a baby, it was going to the moon. When you got on the boat to go to England or wherever none of us knew what would happen whether we would ever come back. When you left it was like dying, everything familiar disappearing in one go, just like that. Everything you were going to see from then on was cold and dark and strange. The dark side of the moon. And most of our lives we've been walking through the dark putting one foot in front of the other.

Maybe that's not what it's really like but that's how it feels, and nobody but us knows what that means . . . To me it's the foundation of my life. I don't understand it, because I'm not that kid anymore and I'll probably never go there again, but it's what I am. *I owe this.* (48)

In this semi-autobiographical extract (he actually did come to Britain at this age) Phillips records an important aspect of immigrant experience for the reader, the careful attention to Dean's racial identity allows for personal anecdote about the young boy's lonely uprooting and its aftermath. It is also important because it is a good example of Phillips's personal agenda of writing about the black experience and bringing this experience to the cultural mainstream in a popular medium. In this manner crime fiction has an important subtext for writers like Phillips who have embraced the genre as a vehicle for foregrounding racial issues.

"Strange thing," I said. "All of us or our parents were born down there, and we live somewhere else." We can travel all over and feel at ease in a lot of places— but anyway, it's not impossible. We're not confined to one country. Sometimes I feel privileged compared to most people, like they're mentally stuck in one place and can't share other people's lives." "That's miserable," Bonny said sullenly . . . "I know that my parents come from somewhere else but this is where I live. I don't want to drift backwards and forwards. That's a punishment man. The Flying Dutchman."

"Wandering the earth for eternity. You crazy?" (*Point* 93)

Interestingly Phillips uses the metaphor of the Flying Dutchman in *Point of Darkness* and in the later text, *An Image to Die For.* The figure of the mythological character is apposite for it outlines the dilemma of the diasporic individual, who on the one hand (in Sam Dean's more optimistic moments) embodies a sort of rootless existential freedom but on the other (in his more gloomy moments) struggles with the vagaries of unbelonging, with a lonely feeling of being outside looking in.

It struck me then that I have been silent for longer than I realised and I struggled to focus on what she'd been saying. We'd both lived in the margins. In her case it was a stronger, more immediate experience, but I also knew how it felt to move in and out of groups whose background or whose instincts I didn't share. Sometimes the sheer mobility we owned struck me as a kind of freedom. Sometimes it felt like the restless and perpetual movement dictated by the curse they laid on the Flying Dutchman. Sometimes you could feel an irresistible tide washing you towards the nearest fixed point—religion, political crazes, prophets of doom—all these shone like beacons home. Every immigrant I knew of struggled in the eddies of this dilemma. How to harness the winds of fate. Where to belong. (*Image* 77)

This extract reminds us of Phillips's intention of reworking the crime fiction mode to include an examination of the diasporic experience. In addition to highlighting racism, the lived experience of black people generally, and racial stereotyping, Phillips is drawing attention to the changing nature of Britishness. In *Point of Darkness* he satirizes a British film which is heavy on stereotype:

I'll turn the TV on and there'll be the latest movie from Britain and they'll all be dressed in flowered hats and lifting tea cups, and all over the world they'll be looking at it and thinking that's what it means to be British, and it will all be the same bloody lies. (283)

Although this is a playful dig at the entrenched idea of Britishness the multicultural agenda which Phillips wants to draw attention to is his real concern. Britishness has been largely reshaped by the large influx of Afro-Carribean peoples in the 1950s and Asian peoples from the 1970s onwards. Again, until comparatively recently British crime fiction simply did not take this on board. What Phillips is insistent upon, it seems, is pointing up racial differences via crime fiction and examining the value in that. He places his narrative firmly in the multicultural world with all the possibilities that that offers him. However there is no neat reversion to type. He does not always make the villain white in order to turn the tables—the real villain in *Point of Darkness* is the treacherous Claude—a Jamaican. In order to enter into the good versus evil battle and final resolution of the text, Sam Dean has to be like him: an intellectual and physical equal.

From the first time I met Claude I'd taken it for granted that he was one of us, a kid just like one of the kids from the village where I'd almost grown up, and which despite everything, lived on as a kind of idyll in my memory. (301)

The idea haunting me was that, in only slightly different circumstances, I might have been exactly the sort of man that Claude had turned out to be. I loved power and money too, and my morality was my own, guaranteed by my own peculiar instinct for what was right and wrong. Perhaps if my life had gone in a different direction I would have been a more ruthless and effective villain. (308)

These extracts show how Sam Dean has idealized the Jamaican character simply because of his origins, because he comes from the same sort of racial background as himself. Phillips has him fall into the racial trap of expectation and stereotyping which he has been cautioning the reader against. In his writing, therefore, there is an insistence upon the importance of reinscribing racial difference within the seemingly innocent project of a crime fiction novel. The black perspective that Phillips builds into the narrative with his protagonist Sam Dean and his insistence upon black experience and positive characterization challenges white moral certainties, but it means that he is continually obliged to have Dean reconstitute his own moral code within a culture where he has traditionally been a moral outlaw and by extension this is Phillips's own position too. His work takes the multiracial world as its location and presents the black characters as ordinary human beings with a full range of human sympathies, using the issue of crime as an instrument for exploring the immorality of racist oppression.

In conclusion, the Sam Dean character in Phillips's fiction is important in "writing black" to a traditionalist, white crime fiction because the boundaries of the detective's racialized personality are permeable and his position is deliberately racially transgressive. There is a proliferation of detectives (of which Mike Phillips's Sam Dean marks the beginning of black British examples) who are adding to the voices who question traditional fixed notions of identity within late twentieth-century texts. The reader maps the shifting relationship between self and the social in a new cultural context where the project of making sense of the contradictions of the modern world is often the detective's central task. This is why writers like Mike Phillips in their refusal to tolerate the status quo are so crucial in undermining and confronting those stereotypes. The crime fiction genre allows him to draw out a lot of arguments about race, to start talking about how that multiracial world works or can work, and what problems there are with it. Such texts, as Hall notes, are a reclaiming of blackness.

. . . resources of resistance and identity with which to confront the fragmented and pathological ways in which that experience has been reconstructed within the dominant regimes . . . of the West . . . Cultural identities come from somewhere, have histories. But like everything which is historical, they undergo constant transformation . . . Far from being grounded in mere "recovery" of the past, which is waiting to be found, and which when found will secure our sense of ourselves into eternity, identities are the names we give to the different ways we are positioned by, and position ourselves within, the narratives of the past. The ways in which black people, black experiences, were positioned and subjected in the dominant regimes of representation were the effects of a critical exercise of cultural power and normalisation . . . They had the power to make us see and experience *ourselves* as "Other." (*Colonial* 394)

Phillips's work is an important response to those crime fiction texts which have previously marginalized the black voice. His work, because it breaks the mold, because it is an important contestation of traditional crime fiction, is in fact a will to power. Phillips embraces a range of racial diversity in his characterizations in order to fully explore those issues which have long been glossed over by the more traditional strand of crime writing. As he says, "I would say I think it is the job of all of us to deal with the multiracial world in which we find ourselves" (Interview).

Note

1. Mike Phillips interview by Claire Wells, Dec. 1995.

Works Cited

Du Bois, W. E. B. *The Souls of Black Folks.* New York: Dover, 1994.
Hall, Stuart. "Cultural Identity and Diaspora." *Colonial Discourse and Postcolonial Theory.* Cambridge: Harvester Wheatsheaf, 1994.
——· "The Local and the Global: Globalisation and Ethnicity." *Culture, Globalisation and the World System.* Ed. Anthony D. King. London: Macmillan, 1991.
——· "Minimal Selves." *The Real Me—Postmodernism and the Question of Identity.* London: Institute of Contemporary Arts, 1987.
——· "New Ethnicities." *Stuart Hall—Critical Dialogues in Cultural Studies.* London: Routledge, 1996.
Mercer, Kobena. "Diaspora Culture and the Dialogic Imagination." *Blackframes: Critical Perspectives on Black Independent Cinema.* Ed. M. Cham and C. Watkins. London, 1988.
Phillips, Mike. *An Image to Die For.* London: Harper Collins, 1995.

——. *Point of Darkness.* London: Penguin, 1995.

Stretton, Jon, and Ien Ang. "On the Impossibility of a Global Cultural Studies."
    Stuart Hall—Critical Dialogues in Cultural Studies. London: Routledge,
    1996.

Symons, Julian. *Bloody Murder.* London: Pan, 1992.

BLACK *NOIR:*
RACE AND URBAN SPACE
IN WALTER MOSLEY'S DETECTIVE FICTION

Liam Kennedy

The streets were dark with something more than night. (Raymond Chandler)[1]

Why is hard-boiled detective fiction a white genre? With this question I do not mean to suggest that only white writers have worked in the genre, but rather that hard-boiled fiction's most distinctive narrative codes, conventions, and characterizations have traditionally been structured around the consciousness of a white subject. Drawing attention to "whiteness" in narrative representation has become a common interest in literary, film, and cultural studies in recent years; Richard Dyer, bell hooks, Toni Morrison, and Eric Lott are only a few of the influential critics who have argued the need to think critically about the concept.[2] Crucial to this critical project is the insistence that whiteness neither exists outside of culture nor transcends race but functions as the invisible norm of dominant cultural values and assumptions while concealing its dependency upon "racial" others. In her *Playing in the Dark: Whiteness and the Literary Imagination* Toni Morrison wonders "whether the major and championed characteristics of our national literature—individualism, masculinity, social engagement versus historical isolation; acute and ambiguous moral problematics; the thematics of innocence coupled with an obsession with figurations of death and hell—are not in fact responses to a dark, abiding, signing Africanist presence" (17). In this article I want to comment on some general features of whiteness in hard-boiled detective fiction to argue that the genre has traditionally responded to "a dark . . . Africanist presence" by adopting a parasitic relationship to blackness. These comments will act as a preliminary to my more detailed study of the distinctively black *noir* which characterizes the fiction of the African American writer Walter Mosley.

Reprinted with permission from *The Contemporary American Crime Novel,* editor P. Messent, published by Pluto Press.

Hard-boiled Detective Fiction and Race

The racialized constitution of hard-boiled fiction owes a great deal to the historical period of its emergence and its generic links with western and adventure genres in the United States. The literary origins of hard-boiled fiction are diverse, and any extensive study of them would have to plot the emergence and reinvention of key elements across nineteenth-century popular literatures. One significant line of development is centered on the myth of democratic heroism, a structural and ideological feature of the frontier romance which is redeployed in later nineteenth-century adventure stories of crime and detection—most notably in the writings of Alan Pinkerton and the red-blooded dime novels of the last quarter of the century—and reemerges in the pulp fiction of the early twentieth century. Richard Slotkin has argued that the dime novels of the late nineteenth century constructed a formula fiction which fused the figures of the outlaw and the detective to produce heroic detectives who defend "the progressive social order, but do so *in the style* of the outlaw, always criticising the costs of progress" (154). In the post-frontier, rapidly modernizing America of the early twentieth century, this hybrid figure takes on a more complex ideological cast in the role of the hard-boiled detective who is "both an agent of law and an outlaw who acts outside the structures of legal authority for the sake of personal definition of justice" and who has no clear class position (219). This hard-boiled hero is invariably represented as a bastard offspring of modernity and democratic individualism. He is at once a liminal, rootless figure—modernist thematics of alienation, homelessness, and melancholia recur in the writings—and a democratic antihero, a classless and self-reliant man able to traverse disparate areas of American society. This antihero reflected many of the social tensions of the 1920s, serving as a populist critic of capitalist powers but also voicing prejudices and fears about racial "others" at a time of heightened nativism. *Black Mask* magazine, which was central to the development of hard-boiled detective fiction as a discreet genre in the 1920s, published a Ku Klux Klan Number in 1923, and throughout the decade published stories in which the presence of African Americans (and selected immigrant groups) connotes pathological violence, sexual license, lack of civilization, and absence of morality (Bailey 41-43).

The racialization of hard-boiled detective fiction is not confined to stereotyping, though, for the presence of race often has a more subtle function in defining the liminal whiteness of the detective hero. It is often noted that as a proto-modernist form hard-boiled fiction renders universal principles of truth and justice subjective and presages moral inquiry as the detective's singular response to the atomized urban scenes of modernity. It is less often noted that the formulation of moral space in hard-boiled fiction privileges a white subject as autonomous agent while devaluing black subjectivity as extrinsic to rights assertion and agency. This devaluation often takes the form of stereotyping, with race ordering conceptions of self and other and categorically rationalizing the "natural" characteristics of black people. But this devaluation is also important as a sign of the white detective's dependency upon racial others. Race functions as a source of psychological and social fantasy for many hard-boiled writers, with blackness often signifying an otherness within the white subject which requires control and mastery. Sin, lack of reason, and absence of discipline not only confront the white detective but are internalized using race as a topos around which images and discourses are organized. In its most simplified form this appears as a juxtaposition of primitive urge and civilizing consciousness, but racial signs are everywhere present. Dashiell Hammett and Raymond Chandler, the writers most frequently identified with the classic mode of urban hard-boiled, provide famous examples. In Hammett's *The Maltese Falcon* Sam Spade is described as a "blond Satan" to indicate an inner darkness due to his associations with criminality. In Chandler's *The Big Sleep* Philip Marlowe is represented as a "knight" who has fallen from purity and become less than white. In both instances the white detective introjects or internalizes the "difference" of the racial other.[3]

What I am suggesting here is that the white detective appropriates signs of blackness to signify his liminal isolation and difference. This appropriation is particularly striking in the urban imaginary of what is variously termed the dark street or mean streets down which the lone detective walks. Chandler's dark street is a romantic image, a fantasy sphere in which ideas of justice, morality, and heroism can be tested out while the psychological focus remains securely on the liminal white subject. The city streets are the site of degeneracy, disorder, lawlessness, and moral corruption, a universalized and fantastical urbanism which elides questions of racial identity. This elision facilitates the white subject's colonization of social spaces traditionally associated with blackness in American culture and these degenerate and anarchic spaces expressively heighten the white detective's transgressions, providing voyeuristic pleasures for white readers. In *The Dain Curse* Hammett's Continental Op follows his investigations to "a Negro neighborhood, which made the getting of reasonably accurate information twice as unlikely as it always was," and Hammett represents this neighborhood as a darktown of easy criminality and degraded passions (152-60). Chandler's *Farewell, My Lovely* opens with Philip Marlowe's observation "It was one of the mixed blocks over on Central Avenue, the blocks that are not yet all Negro." This observation prefaces Marlowe and Moose Malloy's entry into a black club where Moose assaults the bouncer and kills the club manager (7-18). In both instances the white detective transgresses race boundaries into what is depicted as alien and degraded urban spaces, to discover an excessive (passionate, violent) difference in blackness. These transgressions stimulate a white imaginary, for these spaces, though geographically specific, are symbolic repositories of white fears and fantasies.

In this article I am particularly concerned with narrative representation of urban space, for space is a modality through which relations of racial domination and subordination are naturalized. In racialized urban spaces we find metaphorical and material manifestations of the power structures which regulate and constrain the formations of racial identity and knowledge. Terms such as "urban jungle," "ghetto," "inner city," and "underclass" have distinctive racial connotations and in public discourse they function to name and naturalize spheres of racial poverty and immiseration. Universal norms of justice and rights are qualified and delimited in these terms, setting boundaries on recognition of those who are and are not active participants of the civic polis. As David Goldberg notes: "Citizens and strangers are controlled through the spatial confines of divided place. These geometries—the spatial categories through and in which the lived world is largely mapped, experienced, and disciplined—impose a set of interiorities and exteriorities" (186). Spatial categories have a significant presence in hard-boiled fiction where relations between inside and outside, and between depth and surface, interact with the primary dialectic of truth and deception. In classic hard-boiled writings these relations are structured to privilege the perspective of the white subject as a private eye in public space. In the hard-boiled writings of Walter Mosley, as we shall see, these relations undergo connotative defamiliarization and inversion as he plots the urban scene around the perspective of a black subject.

Easy Rawlins, Race, and Urban Space

To understand the significance of the relationship between race and urban space in Mosley's fiction, we need to consider the geographical and historical setting of his texts. The four hard-boiled detective novels he has written to date are set in the Watts area of Los Angeles in the postwar years, and Mosley has very self-consciously appropriated hard-boiled conventions in order to write a *noir* history of black life in the city. Los Angeles is a deeply mythologized city and its mythologizers include detective writers and more broadly those writers and filmmakers associated with *noir*. The category is often thought of in filmic terms but it has broader cultural resonances, for as Mike Davis has argued *noir* is a complex corpus of literary and cinematic production, generally focused on unmasking Los Angeles as a "bright, guilty place." By depicting Los Angeles as "the nightmare at the terminus of American history," Davis observes, *noir* dystopianization of the city has developed as a powerful antimyth countering "the accumulated ideological capital of the region's boosters" (20). Black writers and filmmakers have not figured large in the construction and maintenance of this antimyth, but there are dystopian representations of the city in black culture.

In the early twentieth century, Los Angeles appealed to many African Americans as a locus of opportunity, especially during the boom years of wartime industry, and a place of escape from Jim Crow. The idea of opportunity is apparent in W. E. B. DuBois's confident statement, made in 1913: "LA is wonderful. Nowhere in the United States is the Negro so well and beautifully housed. . . . Out here in the matchless Southern California there would seem to be no limit to your opportunities, your possibilities" (17). But for many African Americans Los Angeles did not prove to be the melting pot under the sun, as opportunities and possibilities were eclipsed by a climate of unremitting deprivation and the luxury of space (highlighted by DuBois) became an experience of spatial confinement and surveillance. The African American writer Chester Himes worked in segregated defense plants in Los Angeles during the Second World War and drew on this experience in writing his first novel *If He Hollers Let Him Go*. The novel details the psychological deterioration of Bob Jones, a skilled shipyard worker, under pressures of white racism. Bob Jones has a utopian wish:

I didn't want to be the biggest Negro who ever lived. . . . Because deep inside of me, where the white folks couldn't see, it didn't mean a thing. If you couldn't swing down Hollywood Boulevard and know that you belonged; if you couldn't make a polite pass at Lana Turner at Ciro's without having the gendarmes beat the black off you for getting out of your place, . . . being a great big "Mister" Nigger didn't mean a thing. . . . I'd settle for a leaderman job at Atlas Shipyard—if I could be a man, defined by Webster as a male human being. That's all I'd ever wanted—just to be accepted as a man—without ambition, without distinction, either of race, creed, or colour; just a simple Joe walking down an American street. (153)

This utopian wish is articulated in spatial terms: what he yearns for is the freedom to move through urban spaces with a sense of belonging and without a fear of violent attack. The idea of "getting out of your place" takes on a double meaning, signifying both geographic location and social prohibition. These meanings converge in the spatial metaphor of place. Himes draws attention to relations between "knowing one's (racial) place" in the city and the social structures of racial space (Goldberg 205). These relations inform the tensions and ironies of his narrative; the desire to be just a simple Joe walking down an American street is a desire for an invisibility and ordinariness which is associated with white subjects. Knowing one's place is not only a geographic imperative but a racial(ized) one, and ultimately an issue of survival for the black subject in a racist society.

The double meanings of knowing one's place are everywhere evident in Walter Mosley's black *noir*. The protagonist of his four detective novels is Easy Rawlins, a migrant from Houston, Texas, who arrives in Los Angeles shortly after the Second World War in which he served in the United States army. The novels—*Devil in a Blue Dress, A Red Death, White Butterfly,* and *Black Betty*—follow Easy's life in Los Angeles from 1948 to 1961, and Mosley plans several more novels in the series. The development of the series has a strong historical impetus which Mosley terms "a migration . . . through time" (Silet 11). He begins in 1948 because it was a period of absolute possibility for the Southern blacks who moved to Los Angeles in great number: "they could go get a good job and buy property and live with some measure of equality. So that was the beginning of a period of transition and hope that didn't quite work out. I want to provide a map through the years of how it didn't" (Maidment 48). In mapping this failure of promise Mosley blends history and memory to produce a critical perspective on the development of race relations in Los Angeles. His novels look both backwards and forwards from the present tense of narrative time, situating Easy Rawlins in a continuum of black diaspora experiences while distinguishing the particular locale and psychological complexity of his protagonist. In Mosley's words, "I wanted to talk about [Easy] as this incredible, complex psyche who comes out of the Deep South into LA with all of these hopes and aspirations and what he can and cannot do for both external and internal reasons" (Silet 12). The external and internal registers of possibility and prohibition are socially formed (if not always consciously recognized) and in Mosley's novels it is the shifting relations between and within these registers which impels the psychological drama of Easy's investigations into the meanings of racial difference and identity in Los Angeles.

Although Easy takes on a range of jobs in the novels (gardener, aircraft mechanic, janitor) he finds himself most consistently, if often reluctantly, employed as a private investigator. As he reflects in *White*

Butterfly, "In my time I had done work for the numbers runners, church-goers, businessmen, and even the police. Somewhere along the line I had slipped into the role of a confidential agent who represented people when the law broke down" (17). As these comments suggest, Easy is within the tradition of the liminal detective hero who operates on the boundaries of the law, but his slippage into this role is notably facilitated by conventional perceptions of black agency and representation. Mosley has observed of his protagonist:

Easy knows how to pay attention to details. He can read the streets as well as a woodsman can read skat. He is educated in the ways of desperation and crime by a lifetime of poverty. Now when Easy gets around white people they may be afraid of him, but they never suspect that he has the smarts of some kind of agent trying to glean their secrets. Turn the coin over: when Easy comes into a bar or church in the Watts community everybody thinks they know by his color that no white man would trust him with a mission. Easy has become invisible by virtue of his skin. (Mariani 132-33)

Mosley makes ready use of the trope of invisibility in his novels to explore the meanings of racial difference and identity. In *Devil in a Blue Dress*, Easy reflects on his first experiences of working as a detective: "Nobody knew what I was up to and that made me sort of invisible; people thought that they saw me but what they really saw was an illusion of me, something that wasn't real" (135). The disparities between illusion and reality signified by the trope of invisibility are complexly figured throughout the novels to depict a social world in which racial perceptions are rarely stable and invariably infused with issues of power and control. Easy's manipulation of his identity affords him (and ironically parodies) the agent autonomy and freedom of movement traditionally associated with the white detective. Yet Easy's movements through Los Angeles are also constrained by white powers. While his role as a detective broadens possibilities for transgressing established racialized and spatial limits, race nonetheless molds the boundaries of social identity and mobility.

Devil in a Blue Dress

Devil in a Blue Dress, the novel I will concentrate on here, details Easy's first experience of working as a private investigator. Set in 1948, it introduces Easy at a point when he has been recently fired by his employer, Champion Aircraft, and is worried about defaulting on the mortgage for his small house in Watts. The investigative narrative is initiated when he is hired by a white gangster to search for a woman named Daphne Monet, a central figure in a local political conspiracy. Easy's search for Daphne takes him on a journey through diverse social spaces in Los Angeles and into conflict with racist police and corrupt politicians. With the help of Mouse, his violent childhood friend, Easy finds Daphne and the bad guys are either killed or outwitted. More compelling than the plot development is what psychologically underpins it: Easy's journey into a paranoid world of illusion, fear, and desire where secure referents of meaning and value begin to dissolve and race is revealed as the most disturbing site of mystery and transgression.

Devil in a Blue Dress opens with a scene of transgression as a white gangster, De Witt Albright, enters a black bar in Watts. His entry is observed by Easy:

I was surprised to see a white man walk into Joppy's bar. It's not just that he was white but he wore an off-white linen suit and shirt with a Panama straw hat and bone shoes over flashing white silk socks. His skin was smooth and pale with just a few freckles. One lick of strawberry-blond hair escaped the band of his hat. He stopped in the doorway, filling it with his large frame, and surveyed the room with pale eyes; not a color I'd seen in a man's eyes. When he looked at me I felt a thrill of fear, but that went away quickly because I was used to white people by 1948. (9)

Opening the narrative in this way Mosley immediately foregrounds the distinctly black point of view of his first person narrator and draws attention to whiteness as a category of identity. The passage is ethnographic in detail and the attention to whiteness is notably excessive, associating it with power. Easy is not only surprised due to the incongruity of the white man's presence in a black space, but he also feels fear in response to this excessive whiteness. This fear is founded on his experiences of racism and the hegemony of white power, and although his experiences in the Second World War have demythologized whiteness ("I killed enough blue-eyed young men to know that they were just as afraid to die as I was" [9]) he retains a residual sense of its "terrorizing" potential (bell hooks). By decoding the meanings of whiteness Mosley interrogates its privileged neutrality at the same time as he establishes the racial identity of his protagonist and his immediate culture. The opening of the novel is a suggestive inversion (and perhaps an intentional critical parody) of the opening of Chandler's *Farewell, My Lovely*. In both novels a white gangster enters a second-story black bar in Watts in search of a woman, a search then taken up by the detective. Whereas Chandler exoticizes blackness in his stereotyping of the bar's inhabitants and assumes the reader's interest in the white character's point of view, Mosley inflates whiteness as a cultural signifier and introduces a black perspective.

Where Chandler treats Watts as alien and exotic territory, Mosley represents it as a living community. In his detailed attention to the black social spaces Easy inhabits—the bars, clubs, churches, barber shops, pool halls, and whore houses—Mosley treats them as the loci of black culture as a way of life, a normative system of behavior and expression, attitudes and values. He is not interested in romanticizing the poverty of Watts nor in exoticizing the violence which marks the lives of many of Easy's associates.[4] He represents the black ghetto as a discreet if immiserated community which offers some insulation from the white world and has its own distinctive history and patterns of life. Easy is a part of this culture and shares with many of its inhabitants a Southern background. His use of dialect, his choice of food, his tastes in music, and much more are influenced by this background. His sense of being a displaced Southerner also sharpens his self-consciousness about racial oppression in a Los Angeles environment. He describes his entry into an illegal nightclub:

When I opened the door I was slapped in the face by the force of Lips' alto horn. I had been hearing Lips and Willie and Flattop since I was a boy in Houston. All of them and John and half the people in that crowded room had migrated from Houston after the war, and some before that . . . being on the bottom didn't feel so bad if you could come to John's now and then and remember how it felt back home in Texas, dreaming about California. (34)

This bittersweet commentary registers the need for a sustaining cultural life for the migrant community of Southern African Americans while recognizing utopian delusion in the dream (articulated by Du Bois above) of opportunity and prosperity.

Easy's strong attachment to, and knowledge of, the culture of the migrant community in Watts distinguishes his role as a detective. He knows where and how to seek information in this culture: "I wanted to find out the whereabouts of Frank Green but it had to come up in normal conversation. Most barbers know all the important information in the community. That's why I was getting my hair cut" (138). Bars and pool rooms are often concealed from public gaze and entry is not open to all: "Ricardo's [Pool Room] was just a hole-in-the-wall with no windows and only one door. There was no name out front because either you knew where Ricardo's was or you didn't belong there at all" (129). It is not only this cultural knowledge which distinguishes Easy as a black detective but his sense of responsibility to a community. Mosley has stressed that this sense of responsibility sets his protagonist apart from the detective heroes of classic hard-boiled fiction:

... the earlier gumshoes who I like, they are White men of European descent who have no mother, no father, no sister, no brother, no property, no job. So they don't have anything that would make them responsible to the world. Easy isn't like that. Easy has a wife, or, at least an ex-wife, he has children, he has friends, he has property, he has things that make him have to do things in the world. ... I think the earlier fiction was necessary, but Easy answers moral questions by being implicated in the world, rather than being perfect. (Maidment 71)

Mosley embeds Easy in local networks of social and cultural relations which play an important part in determining his values and actions.

However, Easy is not only bound within the social and cultural relations peculiar to the black community, he is also subject to a larger and more oppressive system of relations organized by the dominant white world. Transgression, as I noted above, marks race relations in the novel, and Easy's role as a detective frequently takes him beyond the relative cultural security of Watts into white Los Angeles. Although he can play on white ignorance of his role he constantly feels vulnerable to racist perspectives: "It was fifteen blocks to John's speak and I had to keep telling myself to slow down. I knew that a patrol car would arrest any sprinting Negro they encountered" (83). His knowledge of racism and segregation in Los Angeles determines his cognitive map of the city as a racialized landscape of invisible boundaries and prohibitions. When he enters distinctly white social spaces, he is frequently perceived as a threatening presence. The opening scene of the novel is turned around when Easy visits Albright to accept his offer of money to search for Daphne Monet. Albright's residence is "a long drive from Watts" (13) in a white area of the city, and on arrival there Easy is confronted by a white porter who asks

"Who are you looking for?"
He was a little white man wearing a suit that was also a uniform.
"I'm looking for, um . . . ah . . . ," I stuttered. I forgot the name. I had to squint so that the room wouldn't start spinning.
It was a habit I developed in Texas when I was a boy. Sometimes, when a white man of authority would catch me off guard, I'd empty my head of everything so I was unable to say anything. "The less you know, the less trouble you find," they used to say. (21)

The confrontation emphasizes the sense of dislocation Easy experiences due to the interpellating gaze and questioning of the white man. His habit of stuttering and falling silent is learned through everyday experiences in a racist environment and internalized as a survival mechanism.

The association of knowledge with danger is acutely underlined by Easy's transgression into white space for he is—socially as well as geographically—out of place. He reflects: "That little white man had convinced me that I was in the wrong place. I was ready to go back home" (22). Time and again in the novel Mosley explores how discreet social spaces mediate his protagonist's understanding of relations between knowledge and power, morality and justice, in a world in which he is denied "rights."[5]

Easy's desire to go back home is recurrent in the novel, symbolizing a need for security, but to the degree that it announces a desire to escape the racist white world, it is impossible to fulfill. It is important to recognize that Easy is drawn into conflict with this world in part due to his aspirations. While he is skeptical of the African American dream of opportunity and prosperity in Los Angeles, he nonetheless has aspirations which are distinctly material and middle class. This is most clearly articulated in relation to property with his strong desire to own his own house: "I felt that I was just as good as any white man, but if I didn't even own my front door then people would look at me like just another poor beggar, with his hand outstretched" (16). (In later novels he buys several properties and moves to a black middle-class neighborhood.) Easy's house materializes the desire for ordinariness we found also in Chester Himes' protagonist in *If He Hollers Let Him Go*.[6] But this desire, both Himes and Mosley indicate, is also an implicit claim to normative citizenship which is powerfully circumscribed by white society. Easy recognizes that his desire for ownership creates dangerous new relationships: "[W]hen I got that mortgage I found that I needed more than just friendship. Mr. Albright wasn't a friend but he had what I needed" (28). Needing money, Easy's acceptance of Albright's proposition moves him more fully into the system of capitalist exchange and control—to the degree that he may be said to mortgage his black identity. This is clearly indicated when Albright refuses Easy's efforts to return his payment: "Too late for that Mr. Rawlins. You take my money and you belong to me. . . . We all owe out something, Easy. When you owe out then you're in debt and when you're in debt then you can't be your own man. That's capitalism" (108-09). Capitalism, in these terms, is a system of dependency, structured around debt and ownership, and a powerful force in the fashioning of social freedoms and subjugations. In racial terms Easy's debt implies a master-slave relationship: "Money bought everything . . . ," he reflects, "I got the idea, somehow, that if I got enough money then maybe I could buy my own life back" (127).

Easy is caught up in webs of racist social control and coercion from which he cannot easily extract himself. Mosley's depiction of this dilemma is subtly handled and reflects his intention to portray both external and internal factors which mediate the meanings of autonomy and self-sufficiency for a black subject. More particularly, he wants to explore what these may mean for a black *male* subject, for Easy's desire for self-sufficiency has distinctive gender as well as economic connotations. When he decides to accept Albright's money he reasons that he does so not only to pay his mortgage but also because "DeWitt Albright had me caught by my own pride. The more I was afraid of him, I was that much more certain to take the job he offered" (20). Easy is drawn into the complex relationship with Albright as much through a sense of male pride as through economic need. In Easy's responses to Albright and other white men, Mosley emphasizes the intersection of a masculine mystique with institutional racism and draws attention to "the racial dialectic of projection and internalisation through which white and black men have shaped their masks of masculinity."[7] This dialectic is at work in Easy's need for white recognition of his masculinity and demand for "respect" (73) from white men. Mosley's treatment of this dialectic further distinguishes his representation of Easy as a tough guy of the hard-boiled type. Easy's mask of masculinity barely conceals the deep divisions in his subjectivity.[8] In *Devil in a Blue Dress* the instability of his masculine identity is foregrounded in his psychological struggles to come to terms with the violence of his past; throughout the narrative he reflects upon violent experiences and in his dreams is haunted by them as scenes of trauma. His memories of his childhood friend Mouse—"He could put a knife in a man's stomach and ten minutes later sit down to a plate of spaghetti" (55)—and of action in the war frequently puncture the narrative to illustrate his ambivalence about violent assertions of masculinity. Easy's desire for upward mobility represents an effort to escape the horrors of the past but he remains inexorably caught in legacies of racism and violence which have traumatized black male subjectivity.

The divisions within Easy are mirrored in the instability of his narrative authority and the challenges posed to any secure position of truth or knowledge in the construction of identity. This narrative instability is most potently figured in Easy's search for Daphne Monet, the eponymous "devil in a blue dress." Daphne is an excessively enigmatic character whose identity is curiously unstable to Easy's eyes:

Her face was beautiful. More beautiful than the photograph. Wavy hair so light brown that you might have called it blond from a distance, and eyes that were either green or blue depending on how she held her head. Her cheekbones were high but her face was full enough that it didn't make her seem severe. (96)

Daphne's identity appears to shift and change under Easy's gaze—neither hair color, nor eye color, nor facial structure remain constant—and it is with some perturbation that he observes "Daphne was like the chameleon lizard. She changed for her man" (187). Mysterious, sexually attractive, and dangerous, Daphne is very much in the *noir* tradition of the dark woman or femme fatale, but the variable effect of her identity quite literally defamiliarizes the conventional racial encoding of this figure.[9] Daphne, as Easy (and the reader) discovers near the end of the narrative, is a figure of racial masquerade, she is a mulatto who passes as white; her other identity is that of Ruby Hanks, the half-sister of a black gangster. Easy, who experiences a strong sexual and emotional attraction to Daphne, is shocked at the discovery of her double identity: "I had only been in an earthquake once but the feeling was the same: The ground under me seemed to shift. I looked at her to see the truth. But it wasn't there. Her nose, cheeks, her skin color—they were white. Daphne was a white woman" (205). The shifting ground to which Easy refers underlines the arbitrariness of social indicators of racial difference and identity, particularly as these privilege the visible as the surest ground of evidence. There is considerable irony, of course, in Easy's shock at this revelation for he had begun to pride himself in his own form of masquerade: "people thought that they saw me but what they really saw was an illusion of me, something that wasn't real" (135). The figure of Daphne/Ruby Mosley gives a further twist to the meanings of the "interiorities and exteriorities" which structure racial knowledge and identity.

The relationship between Easy and Daphne has significant consequences for the dialectic of truth and deception in the novel. While the perspective of the black detective is privileged, he discovers the inadequacies of his own racial knowledge as well as that of the broader social texts. There is no hidden "truth" of racial being for Easy to discover or uncover, though there is much to be learned in his quest about the indeterminacy of race as a social epistemology and categorical sign of difference. Mosley questions the existence of an essence of racial difference as the secure locus of identity formation. Easy's friend Mouse expresses an essentialist position when he warns Easy

You learn stuff and you be thinkin' like white men be thinkin'. You be thinkin' that what's right fo' them is right fo' you. [Daphne] look like she white and you think like you white. But brother you don't know that you both poor niggers. And a nigger ain't never gonna be happy 'less he accept what he is. (209)

Easy has no answer to this statement but his desires and actions do not reflect the coherence of racial identification Mouse articulates. Mosley does not ascribe an essence to his black subjects, rather he represents them, and Easy in particular, as complexly constituted in both interracial and intraracial relations. He emphasizes his protagonist's urge to self-invention while detailing the powerful racist prohibitions on this process and the dialectics of power, fear, and desire which shape it internally.

Walter Mosley's Black Noir

Mosley has observed of Easy "he does make it here in America. But how he makes it is flawed and scarred" (Silet 12). This statement points up the author's efforts to represent and interrogate utopian and dystopian features of black experiences in Los Angeles. In doing so he defamiliarizes the conventionally white coordinates of *noir*'s counter-mythologizing. Mosley's black *noir* appropriates key elements of classic hard-boiled fiction—the tough guy persona, the femme fatale, the corrupt police and politicians, the quest for a hidden truth, the paranoid imaginary—yet is much more than a critical parody of earlier white writers. If, as Mike Davis, proposes, "L.A. understands its past . . . through a robust fiction called *noir*" then Mosley has used this conduit of historical memory to produce a critical history of race relations in the city and to illuminate the cultural history of people who have come to be pathologized as an "underclass" (15-97). His postwar Los Angeles is observed through cultural and ideological categories of the present time in which he writes. It is a culturally hybrid world, but not a multicultural melting pot, in which racial transgressions haunt individual and collective identities. In the 1990s, Davis argues, Los Angeles is characterized by a "paranoid spatiality which is produced by and reinforces social differences and prejudices" (221-63). Mosley's postwar Los Angeles already shows much evidence of this paranoid spatiality, and, in his revisionist *noir,* race dominates the fantasies, fears, and repressions which shadow the divisions of a virtually apartheid city. In this city's dark streets the black detective's search for freedom, truth, and justice is also an investigation into the meanings of racial difference and identity.

Notes

1. Raymond Chandler, Introduction, *The Smell of Fear* (London: Hamish Hamilton, 1973) 9.

2. See, for example, Richard Dyer, "White," *Screen*, 29 (Autumn 1988) 44-64; bell hooks, "Representations of Whiteness," *Black Looks: Race and Representation* (London: Turnaround, 1992) 165-78; Toni Morrison, *Playing in the Dark: Whiteness and the Literary Imagination* (New York: Random House,

1992); Eric Lott, "White Like Me: Racial Cross-Dressing and the Construction of American Whiteness," *Cultures of United States Imperialism,* ed. Amy Kaplan and Donald Pease (Durham: Duke University Press, 1993) 236-60.

3. For a stimulating analysis of (racial) introjection in "the construction of American whiteness," see Eric Lott, "White Like Me," *Cultures of United States Imperialism,* ed. Amy Kaplan and Donald Pease (Durham: Duke University Press, 1993) 236-60.

4. Mosley has observed "poverty is tattooed on black and brown skins. Ignorance and violence, sex and criminality are deeply etched in Hispanic and African hues. If you're not white it is hard to get out of the slums" (Walter Mosley, "The Black Dick") 132.

5. The issue of rights is made violently explicit when Easy is arrested by two white policemen: "I've got the right to know why you're taking me" [Easy]. "You got a right to fall down and break your face, nigger. You got a right to die" [policeman], . . . Then he hit me in the diaphragm" (75).

6. More than a sign of economic independence, Easy's house is an important site of psychic security. It is a deeply subjective space in the novel where Easy's propensity for self-reflection is often at its most intense. As such it follows a tradition in African American literature of representing the house as "inside space," a semi-autonomous realm of belonging and identity. See Charles Scruggs, *Sweet Home: Invisible Cities in the Afro-American Novel* (Baltimore: Johns Hopkins University Press, 1993).

7. Kobena Mercer and Isaac Julien, "Race, Sexual Politics and Black Masculinity: A Dossier," *Male Order: Unwrapping Masculinity,* ed. Rowena Chapman and Jonathan Rutherford (London: Lawrence and Wishart, 1988) 99.

8. In the hard-boiled genre, the male hero's subjectivity is often split or decentered as a position of narrative authority. See Frank Krutnik, *In A Lonely Street: Film Noir, Genre, Masculinity* (London: Routledge, 1991) 128-29.

9. See Mary Ann Doane, *Femmes Fatales: Feminism, Film Theory, Psychoanalysis* (London: Routledge, 1991).

Works Cited

Bailey, Frankie Y. *Out of the Woodpile: Black Characters in Crime and Detective Fiction.* Westport, CT: Greenwood Press, 1991.

Chandler, Raymond. *Farewell, My Lovely.* Harmondsworth: Penguin, 1949.

——. *The Smell of Fear.* London: Hamish Hamilton, 1973.

Davis, Mike. *City of Quartz: Excavating the Future in Los Angeles.* London: Verso, 1990.

DuBois, W. E. B. qtd. in Lynell George. *No Crystal Stair: African Americans in the City of Angels.* London: Verso, 1991.

Goldberg, David Theo. *Racist Culture: Philosophy and the Politics of Meaning* Oxford: Blackwell, 1993.

Hammett, Dashiell. *Dashiell Hammett: Five Complete Novels*. New York: Avenel, 1980.

Himes, Chester. *If He Hollers Let Him Go*. London: Pluto, 1986.

hooks, bell. *Black Looks: Race and Representation*. London: Turnaround, 1992.

Maidment, Richard, ed. *American Conversations*. London: Hodder and Stoughton, 1995.

Mosley, Walter. "The Black Dick." *Critical Fictions: The Politics of Imaginative Writing*. Ed. Philomena Mariani. Seattle: Bay Press, 1991.

——. *Devil in a Blue Dress*. London: Pan, 1992.

——. *White Butterfly*. London: Pan, 1994.

Silet, Charles L. P. "The Other Side of Those Mean Streets: An Interview with Walter Mosley." *The Armchair Detective* 26.4 (1993): 9-16.

BRIDGES AND BOUNDARIES:
RACE, ETHNICITY, AND THE CONTEMPORARY
AMERICAN CRIME NOVEL

Andrew Pepper

The arrival in the United States of millions of immigrants from non-European countries since changes in the Immigration Act in 1965 has radically altered the social composition, particularly of the American urban population. Cities, it seems, are fast becoming home to a bewildering range of different nationalities and ethnic groups. In New York, formerly dominant Euro-centric groups have been dramatically superseded by arrivals from China, Korea, Jamaica, the Dominican Republic, Colombia, Cuba, and Russia; the city now boasts churches, cultural events, political associations, festivals, shops, and restaurants for all the different groups, together with dozens of foreign-language newspapers and cable TV stations. Los Angeles, its streets dotted with Iranian coffee shops, Korean supermarkets, and Chinese laundromats, and entire neighborhoods where nothing but Cantonese or Spanish is spoken, seems truly to be a multi-ethnic "babylon." As David Rieff notes, "Along Wilshire Boulevard and Melrose Avenue the faces behind the counter were Han and Dravidian, Korean, Persian, Mixtec and Ethiopian, anything, it seemed, except black and white" (144).

On paper, at least, cities like New York and Los Angeles do seem to possess a genuinely multiethnic character. However recent high-profile events, such as the beating of Rodney King and subsequent rioting in Los Angeles, police corruption in New Orleans, the O. J. Simpson trial and more importantly the verdict, and the Million Man March in Washington, DC, have conspired to give the impression that the United States, far from being a kind of multicultural utopia, remains fundamentally split down some kind of racial middle and that cities like New York or Los Angeles, despite their apparent polyethnic character, are in fact organized primarily along black/white faultlines.

This debate has raged with particular intensity in the academy. Scholars like Andrew Hacker, whose book *Two Nations: Black and White, Separate, Unequal, Hostile* highlights the extent of specifically racial divisions in the United States, point out that because race *has* been the fundamental axis of social organization in American society and because the experiences of nonEuropean immigrants have been significantly different to those of European descent, race as a concept cannot be meaningfully discussed under the broader heading of ethnicity. Other scholars, however, like Werner Sollors, while acknowledging the continuing persistence of racially motivated divisions in U.S. society, nevertheless, seek to depict African-Americans merely as "one of many different *ethnic* groups," and race, as "one of the dimensions of the larger cultural and historical phenomenon of ethnicity" (35).

This essay, however, will argue that neither position offers a particularly satisfying portrait of the nature of relationships between different ethnic and racial groups in the United States, because neither offers a suitably complex and flexible model for (group *and* individual) identity formation. To claim that race is indeed the principle axis of social organization and that U.S. society is split down a racial middle leads one towards the inherently dangerous conclusion that black and white necessarily represent something homogeneous, and that in a nation undergoing such a rapid metamorphosis, the population remains simply white- or black-identified. However to deny the claim outright would be to risk trivializing significant divisions in American society that *are* racially determined, and to overlook the simple fact that having dark rather than light skin or certain set of heritable characteristics, as Kwame Anthony Appiah notes, can have very profound social, political and economic consequences (Lentricchia 285).

What is needed, therefore, is an account that is able to entertain at least two apparently conflicting perspectives at the same time, but sociology is, perhaps, less able to offer such an account than fiction, because the novel, as the Russian critic Bakhtin argues, is "heteroglot" and therefore embraces many different voices or languages. Whereas sociology, in Bakhtin's terms, aspires towards a unitary language or an overall perspective that is arguably noncontradictory, the novel welcomes diversity. In fact, the contemporary American detective novel, in particular, has sought to depict society in all its diversity—as the detective attempts to discover who has done what, he or she necessarily comes into contact with individuals drawn from different backgrounds and cultures. And while there might ultimately be only one "language of truth," that of the hard-boiled investigator, his or her voice, according to Bakhtin at least, will necessarily reflect the full diversity of his or her social milieu because language is constructed via a process of what he calls "dialogics" (whereby each voice or utterance only takes its meaning in relation to other voices or utterances and therefore reflects all the voices in a given society).

The article will ask, and at least start to answer, why detective fiction in which the usually alienated, disaffected *Anglo* detective is replaced by an investigator who is part of a socially marginalized group is particularly suitable for this kind of usage. In general, the hard-boiled detective has been perceived to be a positive figure. This does not mean that he or she functions like some kind of morally pure state-sponsored henchman, but simply that in his or her refusal to capitulate to authority and in his or her dogged determination to uncover what has really happened, he or she usually comes across as an attractive figure or at least someone with whom readers can in part identify. This view of the detective has in the past led to one viewing him in dangerously essential and transcendent terms, a man like Chandler's Phillip Marlowe entirely in control of his actions and language. This is not the case with a black or Native American detective, however. In fact, precisely because he or she has traditionally been forced to live in *at least* two worlds (that of his or her culture, which itself needs to be seen in fragmented terms, and that of the so-called "dominant" culture, be it white, Western or Anglo in orientation), he or she will automatically possess an appropriately fractured sense of self; appropriately, because it necessarily problematizes a straightforward model of identity formation. Moreover, such a detective, because he or she understands the kinds of frustration that, to varying extents, define the experiences of all non-white Europeans (ie. having to operate in a white-controlled world) but can also detect differences between various groups and individuals, is arguably better able to view the polyethnic environment in suitably ambiguous terms.

"Race" and "Ethnicity" as Overlapping Yet Diverging Categories

If the "self, as Stuart Hall argues, needs to be conceptualized not in coherent, unitary terms but as a "moveable feast" of usually overlapping and contradictory identities, then what are the implications for different so-called "minority" groups? For just at a time when, for example, Chicanos and blacks in the United States are successfully contesting the perceived dominance of Anglo/white/western culture and promoting or retrieving a sense of their own (previously marginalized) cultures, they are told that the type of coherent and universal identities which might seem attractive are no longer possible. Should one, therefore, be wary of such "post-modern" critiques of the self and simply view this particular challenge as another example of cultural revisionism on the part of a Euro-centric culture intent on maintaining its apparent dominance via blatant divide and rule tactics? Or can this kind of thinking open up our understanding of different African American (and by implication Chicano, Cuban, Jamaican, etc.) experiences and force us to see each group in necessarily heterogeneous, multiplicitous terms?

Again, it seems, this question can be partly answered if one adopts a deliberately self-conscious, flexible approach to the notion of identity construction and before we move onto a more detailed exploration of the crime fiction itself, it is necessary to pause for a moment and consider what this phrase actually means. Terms like race and ethnicity no longer refer to categories that are fixed and stable but to ones that are best seen as fluid and relational, reflecting a growing awareness of the temporary and socially constructed nature of all identities. Yet the temptation to entirely collapse race and ethnicity on top of one another needs to be resisted. One needs to remember that having dark and not light skin can affect what kind of job you have, where you can or cannot live, who your friends are, and that in very many cases, the experiences of non-white European immigrants in the United States *have* been significantly different from those of their Europeans counterparts. Mary Waters makes the point that while an Italian-American might seek to equate the experiences of being black in the United States to being Italian American,

[T]he reality is that white ethnics have a lot more choice and room for maneuvering than they themselves think they do. [But] the situation is very different for members of racial minorities whose lives are strongly influenced by their race or national origins regardless of how much they may not choose to identify themselves in either ethnic or racial terms. (157)

Here the question of how a person defines him or herself, and perhaps more importantly, is defined by the rest of his or her society is crucial. When a fourth generation Italian American tries to be "Italian," where does his or her notion of being "Italian" come from? From an understanding of rituals, traditions, and history, or from family, or even just from watching films and televisions shows? And is it the same for an African American? Benjamin Ringer and Elinor Lawless argue that an ethnic group is besieged by two sets of forces that are in opposition to each other—an internal set that serves to establish a group's cultural distinctiveness or "we-ness" and an external set that serves to establish its "they-ness." Ringer and Lawless, moreover, contend that the latter process is far more pervasive and more actively influences and shapes the character of a particular group if that group is also racially distinctive. Thus, whereas Italian Americans might enjoy considerable choice in selecting which bits of their ethnicity or ethnic heritage to make a part of their lives (because the internal force that serves to establish his or her "we-ness" is stronger than the external force that serves to establish his or her "they-ness"), individuals of nonEuropean descent do not enjoy the same levels of choice when it comes to deciding how to identify themselves. A Jamaican or African American, for example, might similarly try to choose which parts of their ethnicity to make a part of their lives, there is an equal, if not greater, external force that seeks to categorize them merely as black.

The implication, here, is not that American society itself is inherently determined by a black/white model of categorization and the various ethnic groups neatly fit into either category, but rather, there exists a *tendency* to view the United States in this manner; a tendency, primarily on the part of those who have been ascribed a white identity, to want to collapse all differences into the inadequate but dangerously seductive categories of "black" and "white." What I mean is best explained by the African American poet and novelist, Ishmael Reed. Stressing what Sollors calls the "disturbing ability of the categories of 'black' and 'white,' despite their blatant inadequacies to describe a highly miscegenated, polyethnic culture to devour all ethnic differences" (*Invention* xix), Reed argues that despite widespread racial mixing, people have actively sought to retain the racial divide because it serves a useful purpose—to convince blacks not only that they are somehow inferior to whites but also that they are responsible for everything which has gone wrong with American society:

By blaming all of its problems on blacks, the political and cultural leadership are able to present the United States as a veritable utopia for those who aren't afraid of "hard work.". . . And so, instead of being condemned as a problem, the traditional view of the black presence, the presence of "blacks" should be viewed as a blessing. Without blacks taking the brunt of the system's failures, where would our great republic be? (Sollors, *Invention* 229)

If we need to be careful about viewing race and ethnicity as entirely overlapping categories, we should also be aware that neither are they entirely diverging categories. Despite the simple fact that being black in America is *not* the same as being Polish or Italian, scholars have sought to demonstrate that the lines which bind and divide different ethnic and racial groups are not as rigid or as natural as some people might have argued or in fact hoped. William Peterson points out that the terms ethnic and racial have at various times been used to describe the same thing (i.e., the Irish race and the Irish as an ethnicity) and argues that since the word *ethnos* (from which our word ethnicity is derived) "originally pertained to a biological grouping, it was closer to our definition of 'race' (which probably derived from the word *ratio* which, in medieval Latin, was used to designate species)" (Thernstrom 235). He also argues that the separation of the two terms has been inhibited and undermined by confusion in real life between physiological and cultural criteria; an African American, to this extent, can be defined in both ethnic and racial terms—as an individual who belongs to a specific cultural group with its own distinct history, and someone who possesses certain physiological features (Thernstrom 236).

There is pressing evidence, furthermore, to show that racial and indeed ethnic exclusivity in the United States is a falsehood. Writers like Ishmael Reed, Walter Mosley, Henry Louis Gates and Paul Gilroy have strenuously argued that terms like black or African American can no longer be theorized as self-evident but rather as entities whose *essential* character is in fact fluid, fragmented, and defined via a process of negative differentiation (A is an X because he isn't a Y or A is an African American because he isn't Mexican American). Theorists and critics have asked how one can even begin to talk about ethnic and racial groups in essential or transcendent terms given the extent of miscegenation and the growth in crosscultural relationships. If someone is one-fifth Jewish, four-fifths Irish American, half Puerto Rican, or half-African American how does one categorize him? Is it possible? Just as Walter Mosley, a half Jewish, half African American novelist declared, "There's no such thing as a pure black race. We are so intermixed that there is no race. That is, no pure race" (Oxford 4). Ishmael Reed similarly contends that blacks in the United States have a multi-ethnic heritage and argued that "[I]f Alex Haley had traced his father's bloodline, he would have travelled twelve generations back—not to Gambia, but to Ireland" (Sollors, *Invention* 227).

The destabilization of apparently fixed terms like African American or black is perhaps more useful than anything else in helping us to better understand the overlapping and yet diverging relationship between race and ethnicity not least because it asks for, if not demands, a far less rigid approach to the idea of boundary formation. Of course, it is very tempting to view race as some kind of special objective category, not least because having dark skin can affect, in a very real sense, how one is treated, where one can or cannot live and so forth. Furthermore the desire, from within black cultures, to construct some kind of transcendent racial identity in order to counterbalance perceived attacks from "outside" has, according to Paul Gilroy, never been stronger. Yet we must resist this temptation to universalize black or African American experience in unitary terms because such a practice is not only untenable in the light of postmodernist critiques of coherent subjectivities: it also denies or glosses over differences that can, as this essay will demonstrate in the next section, be profoundly liberating.

Walter Mosley's Easy Rawlins: The Detective as Cultural Mediator

To some extent, Mosley's surrogate detective Ezekiel "Easy" Rawlins comes across in the five novels (to date) as a tough and adept character in the mould of, say, Phillip Marlowe—he takes punishment without backing down, isn't afraid of what might happen to him, pursues the truth with a dogged determination, and usually finds out exactly who did what during the course of each novel. Yet his status as African American means that he is constantly torn between what he must do in order to survive and what he feels might be in the best interest of his specific community. Typically, the fact that the hard-boiled detective allows himself to become personally involved in his investigation and adopt some kind of moral position in relation to the crime itself is a key feature of hard-boiled detective fiction. Easy, however, cannot afford to assume such a position because as a black man living in a white-controlled world, he is necessarily forced to compromise his private code of justice (if he has such a code) just to keep his head above water. Rugged individualism, Mouse tells Easy in *Devil in a Blue Dress* is a just myth propagated by white culture in order to falsely valorize its achievements:

"Nigger cain't pull his way out of the swamp wit'out no help, Easy. You wanna hole on t'this house and git some money . . . ? Alright. That's alright. But Easy, you gotta have somebody at yo' back, man. That's just a lie them white men give 'bout makin' it on they own. They always got they backs covered." (158)

One needs to be aware that just as Paretsky's V. I. Warshawski or Sue Grafton's Kinsey Millhone are different kinds of private detectives to, say, Chandler's Phillip Marlowe because they are female, Easy Rawlins is a different kind of private detective because he is African American. (Though one needs to be careful about conflating female and non-white detectives too closely simply on the grounds that they both, in some way, revise existing conventions.) Easy is both part of the dominant white culture, in so far as much of his work comes from white businessmen or families (i.e., Dewitt Albright in *Devil in a Blue Dress* or the Cain family in *Black Betty*), and part of a specific African American community in South Los Angeles. Furthermore he is both inside this particular community and culture (in so far as he has a family and relies on his community to sustain him) and outside it—as an African American struggling to survive in a white controlled world, he invariably finds that he is forced into situations that compromise friendships. In *A Red Death*, for example, he even admits that, "I was on everybody's side but my own" (221). This sense of ambiguity or "doubleness," Mosley suggests, is an inherent part of being African American in the United States. Precisely because Easy has been forced to live in at least two worlds (that of his own African American community, which itself needs to be seen in fragmented terms, and that of the so-called dominant culture, be it white or Western Anglo in orientation) also means that he possesses the kind of fractured identity or subjectivity that enables us to begin to frame black and indeed African American culture in appropriately fluid and fragmented terms.

Bakhtin argues that a single national language is composed of a multiplicity of competing languages, each struggling to assert itself in relation to each other and the dominant or official language. Language, he maintains, is a practice in which there are two forces constantly in conflict with one another; a centripetal force, "working towards a unified and static language" and a centrifugal force, "endlessly developing new forms which parody, criticize and generally undermine the pretensions of the ambitions towards a unitary language" (Tallack 119). This particular battle is an important feature of Mosley's work. Characters like Mrs. Keaton, an elderly librarian in *White Butterfly,* might seek to "colonize" Mosley's African American population and force them "to abandon their own language and stories to become part of her educated world" (56). However the African American characters themselves, specifically Easy, resist such pressures and deliberately choose to express themselves in dialect because to do otherwise would be to negate an entire oral tradition—"folk tales, riddles and stories colored folk had been telling for centuries" (56). Language, here, is not merely a vehicle for communications; it is also a means of connecting people to their history and culture and the fact that most if not all of Mosley's black characters speak in dialect signals the author's intention to challenge, undermine, and even overturn official values.

The centrifugal force in Mosley's writing, therefore, might be stronger, reflecting Easy's claim that he could only truly express himself "in the natural uneducated dialect of [his] upbringing" (*Devil* 17). Yet the impact of the centripetal force or that force which seeks to colonize or appropriate black languages and cultures, cannot be underestimated. Indeed, though Easy himself is proud of his cultural heritage, proud to be black, his identity is not simply constructed from that which is specifically African American. As Mosley starts to question what this kind of term actually means, we start to get a picture of his protagonist as someone whose sense of "self" has, in fact, been constructed from a dizzying range of sometimes conflicting and sometimes interlocking perspectives or subject-positions. Being African American, for Easy at least, is not merely about speaking in dialect and knowing where he came from, but also about holding opinions more often associated with, say, the white/ Anglo middle class, or Mexicans or Jews—like a passion for education and reading that extends beyond wanting to know about his own culture (in *A Red Death* the reader learns that he is taking a night school class in English and European history) and a respect for home ownership, which is seen by some within his community as a specifically white value.

In his language, therefore, we find flexibility, not dogma: a single voice that also represents or reflects an entire spectrum of different perspectives, and utterances. A brief list of examples taken from the novels themselves illustrates the point. In *Devil in a Blue Dress,* the reader discovers, on the one hand that "there were no real differences between the races" (62), and on the other, that no one with white skin actually "thought that we were really the same" (144). Furthermore, while Easy lives in the kind of unequal and racially segregated world where a black man could be arrested or assaulted just for looking at a white women, there are at least some points of overlap between the so-called black and white worlds. Easy might be quick to celebrate certain aspects of black culture(s), like music or storytelling, but he is both aware of its fragmented, heterogeneous nature and he makes friendships and associations with people from other groups and cultures. Moreover, while he can see from his own experiences that black and white America are hopelessly segregated and divided by massive inequalities in wealth and opportunity, he refuses to be ghettoized or isolated simply as a black man who has already been cast in the role of loser. What we find in his character, above all, is a model for boundary formation that is flexible and sophisticated enough to accept that borders, like skin color, exist and have real meaning but that doesn't merely categorize terms like white or black as homogeneous, unitary entities where no kind of interaction takes place.

In his representation of the wider environment—Los Angeles from the 1940s onwards—Mosley paints a similarly complicated picture of racial and ethnic relations. To some extent, I suppose, given that racially motivated segregation even now remains a fact of life in many LA neighborhoods, it is inevitable that Mosley should choose to depict a world where those with dark and light (or black and white) skin live in separate worlds. From *Devil in a Blue Dress* onwards, one is made acutely aware of the fact that just as whites or Anglos rarely venture into Watts, blacks or African Americans hardly ever venture out of Watts, other than for work. Furthermore, this situation seems, if anything, to actually worsen as the novels (and century) progress. By 1962, the temporal setting for the fourth novel of the series, *Black Betty,* Mosley's description of Mofass as being "someone from the old days when there was a black community almost completely sealed off from whites"

(109), implies that events in the wider cultural forum like the election of J. F. K. and the rise of the Civil Rights movement have led to a partial relaxation of strict racial divisions. Yet ghettoization and its inevitable consequences appear to be that much more tangible. Watts, in the first novel of the series *Devil in a Blue Dress* is, to some extent, described as a mecca of opportunity for anyone willing to work—"the promise of getting rich pushed people to work two jobs in the week and do a little plumbing on the weekend" (55-56). However this sense of albeit false optimism has vanished by the 1960s and the same community is likened to a graveyard where hope for the future is little more than a bad joke:

Most of them were black people . . . Women like Betty who'd lost too much to be silly or kind. And there were the children, like Spider and Terry T once were, with futures so bleak that it could make you cry just to hear them laugh. Because behind the music of their laughing, you knew there was the rattle of chains. (*Betty* 216)

Given the extent of social, political, and economic inequalities between black and white, Anglo and African American, in Mosley's fiction (a divide that is appropriately represented in *Black Betty* via a comparison between those described above and the fabulously wealthy Cain family of Beverly Hills), it is difficult not to think of Andrew Hacker's description of the United States in general as a nation fundamentally split down a racial or black/white centre. Yet the author, I think, also wants to suggest that a system of classification based around a straightforward racial binary, cannot effectively come to terms with the extent of diversity in his city. Skin color might well be the most intransigent boundary in Mosley's fiction, but to suggest that race is the *only* axis of social organization would be to ignore other divisions (based on class, gender, and ethnicity, for example) and gloss over those areas where the experiences of those from different cultural backgrounds do, in fact, overlap.

Sole focus on black as a monolithic group, Mosley suggests, fails to take into account the huge diversity of skin color, and by implication miscegenation, within black culture(s). A quick glance though *Devil in a Blue Dress* and *A Red Death,* for example, bears this point out. In the former, just as Coretta James has "cherry brown" skin (44), Odell Jones is colored like a "red pecan" (42) and Jackson Blue is "so black that his skin glinted blue in the full sun" (120). Meanwhile in the latter, just as Etta Mae is described as "sepia-colored" (26), Mofass is "dark brown but bright" (13), Mouse is "dusky pecan" (72), Jackie Orr is "olive brown" (86) and Andre Lavender is "orange skinned" (120). No need, as

Henry Louis Gates says of his similarly "multi-colored" family, to point out that those with lighter skin were part Irish or English because they wore "the complexity of their bloodline on their faces" (Gates 73).

The tendency to see the world in simplistic black/white terms also glosses over significant class and regional differentials within the so-called black community. Most of the black community in Watts, at least in the first three novels of the series (*Devil in a Blue Dress, A Red Death, White Butterfly*), seem to have migrated to the West coast from south Texas and Louisiana, and differences between people from those areas and, for example, African Americans from the northeastern cities, like LAPD officer Quentin Naylor from Philadelphia, are self-evident. There are even noticeable differences between people from Houston and New Orleans, at least in terms of social networks and circles of friends —as Easy explains in *A Red Death,* "Mofass was from New Orleans and though he spoke like me, he wasn't intimate with my friends from around Houston, Galveston and Lake Charles" (18). There are significant differences, too, between those African Americans who work in bars, factories, or who steal for a living, and professional or middle-class African Americans, like Quentin Naylor, who had "an educated way of talking" (*Red Death* 168). Within Watts itself, class differences also prevail. Those who live on Bell Street and "thought that their people and their block were too good for most of the rest of the Watts community" (*Red Death* 197) are part of what might be termed the lower-middle class and seek to foreground differences between their status and the rest of the Watts community as vociferously as possible. Yet it is important to remember that they are no less black for doing so. Countering the idea that black represents some kind of essential state of being that is itself inextricably linked to notions of suffering, "the blues," discrimination and poverty, bell hooks makes the point that while black people from the middle classes may well have been affected by racism in different ways but, "it is not productive to see them as enemies or dismiss them by labelling them not black enough." Rather, she points out, black people in America have multiple identities and that what needs to be stressed is that "our concept of black experience [in the past] has been too narrow and constricting" (37).

Mosley also suggests that an exclusive fixation on those factors which divide different groups, in fact, negates areas of common ground where the interests and experiences of blacks, working-class whites, Mexicans, and given in post-Second World War context, Jews, overlap. In *Black Betty,* for example, we learn that a poor white man called Alamo has forged some kind of allegiance with Easy based on their mutual dislike for the establishment. "He would have hated Negroes if it wasn't for World War One. [But] he felt that all those white politicians had set up the poor white trash the same way as black folks were set up" (30). Similarly, Easy states, in *Devil in a Blue Dress,* that before "ancestry" had been discovered "a Mexican and a Negro considered themselves the same" (182). In *A Red Death,* furthermore, he becomes friends with a Jewish communist activist called Chaim Wenzler. Chaim might have white or light skin, but as a Jew who fled to the United States from Nazi-occupied Europe, he can also understand the painful consequences of violent discrimination. In one passage, he tells Easy that whites [in this case meaning non-Jews] "don't understand being treated like this" (144), and in another, he declares, "Negroes in America have the same life as the Jew in Poland" (111).

This is not, however, a bland multiculturalism that Mosley is espousing, where differences between various minority cultures are, to some extent, collapsed and blacks in America are simply treated as one of many different groups. Discrimination, residential segregation, and racism—all with their roots in the institution of slavery—are a harsh fact of life, even for those with mixed parentage who perhaps do not easily fit into the category of black. Daphne Monet, the object of Easy's quest in *Devil in a Blue Dress,* might appear to have white skin and therefore possess a 'white' identity, but she cannot escape the consequences of her heritage. Her father was an African American and though she desperately wants to marry a powerful Anglo banker and political powerbroker, her concealed racial identity inevitably negates this possibility. "All them years people be tellin' her how she light-skinned and beautiful," Mouse tells Easy, "but all the time she knows that she can't have what people have" (209). Furthermore, though Wenzler's aim is to promote a sense of unity between blacks in the United States and American Jews, Mosley falls well short of exactly correlating their experiences. During the heyday of the 1950s "Red" scare, Easy is told about a list circulating in the business community that identifies not only blacks but also Jews who have been excluded from the work place due to political allegiances. This does not, however, signal some kind of parity—as Jackson Blue ruefully explains to him. "One day they gonna throw that list out. . . . Mosta these guys gonna have work again. . . . But you still gonna be a black niggah. An' niggah ain't got no union he could count on, an niggah ain't got no politician gonna work fo' him" (*Red Death* 230). Given the pre-Civil Rights context of Mosley's first three novels, the fact that Los Angeles is primarily organized along racial or black/white lines is not surprising. However anticipating and reflecting recent theories which dismiss the idea that races are simple expressions of biological or cultural sameness and highlight "the existence of a multiplicity of black tones and styles" (Gilroy 1-2), Mosley works to deconstruct blackness as a singular, monolithic trope.

Ethnic and Racial Divisions in Mike Phillips's Point of Darkness

bell hooks suggests that there is a tendency within the black community in the United States to either essentialize black experience, or, at least, not critique essentialism since many fear "it will cause folks to lose sight of the special history and experience of African-Americans." Yet she stresses that blacks in America have many different identities and "when this diversity is ignored, it is easy to see black folks as falling into two categories . . . black-identified and white-identified" (29). The arrival of blacks from various places in the Caribbean (Cuba and Jamaica, for example) has further accentuated the multiplicitous nature of black identity in the America. Literature and other art forms produced by black artists from these countries, hooks argues, work to deconstruct notions of universalism by affirming multiple black identities and challenging "the colonial imperialist paradigms of black identity that represent blackness one-dimensionally in ways that reinforce and sustain white supremacy" (hooks 28). Indeed, one can perhaps understand why crime novels written by, and about, individuals from, say, Jamaica or Cuba (who do not easily fit into categories like black or white or at least, not in the traditional sense), offer a more complex, flexible, and satisfactory model for identity construction, one that acknowledges both the extent of existing racial divisions and the inability of the old language of race relations to cope with the fragmented nature of black and white identities in the United States.

To claim that race has been, and still is, the fundamental axis of social organization in Mike Phillips's New York is tempting for his Jamaican-born, British-raised investigator, Sam Dean, in so far as the city's Caribbean population, like its African American one, is externally defined or misdefined simply on the basis of skin color. Indeed, the fact that black people in New York regardless of their background, culture, or class are, even superficially, lumped together and viewed by the dominant white European culture in singular terms is some basis for the kind of Pan Africanism that certain politicians want to promote. (Sam notes that blacks of different nationalities and cultures were starting to see the benefits of coming together and "finding common ground" in city politics.) Furthermore it reflects a popularly held desire among some of the city's black intellectuals for a kind of cross-cultural black identity. When Sam's cousin Bonnie, lecturer at a university in Queens, asks him to describe his dark-skinned Latino girlfriend Sophie, the choices she offers him reflect an apparently prevailing view built into many American racial/social attitudes. "You've got two choices," she tells him. "Black or white? Which one is it?" (Phillips 39).

Sam, however, rejects the kind of racial exclusivism that Bonnie is seeking to promote. Though, at the time, he falls into her trap and blurts out, "You'd definitely call her black," later on, he finds himself increasingly dissatisfied with his answer, not least because it fails to take into account the significant cultural differences between Bonnie and Sophie. Indeed, when the two women finally meet and Bonnie disparagingly declares that Sophie is not "one of us," Sam sets out his own position:

I'm loyal to my friends and my memories and want progress for the race. That's how we were brought up, you know that. That don't change. But there's no reason, whether its psychological or sociological or mystical or whatever, that's gonna make me join that exclusion shit. (149)

Sam, then, might be fiercely loyal to what he sees as his race but he uses the term in its loosest possible sense. Just as Henry Louis Gates states in his autobiographical account of his family's history *Colored People,* "I want to be black, to know black, to luxuriate in whatever I might be calling blackness at any particular time—but to do so in order to come out of the other side, to experience a humanity that is neither colorless nor reducible to color" (xv), Sam self-consciously foregrounds his pride in being black but at the same time acknowledges its multiple style and meanings. After all, belief in a pure black identity is something of a misnomer, he suggests, because most black people outside Africa descend from a racial mixture. "Europeans, Indians, and Chinese, all of them at one point or the other stuck their fingers in the New World's black gene pool" (196).

Phillips's point, I think, is that it takes the knowing and perceptive eye of Sam Dean, the novel's investigator, to locate those areas where the interests, experiences, and histories of the different groups either overlap or diverge. As a detective, or surrogate detective, his generic function in *Point of Darkness* is to locate the daughter of an old friend who has gone missing in New York. Yet the plot, as such, I would argue, is something of a Trojan horse, concealing a secondary, perhaps more important agenda, whereby Sam must be able to move among the city's different groups, reading and deciphering people's characters "not only from the physiognomy of their faces but also via a social physiognomy of the streets" (Willet 3). It is a job which he performs admirably. When he visits a Spanish-Caribbean cafe in Queens with Bonnie and Oscar, her African American boyfriend, though many of the faces are black, Sam senses their unease—"as if they were in enemy territory" (212). In another restaurant, Sam is able to precisely identify the identity of the waiters. To his trained eye, they are not simply black or even Caribbean but specifically Haitian—"That is to say, they looked a lot like Jamaicans, but with a kind of prissy smoothness to their style and movements" (139).

Where the lines that bind and divide individuals and individual groups, however, is practically impossible to work out, even for someone like Sam. Far from being a city organized along strictly racial lines Phillips' New York is more a teeming morass of sometimes conflicting, sometimes interlocking alliances. Though Jamaicans and other Caribbean blacks share a nominal racial identity with the city's African American population, differences are clearly foregrounded. The two groups speak differently, think differently and act differently. African Americans, Sam claims, are fixed to one country while Jamaicans, for example, "move comfortably between two countries" (222), and from a cultural point of view, seem to share more in common with the various Latin Americans. Ethnicity does act as a source of conflict between the two groups, especially when perceived Caribbean successes are compared to African American failures, but Phillips is careful to contextualize differences. Though many African American neighborhoods are portrayed as spoilt, rundown and dangerous, and Caribbean ones as dynamic and energetic, differences between the two groups, and the socioeconomic status, are shown to be temporal and based in specific historical circumstance. "African Americans," Sam explains, "had lost it in the grim struggles of the northern cities and then TV had taught them human worth could be measured by possessions and happiness was an escape capsule . . . [but] the Caribbeans still pulled together because that was part of their immigrant heritage" (138).

Ultimately Sam Dean, like Mosley's Easy Rawlins, acts as a kind of cultural mediator whose responsibility or function is as much observational as it is investigative; he moves among the city's different groups, deciphering what he hears and sees in order to decide for himself along what lines the city is divided. The point is that his "self" is not fixed or essentialized but fluid and representative of the fractured environment, as well as his chameleon-like ability to assume different roles and different identities depending on where he is and who he is talking to. In one scene, he is very much a black man, not only struggling to keep his head above water in a white-operated world but also proud of his racial identity and the sense of belonging it affords him as he moves between different black communities. In another scene, he is Caribbean and in another, he is specifically Jamaican—someone whose outlook and indeed entire character is in some way informed by the politics, culture, and climate of one particular place, or defined via a sense of what he is *not* (African American, Haitian, Cuban, etc.). Furthermore, in another scene, he is not so much Jamaican as English or someone who uses his "accent" to help him to elicit information from white or Anglo Americans: individuals who in similar circumstances "might've treated an African-American with a well-rehearsed suspicion" (269).

If Sam's identity cannot be seen to be fixed or "whole" do we view him as less of a man or less of a detective than, say, Chandler's Phillip Marlowe? And just at a time when, for example, Jamaicans and African Americans in the United States are successfully contesting the perceived dominance of Anglo/white culture and retrieving a sense of their own (previously marginalized) identities, can we simply write off attempts to discount or undermine their very existence as another example of cultural revisionism on the part of a Euro-centric culture intent on maintaining its apparent dominance via divide and rule tactics? The answer to both questions has to be an emphatic no. Sam, at least in this situation, is a more effective investigator than Phillip Marlowe could ever be precisely because he can assume different identities to suit different situations (arguably, Marlowe did this, too, but once he stepped outside the Anglo culture to which he belonged, he was always merely a white man). Moreover, to view boundaries (surrounding individual and group identities) in flexible, nonessential terms is liberating for Sam in so far as it allows him to both make connections with those from similar backgrounds and feel pride at the achievements of those who belong to his race and to his specific culture, and, at the same time, move beyond the rather limited essentialist position that dictates who he can and cannot forge friendships with and indeed trust. Once in New York, he inevitably gravitates towards those people who share a Jamaican identity and he feels pride at the dynamism and vitality of the different Caribbean communities, but, at the same time, discovers that a single group identity cannot function as some kind of broad umbrella under which all blacks, or all West Indians, or even all Jamaicans, regardless of outlook, class, and background, can take refuge. Moreover, such a view exactly mirrors a shift that has taken place in contemporary black cultural politics from a discourse of apparent unity, whereby black as a term was used as a means of somehow describing the collective experiences of so-called black people (often in relation and response to having to operate in a white-controlled world) to one of pluralism or fragmentation whereby the diverse and at times contradictory nature of different black experiences and identities has been foregrounded.

Conclusion: Applications

Given that one key purpose of this collection in general is to show how different crime or detective novels can be used to teach cultural diversity both in the classroom and to the general reader, one needs to consider how we can best put some of the ideas outlined in this essay to work. How can they either help us to better understand the relationship between race and ethnicity in contemporary America or, given the extent to which the ethnic and racial composition of U.S. society has altered over the last 20 years, enable us to come to some kind of new appreciation of the American social mosaic? As a conclusion, then, I want to look at the 1992 Los Angeles riots and though such an important event needs a much wider discussion than I have the space to give it, I want to consider how one can *begin* to frame the various conflicts.

That the riots themselves caused widespread damage and loss of life is not in dispute. More than 50 people were killed and over 2,000 were injured. Plumes of thick-black smoke could be seen for miles around as some 4,000 individual buildings were razed to the ground, at an estimated cost of $1 to $2 billion. What does seem to be in dispute, though, is what the violence itself represented. Indeed, though the Watts riots some 25 years before were broadly understood to be a display of frustration and anger on the part of the community's mostly black population, people seemed to be divided as to what the violence in 1992 reflected. For many, the bloodletting was merely the most visible expression of the ever-widening gap between blacks and whites in America and proof that any advances made during the 1960s' Civil Rights upheavals had subsequently been lost. Others, however, saw the disturbances as a chance to attack the old language of race relations and call for a new appreciation of America's social mosaic. Ronald T. Takaki, for example, remarked soon afterwards that perhaps the most important lesson of the explosion was "the recognition of the fact that we are a multi-racial society and that race can no longer be defined in the binary terms of white and black" (Takaki, "Different" 5).

The temptation to view the disturbances in purely black/white terms is of course strong, not least because the initial trigger was undoubtedly the acquittal of four white police officers accused of assaulting a black motorist and the perceived injustice that it represented (especially when their actions had been openly caught by an amateur video cameraman). Yet if one also considers some of the following factors, it becomes increasingly difficult to settle for black/white conclusions. Blacks or African Americans constitute just 10 percent of the city's total population while the various Latino groups make up almost

40 percent; of the 5,000 people arrested during the course of the rioting, only 37 percent were black; blacks in South-Central seemed to vent their anger as much at Koreans as whites; poor whites joined in on the side of Latinos and blacks; blacks fought against other blacks; Koreans accused the mostly white LA police department of deliberately failing to protect them and their interests.

To suggest that American society is fragmented and that the lines which bind and divide various groups are determined not just by straightforward racial or ethnic allegiances but also by, say, class interests, background, and even religion is, of course, nothing new. Yet, in the context of the Angeleno riots, the notion that the black or African American or Caribbean detective operating in a fractured, multiracial environment can function as a kind of cultural bridge is highly relevant. This is not to suppose that Mosley's Easy Rawlins or Phillips's Sam Dean, if put into a hostile real-life environment like contemporary LA, could diffuse tension, successfully mediate between the different groups and bring about stability. It is simply to suggest that via their abilities to deconstruct differences that appear to be natural and, at the same time, to acknowledge those areas where differences cannot be collapsed, they offer some kind of way forward through the morass of U.S. racial and ethnic politics.

The Los Angeles riots, however one ultimately regards them, exposed deep fault lines in American society. Partly the product of specifically black frustration at apparent injustices handed out by the white-dominated judicial system, the riots reinforced the sense that racial divisions, particularly for those in society who are discriminated against and marginalized simply on the basis of where they come from or how they look, are frighteningly real. Indeed, just as it needs to be emphasized that being, say, Chicano and being Cuban are not the exactly same, one also needs to be remember that the predicaments of certain groups (i.e., African Americans), as Richard Rodriguez notes, should not be casually compared to the experiences of other Americans:

My fear is that multiculturalism is going to further trivialize the distinct predicament of black Americans . . . It is my belief that there are two stories in American history that are singular and of such extraordinary magnitude that they should never be casually compared to the experiences of other Americans. One is the story of the American Indian; the other is the story of the black slave. (Takaki, *Different Shores* 281)

Of course, significant advances were made by many blacks as a result of Civil Rights, but the continuing impact of slavery and subsequent institutional discrimination in the job and housing market cannot be underestimated. At the same time, however, it is just as dangerous to erect semipermanent boundaries between the different groups; such a process only naturalizes differences which are often socially shaped and thereby glosses over those areas where the interests and experiences of different groups *do* overlap. As bell hooks argues, "other groups now share with black folks a sense of deep alienation, despair, uncertainty, loss of sense of grounding, even if it is not informed by shared circumstances." She concludes, "Radical postmodernism calls attention to those shared sensibilities which cross boundaries of class, gender, race, etc., that could be fertile ground for the construction of empathy—ties that would promote recognition of common commitments and serve as a base for solidarity and coalition" (27).

Whether or not Mosley's Easy Rawlins novels and Mike Phillips' *Point of Darkness* could ever be classified as radical postmodernist texts is not ultimately clear (and such a statement also depends on exactly where one places the genre in relation to notions of high and low forms of writing). Yet insofar as both authors not only write from the margins but also construct, through their respective protagonists and portrait of the wider community, a fragmented and pluralistic model for black identity formation, their work fulfills two important criteria, as laid down by bell hooks. Such a model, I would go on to add, is useful in helping us to work through the kind of difficulties outlined in the previous paragraph, not just because it is flexible and sophisticated enough to entertain apparently contradictory perspectives; inherent in this kind of model too, is the sense that one can be proud of one's culture and race, as Easy Rawlins and Sam Dean are, but still see them as fractured and multiplicitous categories, and that one can draw sustenance from one's own community and culture, as Easy Rawlins and Sam Dean do, but never so completely immerse oneself in it that outsiders are automatically viewed as enemies. And such a position might be a useful starting point for reconsidering and recontextualizing the 1992 Los Angeles riots.

Works Cited

Gates, Henry Louis. *Colored People*. London: Penguin, 1995.

Gilroy, Paul. *Small Acts: Thoughts on the Politics of Black Cultures*. London: Serpents Tail, 1993.

Hacker, Andrew. *Two Nations: Black and White, Separate, Unequal, Hostile*. New York: Charles Scribners, 1992.

hooks, bell. *Yearning: Race, Gender and Cultural Politics*. London: Turn-around, 1991.

Lentricchia, Frank. *Critical Terms for Literary Study*. Chicago and London: University of Chicago Press, 1987.

Mosley, Walter. *Black Betty*. London: Serpents Tail, 1994.

——. *Devil in a Blue Dress*. London: Serpents Tail, 1991.

——. *A Red Death*. London: Serpents Tail, 1992.

——. *White Butterfly*. London: Serpents Tail, 1993.

Oxford, Esther. The Monday Interview: Walter Mosley,' *Independent* (UK), 9.10.95, 4.

Phillips, Mike. *Point of Darkness*. London: Michael Joseph, 1994.

Rieff, David. *Los Angeles: Capital of the Third World*. London: Phoenix, 1993.

Ringer, Benjamin. *Race-Ethnicity and Society*. London and New York: Rout-ledge, 1989.

Sollors, Werner. *Beyond Ethnicity: Consent and Descent in American Culture*. New York and Oxford: Oxford University Press, 1986.

——. *The Invention of Ethnicity*. Oxford and New York: Oxford University Press, 1989.

Takaki, Ronald T. *A Different Mirror: A History of Multi-Cultural America*. Boston and London: Little Brown & Co., 1993.

——. *From Different Shores: Perspectives on Race and Ethnicity* ed. *in America*, 2nd ed. Oxford and New York: Oxford University Press, 1994.

Tallack, Douglas. *Literary Theory at Work: Three Texts*. London: BT Batsford, 1987.

Thernstrom, S. *The Harvard Encyclopedia of American Ethnic Groups*. Cam-bridge, MA: Harvard University Press, 1980.

Waters, Mary C. *Ethnic Options: Choosing Identities in America*. Berkeley: University of California Press, 1990.

Willett, Ralph. *The Naked City: Urban Crime Fiction in the USA*. Manchester and New York: University of Manchester Press, 1996.

CONTRIBUTORS

Frankie Y. Bailey is an associate professor in the School of Criminal Justice, University at Albany. Her area of research is crime and culture (focusing on race, class, and gender). She is co-editor (with Donna C. Hale) of *Popular Culture, Crime, and Justice* (Wadsworth, 1998). Her most recent publication (with Alice P. Green) is *"Law Never Here": A Social History of African-American Responses to Issues of Crime and Justice* (Praeger, 1999).

Michael Cohen is the author of *Sisters: Relation and Rescue in Nineteenth-Century British Novels and Paintings* (Fairleigh Dickinson University Press, 1995), *Hamlet in My Mind's Eye* (Georgia, 1989), which won the South Atlantic Modern Language Association Studies Award, and *Engaging English Art* (Alabama, 1987). He teaches at Murray State University.

Nicole Décuré is French and teaches English as a foreign language at one of Toulouse universities. She is at the head of a research team in language teaching and learning. Women's fiction, mostly women's crime fiction, constitutes her second (and favorite) field of research.

Frances A. Della Cava and **Madeline H. Engel** teach Sociology at Herbert H. Lehman College, CUNY. Their past writings focused on working women. This research grew out of an earlier study, *Female Detectives in American Novels* (Garland, 1993).

Mary Jean DeMarr is professor emerita of English and Women's Studies at Indiana State University, Terre Haute, Indiana. Her most recent books are *Colleen McCullough: A Critical Companion* and *Barbara Kingsolver: A Critical Companion,* both published by Greenwood Press.

Manina Jones is an associate professor of English at the University of Western Ontario. She is author of *That Art of Difference: "Documentary-Collage" and English Canadian Writing* (University of Toronto Press, 1993), and co-author with Priscilla L. Walton of *Detective Agency: Women Rewriting the Hard-Boiled Tradition* (University of California Press, 1999).

Liam Kennedy is senior lecturer in American Studies at the University of Birmingham. He is the author of *Susan Sontag: Mind as Passion* (Manchester/New York, 1996). He has published articles on American literature and film in *MELUS, Journal of American Studies*, and *Modern Fiction Studies*. He is currently completing *Race and Urban Space in American Culture* (Edinburgh, 1999) and co-editing *Urban Space and Representation* (London, 1999). He co-directs a multidisciplinary project "Literary and Visual Representations of Three American Cities, 1870s-1930s" (http://www.nottingham.ac.uk/3cities/).

Margaret Kinsman is a senior lecturer in the English Studies Department, South Bank University, London, U.K., with research and teaching interests in twentieth-century women writers and feminist crime fiction. She is a contributor to the *St. James Guide to Crime and Mystery Fiction,* the *Oxford Companion to Crime and Mystery Fiction,* and the Scribner Writers Series *Mystery & Suspense Writers*. She is a regular speaker in the Crime and Mystery Fiction caucus of the Popular Culture Association and is a member of The Crime Writers Association (U.K.). A larger work on Sara Paretsky is in progress.

Gina Macdonald and **Andrew Macdonald** teach in the English Department at Loyola University–New Orleans. Both have published widely in popular fiction, detective fiction, and popular culture. They are co-authors of a Prentice Hall Regents writing text for bilingual students. Andrew Macdonald has a book on Howard Fast published by Greenwood Press. Gina Macdonald has two books for Greenwood in the same Critical Companions to Popular Contemporary Writers series, *James Clavell* and *Robert Ludlum*. They are now at work on two books, *Shapeshifting: Images of Native Americans in Recent Popular Fiction* and *The Native American in Recent Detective Fiction: Victim, Guide, Investigator, and Shaman,* both for Greenwood Press.

Andrew Pepper is a lecturer in American Studies at Middlesex University, London, U.K. He is currently completing *The Contemporary American Crime Novel: Race, Ethnicity, Gender, Sexuality* (Edinburgh, 2000).

Priscilla L. Walton is a professor of English at Carleton University. She is the author of *Patriarchal Desire and Victorian Discourse: A Lacanian Reading of Anthony Trollope's Palliser Novels* (Toronto, 1995) and *The Disruption of the Feminine in Henry James* (Toronto, 1992). She has also published articles in such journals as the *Henry James Review, Literature/Interpretation/Theory, Commonwealth, World Literature Written in English, Victorian Review,* and *Ariel*. Her present book, *Detective Agency: Women Re-Writing the Hardboiled Tradition,* is co-authored with Manina Jones (University of California Press, 1999).

Claire Wells teaches at De Montfort University, Leicester, U.K., in the English, Media, and Cultural Studies Department. Her research interests include black British writing, retrieving black British literary history, Diasporic writings, and the reshaping of 'Englishness' and crime fiction.